Covenant of Love

Rev. Richard M. Hogan
Rev. John M. LeVoir

Covenant of Love

*Pope John Paul II on
Sexuality, Marriage, and
Family in the Modern World*

With a Commentary on
Familiaris Consortio

Ignatius Press San Francisco

First edition printed by Doubleday, Inc.
Published with ecclesiastical approval

Cover photograph: CNS/Arturo Mari

Second edition 1992, Ignatius Press
ISBN 0-89870-399-9
Library of Congress catalogue number 91-76516
Printed in the United States of America

Contents

PART ONE
THE FAMILY IN THE TEACHINGS
OF POPE JOHN PAUL II

CONTENTS

PART TWO
A COMMENTARY ON THE APOSTOLIC EXHORTATION
Familiaris Consortio, "The Role of the Christian
Family in the Modern World"

Foreword

And now the most eminent cardinals have called a new bishop of Rome. They have called him from a distant country, distant but always so close through the communion in the Christian faith and tradition.

Talks of John Paul II

Karol Wojtyla was neither a recluse nor a stranger to much of the world when he accepted the duties of the Vicar of Christ on October 16, 1978. He had played a strong role in the proceedings of the Second Vatican Council and had served as a representative from his native Poland in each of the synods of bishops from the time of the institution of that forum.

It is unlikely, however, that anyone could have anticipated the extraordinary impact he has had on the world in these past six years. In part because of his travels and in part because of his obvious attractiveness to people, what he says and does receives the greatest possible attention.

What is becoming increasingly clear to me is that it is impossible to divorce the person of John Paul II from his teaching. In a world of personality peddlers, he comes through as integral and a person totally informed by his unwavering faithfulness to the Church of Christ.

Concern for truth is the Holy Father's basic preoccupation. He is able to teach people hard truths. He preaches chastity to an age that has pretty much rejected chastity. He teaches the values of family life to a world that is pretty cavalier about those values. There is an extraordinary consistency about John Paul II, the man and the teacher. He is the product of a living, growing faith, and his roots are set solidly not only in his native Poland but in the Second Vatican Council. His mission in life is to share his vision of faith and the vision of that Council with all who will listen.

As early as 1972, when he published *Sources of Renewal*, the cardinal archbishop of Cracow patiently explained what the teaching of the Council was. Now, with a much larger platform, he brings that same message to the entire world. The secret of John Paul II's consistency in teaching is that today he is guided by the same Holy Spirit who inspired him and his brother bishops when they drafted the conciliar documents.

In an extraordinary statement, the conciliar fathers taught that our Lord Jesus Christ "fully reveals man to himself" (*Pastoral Constitution on the Church in the Modern World*, no. 22). Of course, within John Paul's new and most interesting theological system this statement is clearly associated with God's revelation in Genesis that human beings are made to the image and likeness of God. Obviously, if we are like God, we do not know ourselves unless we know God.

That central insight in the Holy Father's approach to faith lies in God's revelation in Genesis and Christ's fulfillment of creation. This insight has dictated his teachings on sexuality and family life.

It is not possible to fragment the teaching of this pope. You really don't understand what he says about sexuality and the family without understanding his entire system of thought.

It is my belief that Fathers Hogan and LeVoir have not only provided this background in the first part of this volume, but they have also applied their studies of his thought to the most important document the Holy See has issued on the family, *Familiaris Consortio, The Role of the Christian Family in the Modern World*. It is my hope that this volume will be an enrichment to the many who look for truth from a man who spends his life in the cause of truth.

THE MOST REVEREND JOHN R. ROACH
Past President, National Conference of Catholic Bishops

Preface

The authors of this volume have incurred a responsibility toward John Paul II. They have received the priceless gift of the truth in the teachings of the present successor to Saint Peter. In accepting such a gift, the authors have incurred an obligation to make some repayment. In a sense, they have a debt to John Paul II—a debt which they now desire to discharge. Since the Holy Father wishes his teachings to be made known to all people, the authors, through this work, wish to repay the Holy Father in a small way by making his masterful preaching of the gospel better known and understood, especially as it relates to sexuality and family matters.

This volume is divided into two parts. The first part, in five chapters, is an analysis of John Paul II's new synthesis as applied to sexuality and family life. The first chapter briefly examines John Paul's revolutionary new synthesis of faith and reason. The next four chapters consider the human person as an individual, as a member of the *communion of persons* of the family, as a member of the *communion of persons* existing among all workers, and as a member of the mystical person of Christ, the Church. Sexuality and family life are discussed extensively in the second and third chapters. The second chapter considers the individual human person as an image of God called to love in and through the body. The third chapter examines the expression of love within the family. Clearly, these chapters are closely related and a few of the same topics are discussed in both. However, we have striven to limit the duplications. The second chapter will discuss those areas that pertain more to the individual, e.g., sterilization, and the third, those that pertain more to a couple, e.g., premarital sexual contact. But since the family in many modern societies has been devalued by a fundamental misunderstanding of the relationship of man and work, John Paul II's view of sexuality and family life is incomprehensible without an understanding of the Holy Father's considerations on work. The application of John Paul's new synthesis to work corrects the false understanding of work and situates it within the context of human and family values. Thus, it is only through a comprehension of the Holy Father's revolutionary view of work that the family can be restored to its proper position in society. Therefore, the chapter on work is essential to this study of John Paul's vision of family and family life. Finally, the Holy Father describes the family as the domestic church. As such, it cannot be understood without knowing who the Church is.

The second part of this volume applies the principles analyzed in the first part to a key document of John Paul II's pontificate, *Familiaris Consortio, The Role of the Christian Family in the Modern World*. The commentary on this document will serve to highlight a brilliantly written work, which has, for the most part, not received the attention it deserves.

Of course, the second part depends on the first. The same ideas and some of the same arguments are found in both parts. However, we have tried to avoid unnecessary repetition. Thus, in the second part, an idea might be sketched briefly in a few sentences because it has been extensively explained in the first part. Since we did not want to burden this work with numerous notes, we have not included citations to previous or subsequent discussions of a topic. However, the index should prove helpful in locating all the references to a particular topic. We have also avoided other notes except in the case of direct quotes. The references in the notes are abbreviated. The full titles of those works cited and abbreviated in the notes, together with their abbreviations, are listed following this preface. The Scripture quotes are taken from the Revised Standard Version (Catholic Edition).

One further note is important. The Holy Father is almost

exclusively addressing the normal situations. For example, he teaches that the body expresses the person as God gave it to us. This is true for all those born without handicaps. However, if a child is bodily handicapped from birth, his body does not adequately express his person. Not only *may* the medical profession do what it can to restore normal health, i.e., the normal bodily expression of the person, it *must* (provided the medical means employed are ordinary). The Holy Father does not address this case precisely, but, in his principle, he does not mean to exclude ordinary medical intervention to restore the health of handicapped infants. The Holy Father addresses normal situations. He expects us to apply his principles to the less than ordinary cases without doing violence to his basic system.

The authors owe a debt to many people, not the least of whom is Pope John Paul II. Others who have encouraged this work at various stages include Monsignor Richard J. Schuler, Reverend Leo Dolan, Mr. Alphonse J. Matt, Mr. Paul W. Le Voir, Dr. Richard H. Berquist, Dr. Thomas Sullivan, Dr. William May, Mr. John (Jack) G. Quesnell, Mr. and Mrs. Patrick Shannon, Mr. and Mrs. Donald Kramer, Mr. Douglas G. Bushman, Mrs. Mary Jo Smith, Mrs. Karlee Gardner, and Mr. John Gries. We are particularly grateful to the Most Reverend John R. Roach, Archbishop of Saint Paul and Minneapolis for writing the foreword, and to our pastors, Monsignor Stanley J. Srnec and the Reverend Francis R. Kittock for their encouragement. We wish also to express our gratitude to our families, who have helped us in many intangible ways while this work was prepared.

Further, we are grateful to the many people who allowed and even invited us to present to them the ideas found in this volume. This group would include the parishioners of both Saint Raphael and Saint Charles parishes in Minneapolis. In a special way, it includes the members of the Saint Raphael Inquiry classes of 1982, 1983, and 1984. We also want to thank Mr. John Hamlon and the Family Life Bureau of Saint Cloud.

This bureau has invited one or both of us to speak at various meetings and conventions. Similarly, we wish to thank Mr. and Mrs. Michael Marker of the Human Life Center at Saint John's University in Collegeville, Minn., for their invitations to speak. We have also experienced the hospitality of the Reverend Richard Villano and Mr. John Sondag of Saint Helena's parish in Minneapolis. We are grateful to Mr. Paul Sellors, who invited us to speak at De La Salle High School, and to the Reverend Patrick Ryan and Mrs. Nancy D'Heilly, who invited us to speak at their parish, Saint Rose of Lima, in Saint Paul. We will never be able to repay the kindnesses of these and many others who contributed to this volume. Lastly, we must end with a note of thanks to those who made this published work a reality. We wish to thank Mrs. Roberta Nathe and Mrs. Michaeline (Ondrey) Loomis, who typed portions of this volume. Without our editor, Patricia Kossmann, this work would never have appeared.

John Paul II is the answer to modern man's question, "To whom should I go for the truth?" If this book aids others to see the truth that the Pope is teaching, the authors' labors will not have been in vain.

Finally, let it be said that the authors of this volume submit *in all things* to the Holy Father. It is their intention to present *his* thought, not their own. With this hope, they place this book into your hands.

RICHARD M. HOGAN
JOHN M. LEVOIR

Preface to the Second Edition

The second edition of this volume is substantially the same as the first edition. Readers familiar with the book will notice that the "Introduction" to the first part has been expanded. Actually, this chapter now stands as it was originally written. During the editing process for the first edition, some materials were cut from the first chapter. These have been restored in this edition. Familiar readers will also recognize that an effort has been made to eliminate the awkward he/she language. In some cases, we have used the plural. In a few cases, where it is absolutely necessary for the sense, we have decided to say he or she. There were one or two references to the Soviet Union in the first edition. Where necessary, we have changed these to account for the different world we see today.

We both are firmly convinced that this book is as timely today as it was when it was first published. Pope John Paul II continues to teach the world his new synthesis of faith and reason. Even today, in the second decade of his pontificate, many, many people do not seem to grasp the extraordinary new way that John Paul II is using to present the Faith. This new synthesis of the Faith can be the means of renewing the Faith of all Christians and of bringing more people to Christ. If this second edition promotes that process, then it will have fulfilled its purpose.

RICHARD M. HOGAN
JOHN M. LEVOIR
November 8, 1991

15

Abbreviations

The following are works of John Paul II:

DM   *Dives in Misericordia, On the Mercy of God.* Boston: Saint Paul Editions, 1981.

FC   *Familiaris Consortio, Apostolic Exhortation, The Role of the Christian Family in the Modern World.* Boston: Daughters of Saint Paul, 1981.

LE   *Laborem Exercens, On Human Work. L'Osservatore Romano* (English Edition.) Vol. 14, no. 38, (September 21, 1981), pp. 1–13.

LR   *Love and Responsibility.* Translated by H. T. Willetts. New York: Farrar, Straus & Giroux, 1981.

RH   *Redemptor Hominis, The Redeemer of Man. L'Osservatore Romano.* (English Edition.) Vol. 12, no. 12 (March 19, 1979), pp. 3–14.

SC   *Sign of Contradiction.* Translated by Saint Paul Publications. New York: Seabury Press, 1979.

SR   *Sources of Renewal: The Implementation of Vatican II.* Translated by P. S. Falla. New York: Harper & Row, 1980.

TB   *Theology of the Body.* (A series of sixty-three addresses at the Wednesday papal audiences. These are cited in the notes by number, 1–63. The numbers are given in parentheses after the dates in the following list.)

All the addresses are found in *L'Osservatore Romano*. (English Edition.) Vol. 12, nos. 37–40, 42, 44–48, 51–53 [September 10 (1), 17 (2), 24 (3), October 1 (4), 15 (5), 29 (6), November 5 (7), 12 (8), 19 (9), 26 (10), December 17 (11), 24 (12), 1979.] Vol. 13, nos. 1–3, 5–8, 10–11, 13–14, 16–18, 20, 22–23, 25–26, 30–46, 49–50, 52. [January 7 (13), 14 (14), 21 (15), February 4 (16), 11 (17), 18 (18), 25 (19), March 10 (20), 17 (21), 31 (22), April 8 (23), 21 (24), 28 (25), May 5 (26), 19 (27), June 2 (28), 9 (29), 23 (30), 30 (31), July 28 (32), August 4 (33), 11 (34), 25 (35 and 36), September 1 (37), 8 (38), 15 (39), 22 (40), 29 (41), October 6 (42), 13 (43), 20 (44), 27 (45), November 3 (46), 10 (47), 17 (48), December 9 (49), 15 (50), 29 (51), 1980.] Vol. 14, nos. 2–3, 5–7, 12, 14–19. [January 12 (52), 19 (53), February 2 (54), 9 (55), 16 (56), March 23 (57), April 6 (58), 13 (59), 21 (60), 27 (61), May 4 (62), 11 (63), 1981.] These addresses can also be found in the two-volume series: *Original Unity of Man and Woman: Catechesis on the Book of Genesis* and *Blessed are the Pure of Heart: Catechesis on the Sermon on the Mount and Writings of Saint Paul*. Boston: Saint Paul Editions, 1981, 1983.

The following works of the Second Vatican Council are cited from *Documents of Vatican II*. Edited by Austin P. Flannery. Grand Rapids, Michigan: William B. Eerdmans Publishing, 1975:

GS   *Gaudium et Spes, Pastoral Constitution on the Church in the Modern World*. (December 7, 1965), pp. 903–1001.

LG   *Lumen Gentium, Dogmatic Constitution on the Church*. (November 21, 1964), pp. 350–432.

PART ONE

The Family in the Teachings of Pope John Paul II

INTRODUCTION

Pope John Paul II
A Man for Our Times

A. The Papal Elections (1978)

"*Annuntio vobis gaudium magnum: Habemus Papam!*" These historic words were spoken from a Vatican balcony in Rome by the then dean of the College of Cardinals, His Eminence, Pericle Cardinal Felici, at 6:43 P.M. on October 16, 1978. Through the miracle of modern satellite communication, the whole world watched and listened in anticipation as the cardinal appeared from behind the balcony doors. All was quiet as he gave voice to the conclave in the official and venerable language of the Roman Church: "I announce to you a great joy: we have a Pope, the Most Eminent and Most Reverend Lord, Cardinal of the Holy Roman Church, Karol Wojtyla, who has taken the name, John Paul II."

Profound mystery, inspiring nothing less than awe—even in the eyes of nonbelievers—surrounds the passing of the keys of Saint Peter to a new pope. The drama and ritual of this event include the funeral of the deceased pontiff, the conclave, and the election and installation of a new pope. But present in addition to all of this, is the awesome and even fearful hand of God. For, as Catholics believe, it *can not* be that God would abandon his Church at such a time. Quite the contrary is true. The exterior pomp and ceremony are merely the visible signs of the hidden and subtle workings of the Holy Spirit. What does not appear to the senses must be seen through the eyes of faith, and it is usually in retrospect only that these eyes can be focused enough to see how the invisible God has inspired visible results. What does such a retrospective view of the election of Karol Wojtyla disclose?

First, the papal elections of 1978 were somewhat unusual because most observers did not expect the two popes chosen after Paul VI to become the successors of Saint Peter. In past papal elections of this century, there have often been one or two cardinals who were the obvious candidates. Since speculation about an upcoming conclave had started long before Pope Paul VI had died in August 1978, the lack of two or three clear candidates is especially noteworthy. With the increasing age of Pope Paul, everyone knew that there would soon be a conclave, and many were preparing for it by publishing and discussing the biographies of the cardinals. From these biographical sketches and discussions there emerged a list, as there always does before a conclave, of the *papabili*, that is, the cardinals from whom most observers thought the next pope would be chosen. But in 1978, the list was extraordinarily long. Of course, no one at the time knew what the cardinals were actually thinking. Nevertheless, the *papabili* lists in the past had been reasonably accurate.

Immediately after the death of Pope Paul VI, and continuing until the election of Pope John Paul I, the mass media made the varying *papabili* lists known. Everyone was confident that the new pope would be chosen from among those on these lists because they were *so long*. The observers could not be completely wrong, or so thought most people.

Imagine then the frustration of the observers and the newscasters when, in August 1978, the cardinals elected the Patriarch of Venice, Albino Cardinal Luciani, a man almost unknown, and, of course, not on anyone's *papabili* list. The television newscasters in New York covering the papal election had to apologize to their viewers for not having a dossier on the new Pope immediately available. After all, they had thought that one of the *papabili* would be chosen. Dare it be suggested that the Holy Spirit was clearly letting everyone know that a papal election was his business, and that he was not limited to prepared lists of *papabili*?

After the untimely death of Pope John Paul I, the second papal election of 1978 took place. An identical situation arose. Again, the same lists as before appeared, with amateur political guesses as to what had "gone wrong" in the previous conclave. A general consensus seemed to be that the smiling Pope John Paul I was a compromise candidate. Now, of course, the pundits seemed sure that the cardinals would choose someone from the *papabili* lists. Still, they were more cautious than before.

Remembering their previous embarrassment, at least some of the television news organizations added dossiers on cardinals who were not on the previous *papabili* lists. One newscaster proudly announced that he and his staff could not be caught off-guard this time because they had prepared dossiers on *all* the *Italian* cardinals. Furthermore, they still had on file the dossiers of the *papabili* cardinals who were not Italian.

Imagine then, this news staff's frustration when Cardinal Felici made his historic and striking announcement of the election of Wojtyla. They were in the same situation as before. They did not know at first where this new Pope had been bishop. They had to ask their viewers to be patient until they could assemble some information on this obscure Polish cardinal.

Of course, one cannot blame them. By any normal human assessment, the election of Karol Wojtyla had to be regarded as a very poor bet. But the transfer of the keys of Saint Peter is not merely a human affair. The Holy Spirit guides the cardinals in their choice, and in this particular instance—as with John Paul I—the hand of the Holy Spirit seems quite apparent.

Second, the events of August and October 1978, were striking because of the new double name that each of the new popes took. For John Paul I, this was either an attempt to ward off a comparison between his pontificate and those of his predecessors, John XXIII and Paul VI, or it was a unique way of showing his continuity with these two popes of Vatican II. In either case, it was nothing short of revolutionary. It was comparable to the move in the late tenth century when the popes first began to take new names when they were elected to the chair of Saint Peter.

One television commentator noted the significance of the new double name when he spoke of the "John Paul Revolution" on a newscast after the election of Karol Wojtyla. Perhaps some would argue that this was an exaggeration, but in fact it was not. The incredible force of ritual and tradition in papal elections, even in the post-Vatican II Church, must be remembered when addressing this development. It was indeed a departure from previous practice, and it will probably change the names that the popes take in the future. Thus, it qualifies as a revolution.

Third, the most striking and unusual feature about the events leading to the election of Pope John Paul II was that his was the second election in a single year; 1978 was the year of three popes. Not since 1605, with the election and death of Pope Leo XI, had there been three popes in one year. For some reason known to God alone, it was divinely ordained that Karol Wojtyla should succeed not Paul VI, but John Paul I.

The world reacted to the death of the smiling Pope John Paul I with shock and disbelief. In America, the news came in the middle of the night and many were wakened by friends calling early in the morning. Still others heard about the Pope's passing on the morning radio or television newscasts. More than a few initially thought that this was old news. Since the Pope had died almost two months previous, why were their friends disturbing them in the middle of the night with such old stories? Why were the newscasters so excited about what everyone already knew? In short, the world could not comprehend the death of the sixty-five year-old Holy Father less than a month after he had been elected. The news was simply extraordinary! (In Germany, the initial reaction was that the Pope had been poisoned by the Italians!) Why God called John Paul I to his eternal reward is not for us to know, but it is clear that such an event is evidence of God's activity in his Church.

In addition to the extraordinary events already mentioned—the election of two unexpected candidates as pope; the choice of a double name by both popes; and two papal elections in one year—there was the choice of a non-Italian as the Vicar of Christ. Not since the pontificate of Adrian VI (1522–1523), who was a Dutchman, had a non-Italian been elected to the chair of Saint Peter. Of course, after the Second Vatican Council, many had expected that a non-Italian would be elected pope, if only to demonstrate the international character of the papacy. Some thought that this would happen after the death of Pope Paul VI. Others thought it would occur only after his successor's pontificate. Of course, the latter were correct, but they never foresaw the short reign of Pope John Paul I. Astonishingly, however, Wojtyla was not only *not* Italian, he was Polish. This fact in itself is significant and deserves an in-depth look.

Never has there been a Polish pope! Few, if any, ever expected the first non-Italian pope in four centuries to be Polish. Some speculation (rather far fetched and irresponsible, or so it was thought), stimulated partly by the famous movie, *The Shoes of the Fisherman*, held out the possibility that a man from the Eastern-bloc nations would be elected pope. But even the most outlandish of these opinions never considered a Polish cardinal as a possible successor to Saint Peter.

Furthermore, such an election of an Eastern-bloc cardinal was envisioned as ending the difficulties between the Church and the communist governments. Instead, we have Wojtyla who, it seems, has completely opposed the Polish communist government with some success. Far from a rapprochement, his election was clearly the beginning of a new phase in the struggle between the Church and the communist governments, especially in Poland.

There is no doubt today that Karol Wojtyla, as Pope, is the

spiritual father of the solidarity union movement in Poland. The very name, solidarity, reflects one of the major components in John Paul II's new synthesis of philosophy and the gospel, the *communion of persons*.[1] However, what many do not realize is that the term, solidarity, was used as a leftist-Marxist slogan in 1973–1974, especially with regard to the difficulties in Chile in those years. The communists of the world were to rally in solidarity with their comrades suffering in Chile. Now, an anti-Marxist Polish union, inspired by the Pope, is using the same word to signify opposition to the Marxists.

The communist governments of the East face a man wielding enormous influence extending far beyond the borders of their nations. They face a man who knows their mode of operating intimately and who uses their own ideas against them. Never could such a forceful and effective Polish anti-communist Holy Father have been predicted in 1978. In such there is clearly the hand of God.

It was probably because of our Holy Father's anticommunist stance that a tragedy, unknown for centuries in the history of the papacy, occurred. On May 13, 1981, less than three years after his election, an assassin's bullet struck the Pontiff while he was greeting the people assembled in Saint Peter's square for his weekly Wednesday audience. Was the assassin part of an elaborate plot to kill the Pope? Was there a conspiracy having ties with the communist governments? These are certainly possibilities. At any rate, it appears that the attempted assassination was done by professionals and that *it should have succeeded*! As it was, the Pope was rushed from the square, slumped over in the rebuilt jeep that he uses for transportation around the crowded square on Wednesdays. If it was surprising that the professional assassin did not succeed in killing him instantly, it was equally surprising that he did not succumb to his wounds. For it now seems clear that these wounds were much more serious than originally reported in those long hours immediately after the

---

[1] See below, "The Family and Sexuality", pp. 71–102.

shooting. As our Holy Father himself has acknowledged, he was saved through the intervention of God and the Blessed Mother.

Besides these extraordinary occurrences, one must take account of the tremendous mobility and popularity of Pope John Paul II. It seems that the world knew, from the very first month of the new pontificate, that the face of the papacy would be changed by this man from behind the Iron Curtain. In the person of Karol Wojtyla, a fresh breeze off the Carpathian mountains had blown into Rome. He was elected on October 16, 1978, and by the end of the following January he was in Puebla, Mexico, with plans already formulated for a visit to Poland the following May. Literally millions from around the world have seen this Vicar of Christ on his visits to the British Isles, the United States, South America, the Philippines, Japan, Australia, Africa, Germany, France, Spain, and his many visits within Italy. Countless other millions have watched him on television. No other pope has traveled so much or as widely. Never has a pope been as well known or as famous as John Paul II. But the people of the world not only know him, they love him. There are numerous manifestations of the affection with which the people of the world regard the Pope: the recording "Vatican Rock", which appeared shortly after his election; the cry "J. P. II, we love you" heard in the English speaking world; the chanting of Polish hymns to honor the Pope; and the comic book published about his life. The papal trips, together with the response of the people, could never have been predicted or foreseen. They are, by any human standard, absolutely extraordinary.

Of course, not every Holy Father could have made such a success of these travels. It is part of the genius of Karol Wojtyla that he is able to use this method of bringing the message of Christ to the world. As the Holy Father constantly repeats, the purpose of everything that he does is to make Christ better known and better loved. The initial words of his first encyclical manifest the same attitude. "The Redeemer of man,

Jesus Christ, is the center of the universe and of history."[2] There is nothing new in this statement or in the desire of a pope to make Christ better known. Every pope has believed this and every pope has tried to spread the gospel of Jesus Christ. Still, most realize that the message of this Holy Father has a different emphasis from that of his recent predecessors. Even such little gestures as kissing the ground in all of the countries that he visits betray this different emphasis. It seems that John Paul's way of teaching the gospel, and (this is crucial) his absolute fidelity to it in his own life and in his activities as Vicar of Christ, are what account for his widespread popularity. In short, we see in him—in what he does and teaches—the reflection of Christ. Just as the gospel attracted people at the time of Christ, in the early Church, and in every succeeding age, so it is attracting people now. Absolute fidelity to the gospel, coupled with a teaching of that gospel message in a manner suited to our age, is the gift that John Paul is giving to the world. Thus, John Paul II's success in his travels rests on his new presentation of the gospel to today's people, and on his own witness to that gospel in his life.

Now and then one reads that it is John Paul's personality which is winning the people of the world over to him. But it is impossible to divorce the personality of the Holy Father from his deeds. A person is manifested by his acts.[3] When we speak of a personality, we are referring to the acts that we see. John Paul's acts and deeds, each and every one of them, are informed by his unwavering faithfulness to the truth of Christ. To speak of a winning personality as the reason for the outpouring of love and devotion given to this Pope, wherever he goes in the world, minimizes and cheapens what is a profound message expressed in both the words and deeds of John Paul II.

The world is literally starved for Christ. People see Christ in everything that John Paul does. Therefore, they respond. Any

[2] See RH, no. 1.
[3] See below, "The Theology of the Body", pp. 39–70.

other explanation of his popularity is a denial of the effect of the Christian message. Of course, it is in the interest of our secular age to attribute the Pope's success to anything but the gospel. The gospel has been denied, both in and out of the Church, and therefore no success can be attributed to it! But, in effect, there is no other reasonable or possible explanation for the popularity of the Holy Father. Even those who speak of the Pope's personality also admit that they cannot understand how he can, for example, demand chastity before and during marriage, and still be popular with people in an age that has rejected chastity as something belonging to the Puritans. The reason is that he is simply preaching the true message of Jesus Christ, adapted to our age, for which the world is thirsting.

B. Wojtyla and the Council

The response to the teaching of this Holy Father is exactly what Pope John XXIII had hoped the teaching of the Second Vatican Council would receive. The purpose of that gathering of the world's bishops was to present the gospel message to the modern age, and it did just that. John Paul II is a faithful son of that Council; thus everything that he does, writes, or speaks springs from it. In other words, he is teaching what the Council taught. The only reason the conciliar teaching appears new is that in the nearly twenty years since the end of the Council, its fundamental and vital message has been ignored or obscured. The Council was not primarily about superficial structures in the Church, e.g., parish councils, priests' senates, and national episcopal conferences. This was not the vision of John XXIII, nor was it the vision of the Holy Spirit as expressed through the bishops in the documents drafted by the Council. The Council was concerned with enriching the faith of the Church by formulating the gospel message of Christ for the modern age. "The council does not merely outline an external plan for the renewal of the Church, based on new structures that correspond more completely to the present-day demands of communal sociology; it also outlines a real plan for the enrichment of faith."[4]

The Second Vatican Council was not only pastoral, it was also a doctrinal council (despite all the protestations to the contrary). "The doctrine of faith and morals (*doctrina fidei et morum*) is the content of the teaching of the pastors of the Church, so that on the one hand doctrinal acts of the magisterium have a pastoral sense, while on the other pastoral acts have a doctrinal significance, deeply rooted as they are in faith and morals."[5] In concentrating on the Council's superficialities, some have failed to see that it did accomplish a new presentation of the Faith vital to modern man. Now John Paul II is teaching us what the council was all about.

Karol Wojtyla is the first pope who as a bishop participated in all of the conciliar sessions (with the exception of course of John Paul I, who did not have a chance to share his vision with the world in any depth). Although Pope Paul VI participated in the Council, first as a bishop, and then as the Pope, the participation of a pope in an ecumenical council is radically different from the participation of a bishop in a council! Furthermore, Karol Wojtyla had an important role in drafting the constitutions on the Church: *Gaudium et Spes*, the *Pastoral Constitution on the Church in the Modern World*, and *Lumen Gentium*, the *Dogmatic Constitution on the Church*.[6] Who is better qualified to explain to us the documents of the Council than one of its major participants who played a crucial role in formulating its statements?

As early as 1972, when he published *Sources of Renewal* in Polish, the Cardinal Archbishop of Cracow told the Polish people that many had missed the point of the council. He logically pointed out that a man must know what to implement

---

[4] See SR, p. 218.
[5] Ibid., p. 17.
[6] Ibid., p. iv, and also SC, p. x.

before he can begin to implement it. He patiently explained what the teaching of the Council was. Now, as Pope, he is bringing that same message to the entire world. Of course, in doing so he is guided by the same Holy Spirit who inspired him and his brother bishops when they drafted the conciliar documents. One can only say, "Thank God for this Pope!" Thank God that we will finally have the riches that Pope John XXIII foresaw and wanted!

As was stated above, Karol Wojtyla was an active participant in the Council who, under the inspiration of the Holy Spirit, significantly influenced the conciliar teaching. In fact, through Wojtyla and the other Polish bishops, a new Christian synthesis of the Faith and reason (developed in Poland at the University of Lublin/Cracow) was received into the conciliar documents. This synthesis was practically unknown in the mainstream of Western philosophical and theological thought before Pope John Paul II's election. Therefore, it is difficult for many who are not trained in this new synthesis to understand fully the conciliar documents—documents which are imbued with it. Nevertheless, the writings of this Lublin/Cracow school form a necessary background to many of the major conciliar documents. It is as though the Holy Spirit wished to catapult this Christian school of thought into world prominence through John Paul II, so that the new Christian synthesis developed in Poland and expressed in the writings of the council might become the property of the entire world. For it is in light of this school of thought that the conciliar teaching becomes clear, and that the vision of Pope John XXIII for a re-presentation of the gospel in tune with the modern age becomes a reality.

Still, one might question why the Holy Spirit did not do this sooner. Why wait for almost twenty years? The answer might be that the Lublin/Cracow school not only influenced the Council, but the Council influenced it. There had to be a period of time while the new Christian synthesis in Poland digested and made its own the teaching of the Council. For it is too much to claim that the Council simply reproduced the teaching of the Lublin/Cracow school—far from it. There was a genuine development stimulated by the Council in the Lublin/Cracow Christian synthesis (especially in the teachings and writings of Karol Wojtyla, as is clear from a comparison between his earlier and later works). However, that does not change the fact that large segments of the conciliar documents are nearly impossible to understand without a knowledge of the activity of the philosophers and theologians at the University of Cracow.

C. A New Presentation of the Gospel

The leading representative of the Lublin/Cracow school is none other than Karol Wojtyla. He was eminently suited to wed the teachings of Saint Thomas Aquinas with modern phenomenology, because of his background in Thomistic theology and philosophy, and because of his knowledge of the Lublin phenomenological realist philosophers, especially Roman Ingarden. The result of his work and the work of the Lublin/Cracow school is a new synthesis which speaks to modern man. This new synthesis is found already in a highly developed form in Wojtyla's book, *Love and Responsibility* (1960). As was mentioned previously, it is found in the conciliar documents. The philosophical underpinnings of this system of thought are disclosed in Wojtyla's magnificent work, *The Acting Person* (1970). Furthermore, his *Sources of Renewal* (1972) applies the phenomenological conclusions of the Lublin/Cracow school to a difficult topic of the Faith, namely, the Church—the same topic to which the Council devoted so much attention. Finally, and more importantly, this synthesis is present in everything that Karol Wojtyla has written as Pope.

It is, then, absolutely crucial to understand this new Christian synthesis of faith and reason. At the heart of this new synthesis is the concept of personhood. Of course, Christianity has employed this concept since Tertullian. In fact, Christianity, confronted with the mysteries of the Trinity and the

Incarnation, developed the category of the person as a tool for understanding, as far as possible, the Holy Trinity and the God-man, Jesus Christ. Thus, it is hardly startling that the Holy Father should emphasize personhood. It is at the center of our Christian heritage.

It is precisely because the person is vital to revealed truth that there can be a synthesis of phenomenology and the Faith. Phenomenology begins its investigation with the individual human person. It begins with our conscious experience of ourselves as acting agents. Of course, this subjective, individualistic approach is not without its perils. Often, the result is the annihilation of all objective truth or criteria. The only valid "truth" is my own experience which (I claim or could claim) is absolutely unique. Such rampant subjectivism could never be reconciled with the Faith.

The problem for Wojtyla and the Lublin/Cracow school was to employ the essential discoveries of phenomenology in the service of the Faith without sacrificing the objectivity of ethical norms and the teaching of the gospel. The difficulty was resolved through the text in Genesis: "Let us make man in our image."[7] Man is a person (has an awareness of his own acts, one of the most important marks of personhood) because he is like God, made in God's own image. This is an objective truth which is at the same time central to man's experience. Every human being knows that he is different from the animals and the plants. This is at the heart of his subjective experience. The reason why he is different is revealed in the objective order, but it explains the subjective experience of every human being. At one and the same time, the truth that man is created in the image of God is both objective and subjective. It saves the subjective insight of the phenomenologists without losing the objectivity of the gospel. For, if a man is in God's image, then his only hope, if he is to be true to his very self, is to function as God does! The revelation of God, especially the revelation

[7] See Gen 1:26.

shown to man by the Incarnation, thus becomes crucial if man is to be true to his own self.

This subjective turn has immense consequences and is fundamental to the new Lublin/Cracow synthesis. Most importantly, as is clear in the teachings of John Paul, there is a renewed, almost vehement, insistence on the dignity of each and every human person. The dignity we possess is inherent in us because, first of all, we are created in God's own image. This dignity is not granted to us by some law of a higher authority, even of the highest authority. It pertains to us by creation. It is a personal, subjective attribute proper to each and every human being.

Second, this dignity, as full of wonder as it is, was enhanced even further when God the Son took to himself our human nature. "For by his incarnation, he, the Son of God, has in a certain way united himself with each man."[8] Thus, the infinite dignity which is ours by the Incarnation is also subjective, i.e., it pertains to the individual subject. The union is not external, but within the human heart. As with our creation, the dignity which finds its source in our redemption is not conferred on us from the outside, but is part of who we are.

There could hardly be a message more important for the twentieth century to hear. Our century has seen millions of men and women killed in war and in concentration camps; millions of homeless and abandoned refugees driven from their lands; countless millions of unborn children killed in their mothers' wombs; women, children, and even men treated as sex objects for the use of others; and workers treated worse than machines —their lives being measured by their usefulness.

In addition to the new emphasis on man's inherent dignity, the subjective turn of the new synthesis provides a better understanding of the relationship between the creation and the redemption. We are created in God's own likeness. However, original sin made it impossible for us to live and act as God in-

[8] See GS, no. 22.

tended. We could no longer function as human beings because we could no longer fulfill the role for which God had created us. We need Christ, the God-man, to show us what it means to be in God's image and to make it possible for us again to live as images of God. Christ "fully reveals man to himself" because he shows us who God is and thus shows us who we are.[9] The redemption is therefore essential to each and every human being because without Christ and the grace he won for us, it is impossible to live even as human beings, as creatures made in God's image. Christ restores creation and is therefore "the center of the universe and of history".[10]

A corollary to this view of the creation and the redemption is that grace was given to Adam (man) in God's creative act, and thus pertained to him "from the beginning". Lost by original sin, God's grace is crucial if man is to live as God intended, i.e., in his image. Thus, after original sin, living without grace, man is not living in a natural state, if by natural we mean what God intended through creation. Rather, man is now less than natural. Christ restores grace to man and thus restores man. It is clearly impossible then to disassociate grace and nature in historical man, i.e., it is impossible for fallen man to be fully human without grace. Further, it is even clear that there is no such thing as a two-story universe as some would have it. Rather God created man with grace and intended that he possess it in this life as the seed of glory. Man's sin caused him to lose it, but the state of man after sin is hardly natural. The only natural state is that willed by God in his creative act. Saint Thomas Aquinas taught that "the soul is naturally capable of grace because it is made in the image of God."[11] Thus, the Pope's subjective turn recovers an important insight found already in Saint Thomas.

The third result of the new synthesis is a new unity between

---

[9] Ibid.

[10] See RH, no. 1.

[11] See *Summa Theologiae*, I IIae, Q. 113, art. 10. The text reads: "naturaliter anima est gratiae capax: eo enim ipso quod facta est ad imaginem Dei, capax est Dei per gratiam, ut Augustinus dicit."

philosophy and the Faith. This new unity is at the same time a new theology. Theology is the study of God, but, since man is made in God's image, the study of God is also the study of man. Of course, the opposite is also true. The proper study of man, one which acknowledges the full truth about man, is also the study of God because man is made in God's image. Therefore, in the Holy Father's thought, there can be found two fundamental progressions: one beginning with man and moving to God, and the other beginning with God and moving to man. Obviously, Christology, the study of the God-man, is at the center of both these movements.

Even if Cardinal Wojtyla had never been chosen for the papal office, his work would have represented a new and original milestone in man's reflections on himself and on the gospel. Wojtyla has linked the "insights of modern phenomenology (especially Schelerian) philosophy to discoveries of the Aristotelian-Thomistic and Augustinian tradition of philosophy".[12] His philosophical insights, when applied to the truths of the Faith, produce a new theological synthesis founded on a new and revealing subjective turn. The unifying element in this synthesis is the individual subject—the human person—created by God in his own image and redeemed by the God-man. Can it not be suggested that such a synthesis is comparable to the previous syntheses of Saint Augustine and Saint Thomas?

But the chief representative of this new synthesis is now the Pope! We have an eminent theologian as Pope. What he has written and will write as the Vicar of Christ has a much greater authority because of his position than what he wrote as a cardinal or as a bishop. What force do theological arguments in papal documents have? Many previous popes did not make new or startling theological arguments in their writings. This Holy Father does, and he is qualified academically for this task. He is also guided by the Holy Spirit in this work. The theological

---

[12] See Josef Seifert, "Karol Cardinal Wojtyla (Pope John Paul II) as Philosopher and the Cracow/Lublin School of Philosophy", *Aletheia*, vol. 2, (1981), p. 132.

arguments found in his papal writings are representative of the new synthesis. They certainly cannot be ignored as the Lublin/Cracow school has been ignored in the past. They are clearly willed by God. Why else would a Polish theologian have been elected Pope? How else can one explain the other extraordinary events surrounding the recent papal elections and the early pontificate of Pope John Paul II? How else can one explain the global, positive response which our Holy Father has enjoyed when he has traveled around the world and taught the "hard sayings" of the gospel?

The Pope is teaching us the gospel, the message of Christ, clothed in a garb we can understand. Our age desperately needs a voice—the voice of Christ—which will persuade the world that the God-man is important to them individually, that religion (theology) should have a part in their lives, and, most of all, that each and every human person is endowed with an incomparable dignity. We have this voice in John Paul II. Will we listen?

Since the teaching of Pope John Paul II does not (and according to the Catholic Faith could not) contradict previous authoritative pronouncements of the Magisterium, some wish to dismiss him as a conservative. Others, noting an emphasis on the issues of war and a proper distribution of the world's goods, want to label him a liberal. However, his preaching is centered on Christ and on a new presentation of the gospel which appeals to the men and women of our age. Thus, it is the truth, which is neither liberal nor conservative. Those who wish to categorize him and his teaching into either of these groups simply have failed to see the significance of his new synthesis. In effect, they deny the new interpretation by insisting that it fit into categories established in the 1960s or earlier. His view of Christ and the gospel is new and, in a sense, revolutionary.

John Paul II was elected to the chair of Saint Peter to teach the world what the Second Vatican Council really intended. He is eminently qualified for this task because he was an active participant in the Council and its preparations. He had an important hand in the formulation of some of its most crucial documents.

Cardinal Wojtyla was also elected to teach the world a new synthesis of the gospel and modern philosophy—a synthesis grounded in the Christian tradition represented by Saint Augustine and Saint Thomas Aquinas. This synthesis was developed in Poland and shaped some of the conciliar documents and in turn was shaped by them.

The extraordinary events before and during the pontificate of John Paul II point to the significance of the age in which we live. The new adaptation and presentation of the gospel is nothing less than the beginning of a new era for the Church. Just as Saint Augustine and Saint Thomas ushered in new eras, so is John Paul. As such, his teaching represents the fulfillment of what Pope John XXIII envisioned for the Church when he called the Council. Let us apply this teaching to the vital area of family life! However, we must begin with an analysis of the individual human person as an image of God.

The Theology of the Body

A. The Human Person as an Image of God

All human beings have an interior, subjective need to reflect God because when God created us he said: "Let us make man in our image."[1] This insight, i.e., this subjective turn, is the pivot on which John Paul II's new presentation of the Faith turns. To understand John Paul and, therefore, to understand the Council, it is necessary to comprehend our existence and proper activity as the only earthly creatures that are called to reflect the Creator. An examination of the individual human being in his interior (mind, will, consciousness) and his exterior (body) structures will establish the necessary foundation for the subsequent investigations of the "places" where he loves as God loves, i.e., in the family and in the workplace.

We mirror God primarily as persons, as beings endowed with intellects and free wills. Just as God has an intellect, so does his image, the human person. (There is, of course, an infinite difference between what God knows with his intellect and what we know with ours.) Secondly, God wills and therefore human beings, made in his image and likeness, also will. Free will and intellect constitute the human person as an image of God.

Thus, the human person, as an image of God, is a thinking and a choosing being whose very thoughts and whose very choices are integral functions of his spiritual inner self. Mind and will make a human person his own master in a way similar to God, who is his own master *par excellence*. No other person

[1] See Gen 1:26.

39

can think for an individual and no one else can choose for him. In this sense, human persons, as the divine Persons, are incommunicable—they are *sui generis*.

There is no doubt that God is a conscious being. In other words, God has a consciousness or an awareness of himself. God's consciousness is a kind of inner image which he has of his acts of knowing and willing. The human person, as an image of a conscious God, is a conscious being too. The consciousness of an individual human being mirrors or images every conscious act which he does. Further, every deliberate act of a person is present in his consciousness. Thus, as human persons, we become what we do. We determine ourselves through our consciousness.

Our consciousness not only allows us to determine ourselves, it also is the source of our self-knowledge. God knows himself as a Trinity through his awareness of his own acts of knowing and loving. Similarly, we know ourselves through our awareness of our own acts.

For example, in writing a letter to a friend, a person has a consciousness of his act of writing. In other words, he has a consciousness of his act of knowing the contents of the letter and a consciousness of his act of choosing to write the letter. The author has determined himself as a writer. Even after his letter is finished and mailed, his consciousness "contains" or remembers all that he consciously did in writing the letter. The author's consciousness also remembers that he was the one who wrote the letter. This latter function of consciousness is the source of self-knowledge. In this case, the author comes to know himself as one who writes.

However, a human person is not just a spiritual being. A human being has a body. Therefore, the interior acts of knowing and willing, powers of a person's soul, should find expression in and through the body. Further, a human person's consciousness will mirror or reflect everything he does within himself (interior conscious acts: knowing and willing) and the expression of his interior acts through the body.

In addition to consciousness, the concepts of efficacy, freedom, transcendence, and truth are vital in the theology of John Paul. As creatures made in God's own likeness, we are capable of experiencing moments of efficacy. John Paul distinguishes efficacious acts from those occurrences which merely happen in us, e.g., the beating of one's heart as opposed to the choice to marry. Efficacious acts are freely chosen ones. When a person acts through his own choice, he is acting efficaciously. Freedom, then, is essential to us if we are to be the cause of our own acts as God is the origin of his acts. We should, as images of God, experience efficacious moments.

Transcendence, the exceeding of a certain boundary, applies, for the human person, to both the intellect and the will. Our intellects are made to reflect God's intellect. Since God knows truth, we should come to know the truth. When we increase our knowledge of the truth, we reach beyond ourselves and reflect God more perfectly. We cross the boundary of our former knowledge. We transcend ourselves. John Paul calls this horizontal transcendence.

As images of God, human persons should choose to act as God acts. By making such a choice, we are stepping beyond the boundary of our natural physical processes. By deciding to act in this way, we are willing an action which our physical nature would never do on its own account in and of itself. In this way, a person transcends or rises above his nature. Thus, he decides not to be bound by the merely natural and instinctual as animals are. John Paul calls this vertical transcendence.

It is quite clear that truth is absolutely essential to horizontal transcendence, but it is also vital to vertical transcendence. Vertical transcendence occurs when a person acts the way God acts. God acts only in conformity with the truth. Therefore, a person does not experience vertical transcendence (does not act as God acts) without the truth.

A human person is an image of God because he possesses a mind and a will. Through the awareness (consciousness) of his freely chosen (efficacious) acts of knowing and willing, a human person knows himself and determines himself. Transcendence is the effect of our acquiring the truth, i.e., the way things are in reality (God and the created world), and our choices made in accordance with the truth. These interior spiritual realities reflect God and when they are expressed through the body, it becomes a physical image of God in the world.

B. Adam and Eve: The Body and Three Original Human Experiences

From September 5, 1979, to May 6, 1981, Pope John Paul gave a series of sixty-three Wednesday audiences entitled the *Theology of the Body*. It was in these audiences that the Holy Father set forth some of his essential teachings on the human person, the body, and Christian marriage.

At the time when John Paul began this series of talks, he stressed that he was beginning "the work of preparation for the synod [of bishops, which met in the fall of 1980 in Rome and studied the family] from afar". He took as his starting point the response of Christ to a question raised by the Pharisees: "Have you not read that he who made them from the beginning made them male and female, and said, 'For this reason a man shall leave his father and mother and be joined to his wife, and the two shall become one flesh'? So they are no longer two but one flesh. What therefore God has joined together let no man put asunder."[2] Reflecting on these words of the Divine Master, Pope John Paul II noticed that Christ referred to "the beginning". "The beginning" is recorded in Genesis and in fact, in his response, Christ quoted Genesis.[3] The Holy Father, therefore, turned to Genesis and the experiences of Adam and Eve in the Garden of Eden. With amazing insights into the original human experiences, original sin, lust, and grace, Wojtyla revealed much to us about ourselves.

[2] See Mt 19:3–6.
[3] See Gen 2:24.

The Pope argues that the Scriptures and especially the text in the second and third chapters of Genesis speak of "original human experiences", which "are always at the root of every human experience".[4] The Pope's insight seems to be that the Scriptures explain and describe original human experiences, which, upon reflection, everyone realizes that he has had.

In defense of this amazing view of the Scriptures, the Pope reminds us that we are made in God's own image. We do not know who we are unless we know who God is. It is only in understanding who God is that we are able to understand who we are as reflections of God.

The Old Testament was a preparation for the coming of Christ. In the words of the Old Testament, the Holy Spirit inspired the human authors to reveal more and more about God. This revelation was a preparation for the fullness of revelation which was to come in and through Christ. Still, in revealing God, the Old Testament reveals man to himself. Therefore, the Scriptures have a totally universal application to every man and woman and even to non-Christians and non-Jews. The Pope has described the means to teach the Scriptures to everyone.

In the Garden of Eden, there were three "original human experiences": solitude, original unity, and nakedness. Solitude was the result of Adam's realization that he was unique among all the creatures of God's Kingdom. In other words, Adam experienced solitude, the first original human experience, because he discovered that only his body among all the bodies in the universe expressed a person.

In the second chapter of Genesis, the second account of creation, God created Adam first. God asked Adam to name all the animals. Adam gave the beings of God's creation names, but, in doing so, he realized that no other body was informed with a human soul. Adam discovered that no other bodied being was a person. No other body was like his. During this naming

---

[4] See TB, no. 11.

"man becomes aware of his own superiority, that is, that he cannot be considered on the same footing as any other species of living beings on earth".[5]

As part of the gift of life, the body (Adam's body and our bodies) participates in the dignity we have as beings made in the image of God. The human body is the only body in the world which manifests in the physical world how a person acts. We, as human beings, are unique in all of God's creation because we are persons with bodies. Of all the persons in the universe (the three divine Persons, the angels, and human beings), only the human person has a body. (Of course, our Lord Jesus Christ possesses a body, but that is because he assumed a human nature and became man. He has a body because he is a man, not because he is God.) Of all living bodied beings in the world (the plants, the animals, and human beings) only the human body is united to a person. Therefore, only the human body expresses a person. The human body then is a sign or a sacrament of the person. We are called to act as God acts. When we act as God acts and manifest those acts in and through our bodies, the body is not only a sacrament of our own persons, but is also a physical image of God, an outward sign of how God acts. We are not just images of God in our interior structure, in the powers of thinking and choosing, but also physically in the body.

The human body expresses the human person as God gave it to us. The Creator decided how our bodies should express our persons. Any substantial alteration of the body, except for the sake of health or, in certain cases, to correct a quirk of nature, e.g., cosmetic surgery, is to attempt to improve on God's handiwork. In effect, to alter the body (except for the instances noted) is tantamount to telling God that his work is not good enough. Further, since the body is part of the gift of life, an unauthorized alteration is an attack on life itself, our life. For example, it is not permissible to amputate a healthy,

[5] Ibid., no. 5.

functioning arm. The arm is part of the body, part of the gift of life. It contributes in its own way to the body's expression of the human person.

Just after he was created, Adam experienced an agonizing loneliness because he discovered that he could not fulfill himself as God intended. Adam was created in the image of God to do what God does, i.e., love. He longed to love. But since Adam was composed of body and soul, he needed to express love for someone (another human person) in and through his body. However, when Adam was first created (in the second account of creation in Genesis), he was the only human being. He had no one like himself to love. He could not truly love the animals because love is a mutual self-donation of at least two persons to one another. It was the discovery that only he was a person called to love in and through a physical body which led directly to his loneliness. As God knew "from the beginning", it is not good for man to be alone. But Adam had to experience solitude, i.e., he had to discover the mystery of his enfleshed personhood, his unique call to imitate God in love expressed through the body, before he could realize his need for other human persons. Only then, when Adam felt the need, would he treasure the gift of another human being.

It would seem that most of us have experienced loneliness at one time or another. However, the usual loneliness we experience is not comparable to the profound solitude which Adam felt. It seems though that each of us does experience something akin to the solitude of Adam. At one time, we were all children. A child longs to love, to imitate God through a total self-donation to others. As children, we had not yet learned how to love. Of course, we were not alone as Adam was. We had our parents, our brothers and sisters, grandparents, uncles and aunts, friends, and teachers. Still, we were alone because we could not love in the true sense. The result was a profound loneliness, which, often, we only realize existed when we, as adults, reflect on our childhood.

Children desire to love and they cannot. Love is a mutual self-donation of at least two persons to one another. Each possesses the other through the other's self-gift. Often children try to satisfy their longing to love by possessing things. The almost universal phenomenon of a child clinging to a favorite blanket, doll, teddy bear, or some other object he claims as belonging exclusively to him testifies to the child's need to love. Unable to love in the true sense, the child substitutes the possession of an object in the (unconscious) hope that this will alleviate the loneliness. Of course, the ownership of an object never quite satisfies the child's longing for a true loving relationship. Other children solve their need by fabricating mythical friends who are their constant companions. They know these "friends" intimately because they have created them from their own experiences. They can possess these "friends" completely. Of course, this is also a poor counterfeit for true love. Both these recurring phenomena point to the loneliness of childhood, to the solitude which Adam felt and children feel. Still, it must be emphasized that this loneliness is only clearly understood from the vantage point of the adult. The child does feel a certain loneliness, but he does not understand it and could not identify it. It is only as adults that we can fully appreciate the tribulations of childhood.

"So the Lord God caused a deep sleep to fall upon the man and while he slept, took one of his ribs and closed up its place with flesh; and the rib which the Lord God had taken from the man he made into a woman."[6] We can hardly imagine the joy Adam must have experienced when he finally saw Eve. Genesis records the event with the simple statement, "This at last is bone of my bones and flesh of my flesh."[7] The joy of that first man at the sight of Eve was total, both spiritual and physical. If human beings are made in the image of God to give themselves as God gives himself and if the human body is the expression of the human person, then there ought to be a physical means for

[6] See Gen 2:21–22.
[7] Ibid., 2:23.

a human person to express love to another human person. It is precisely masculinity and femininity which allow this unity (love) between human persons to be realized in a bodily way. Without sexuality, there would be no physical union because we would be without the bodily means of expressing a loving self-donation, our most noble and important activity. After the original loneliness, encompassing as it did, the longing for another human being, Adam and Eve discover the immense joy of a loving union expressed in and through their bodies. They experience the profound unity of a reciprocal self-donation in love. This is the experience of original unity.

The experience of original unity is (as is the experience of solitude) common to all of us. The Holy Father writes that "the man (*adam*) falls into that 'sleep' in order to wake up 'male' and 'female'".[8] Is not adolescence a "waking up" to the realities of femininity and masculinity? In adolescence, each individual repeats the wonderful discovery which Adam made when he saw Eve, i.e., the discovery of the marvelous gift of our sexuality. It is in the "waking up" to sexuality that each individual should realize the irreplaceable role which the body has in a human person's fundamental vocation to love. During adolescence men and women should come to appreciate God's wonderful invitation to reflect his love in a self-donation expressed through the body. Further, every spouse certainly must experience the joy Adam felt when he first saw Eve. Adam's cry of joy at the sight of Eve must express the joy of each and every spouse as he meets his future wife or she meets her future husband. Even virgins and celibates share Adam's joy as they gradually come to a greater and greater understanding of God's love for them.

The experience of original unity was possible for both Adam and Eve because both were able to express their persons in and through their bodies. Personhood is characterized by the faculties of thinking and choosing, by the mind and the will.

[8] See TB, no. 8.

If God created Adam and Eve to express their persons in and through their bodies, then God, if he were not to frustrate his own creative act, must have given the minds and wills of our first parents a dominion or control over their bodies. If the human body is not governed by the faculties of thinking and choosing, then it is no longer capable of expressing the human person.

God did indeed create the human body to express the person. Therefore, God gave the minds and wills of our first parents a certain control over their bodies. They were able to express their persons in and through their bodies because their bodies, unlike ours, were under the rule of their minds and wills. Consciousness, efficacy, freedom, transcendence, and truth were expressed in and through their bodies. In other words, they were integrated. The wills of our first parents did not have to struggle against the desires of their flesh. Our first parents had no need of will power as we do. The experience of original unity was possible for our first parents because both, within themselves, were completely in harmony. There was no opposition, as there is in us, between the mind and the will, on the one hand, and the body, on the other.

Since Adam and Eve were perfectly integrated when they first saw one another, the elements of their love were in perfect harmony. In an enfleshed person, love includes bodily realities. Adam and Eve felt a sensual pleasure toward one another. Secondly, they felt an emotional delight in each other's presence. However, both these bodily expressions of love were under the dominance of their minds and wills. Phenomenologist that he is, John Paul analyzes these facets of love as follows.

A man or woman has a sense impression, usually a very powerful one, when he or she meets a person of the opposite sex because the other has a bodily, sexual value for him or her. Each perceives the other as a being who can complete him or her. From the sense impression experienced through the presence of a person of the opposite sex, there arises, quite naturally, a desire for the other, a desire to be completed through the other.

Each longs for something which is a good for him or her, i.e., the gift of the other's body. One can only imagine the power of the sense impression when Adam and Eve saw one another for the first time. It certainly was not the gradual "waking up" to sexuality which most of us experience in adolescence.

Sentiment or the emotional delight which Adam and Eve experienced when they first saw one another should be distinguished from the sense impression, from the sensuality, which they both felt in each other's presence. Sensuality engenders an attraction to the bodily sexual value which resides in all persons of the opposite sex. Sentiment is an emotional reaction to the totality of a particular person of the opposite sex. It is a particular individual who is charming or strong and not all men or all women. The sentimental emotional reaction of a woman will be to the value of masculinity, and of a man to the value of femininity. "The first may be connected with, for instance, an impression of 'strength,' the second with the impression of 'charm,' but both are connected with a whole person of the other sex, not only with that person's 'body.'"[9] Still, sentiment is a bodily reaction. As yet, for the one attracted, there is no involvement of the whole person, of the mind and will. Adam and Eve must have felt sensuality and sentiment when they first saw one another.

Although sensuality and sentiment are good because they are given to us by God, they cannot be the basis for love. Love is a mutual self-donation of two persons. The lover does not desire anything selfishly from the other, but rather seeks the good of the other person. The other makes a total self-gift to the beloved. Anything other than a true self-gift for the sake of the other would not be love. It would be using. We use things for our own benefit. We dare not use as a thing another human person who is endowed by God with an infinite dignity.

Sensuality and sentiment both tend to make the other into

[9] See LR, p. 110.

someone or even, some thing, *for* me. They tend to reduce the other, i.e., the other's body, to an object of use. In effect, sensuality and sentiment in seeking only a bodily good from the other separate the other's body from his person. This attack on the other occurs when sensuality and sentiment are not integrated into a total self-donation made in the will. As John Paul puts it, "The route from one 'I' to another leads through the free will, through a commitment of the will."[10] In Adam and Eve, sensuality and sentiment, bodily realities, were subject to their minds and wills. In other words, since our first parents were integrated, neither sensuality nor sentiment dominated them. Their love was a mutual self-donation of their persons made through an informed choice of their wills (efficacy and freedom). They gave not just their sexual powers or their masculinity and femininity, but their whole persons, their "I's" to each other (transcendence). Their sensuality and sentiment, their desire and attraction for one another, were important, but these feelings were put at the service of their reciprocal self-donation. Further, the love of our first parents was an unselfish love. They did not embrace because they wished something in return. Rather, each desired, more than anything else, the good of the other. Each desired the good of the other's whole being. In the experience of original unity, our first parents loved one another totally. They did not use one another by reducing each other to an object. They did not separate each other's body from each other's person.

Genesis records the third original experience of Adam and Eve in these words: "And the man and his wife were both naked, and were not ashamed."[11] These words "do not express a lack but, on the contrary, serve to indicate a fullness of consciousness and experience . . . That nakedness corresponds to that fullness of consciousness of the meaning of the body."[12] In other words,

[10] Ibid., p. 85.
[11] See Gen 2:25.
[12] See TB, no. 12.

their bodies fully and perfectly expressed their persons. They had given themselves in a total self-donation to each other and this was expressed through their (naked) bodies. Far from being disturbing, nakedness was the opportunity for our first parents to do what God had called them to do: to express their love in and through their bodies. Integration enabled all aspects of the body under the governance of the mind and will to express love. Shame exists with sin. But the expression of true love is not a sin. Therefore, our first parents rejoiced in their mutual self-donation expressed through their (naked) bodies.

Lacking integration because of original sin, it is impossible for us to experience nakedness as our first parents did. However, we do experience shame when naked. This negative common phenomenon points to the disorder in us caused by original sin and allows us to realize how things should be. Through our shame, we certainly can understand what the lack of shame in the state of original innocence might have been like.

C. The Body and Original Sin

The ability of the body to express the person and the capacity to give oneself to another were diminished with the advent of sin into the world. The Pope calls this a "fundamental disquiet in all human existence". There was a "constitutive break within the human person, almost a rupture of man's original spiritual and somatic unity". "The human body in its masculinity/ femininity has almost lost the capacity of expressing" love.[13] In other words, the human person lost the gift of integration which was his in God's creative act.

In the beginning, Adam and Eve had perfect control over their bodies. Their minds and wills, their persons, were perfectly expressed in and through their bodies. There was no inward struggle between the desires of their bodies and their

---

[13] Ibid., nos. 28, 32.

minds and wills. For this reason, the devil could not tempt them, as he might tempt us, with sins of the flesh. The flesh and its passions could never compel the wills of our first parents. Therefore, for example, the serpent did not attempt to describe the delicious characteristics of the fruit of the forbidden tree. Such an approach would not have altered the wills of Adam and Eve at all. The devil's only hope of success lay in a temptation directed at the intellects of our first parents.

The serpent suggested that Eve could become like God if she ate the fruit God had forbidden her to eat. The implication is, of course, that God had asked our first parents not to eat this fruit because he did not want to share his dominion over the earth with them or anyone else. According to the devil, God was jealous and did not want Adam and Eve to have the power and position he had. It is clear that this was a stupendous lie, but it had a chance of success because it was a temptation directed at Eve's self-concept, at her intellect. Eve believed the devil's lie and succumbed to the temptation. She may have believed that she deserved more than what she had. She probably had an inflated self-concept and believed that she deserved to share dominion with God.

As a direct result of this sin of pride, our first parents lost the gift of God's life, his grace. Sin and grace are directly opposed to one another and cannot exist together. When the sin was committed, the loss of grace was immediate and predictable. Of course, the loss of the trinitarian life meant that Adam and Eve no longer shared the life of heaven. They no longer had anything in common with God and could not, should they die, enjoy eternal life with God in heaven. But God had made them for himself. Adam and Eve were made to be with God forever in heaven and now, seemingly, that could never be. Unable to fulfill the very purpose of their creation, our first parents must have been extraordinarily frustrated.

However, in addition to the loss of divine life, Adam and Eve damaged themselves through the sin they had committed. As a result of their sin, our first parents lost the gift of integration. Now their bodies no longer would express their minds and wills as they had before. Rather, they and their descendants would be subject to the desires of the flesh. This dis-integration, the lack of control over their bodies, was certainly suitable. They who had wished to rule the world by achieving equality with God through the forbidden fruit now could not even rule their own flesh.

After their sin, Adam and Eve discovered their lack of integration almost immediately. Genesis records that "they knew that they were naked; and they sewed fig leaves together and made themselves aprons".[14] The experience of nakedness had changed. Now they were ashamed in their naked state. The Holy Father points out that "This . . . passage speaks of the mutual shame of the man and the woman as a symptom of the fall."[15] Shame existed because the bodies of our first parents no longer expressed their persons. Naked and without integration, Adam and Eve confronted one another and they experienced lust for one another. In other words, their bodies no longer were the means of their mutual self-donation. Instead, their bodily desires, i.e., lust, sought the other as a means of gratification. Their feelings of sensuality and sentiment were no longer under the control and domination of their minds and wills. With these bodily desires compelling their wills, Adam and Eve were sorely tempted to use one another to satisfy their own needs. To use, however, is not to love.

They were ashamed of their own desires to use one another. According to John Paul, "Man is ashamed of his body because of lust. In fact, he is ashamed not so much of his body as precisely of lust."[16] The feeling of shame occurs when we do something we realize is wrong or sinful. We are ashamed only when two simultaneous conditions are met: (1) we are incapable

---

[14] See Gen 3:7.
[15] See TB, no. 27.
[16] Ibid., no. 28.

of the proper activity even though (2) we wish to do the right thing. Since our first parents felt shame when they were naked after original sin, they could no longer compel their bodies to conform to the proper activity which they knew and had chosen. Our first parents knew what was right and willed it, but they could not compel their bodies to act accordingly. They were no longer integrated. Shame thus testifies to the rupture within the human person. But shame not only shows that our first parents were incapable of controlling their bodies, it also shows that they retained God's original plan in their minds: the body should be subject to the mind and the will, i.e., it should express the person. Most of all, it should be the means of expressing love, a self-donation, to another. If they had not believed that, they would not have been ashamed because their lust would not have been contrary to their own values. Shame encouraged our first parents to attain the status they had before original sin. Of course, this was impossible for them. They had lost the gift of integration.

After original sin, the mind and will could no longer dominate the body. The body with its passions and desires is now a counter force to the will. Not only is it a counter force, but it is often the stronger force. But man "is the one who can fully discover his true self only in a sincere giving of himself".[17] This "sincere giving" is, as we have seen, accomplished for man through an act of his will and then the gift should be expressed through the body. Original sin broke the unity within us. No longer is the body subject to the will. Rather, the body and its passions are often able to sway the will. Instead of the body subjected to the will, it is the will which is, in many cases, subject to the desires of the flesh. For the man or woman driven by lust, the gift of love to a person of the opposite sex is almost impossible. Rather than a self-gift, the person driven by the lust of the flesh seeks gratification from the other. This is selfish desire. It is certainly not a self-donation for the sake

[17] Ibid., no. 32.

of the other. Therefore, lust makes the sincere gift of oneself almost impossible.

Lust and the other desires of the flesh have an incredible power within us. They influence the will to the point that we sometimes act on their impulses. It is lust, caused by the loss of integration, which impels us to seek sexual gratification from other people rather than to give ourselves to them in love. In turn, we justify these acts by the claim that the body is not part of the person and that it is a machine which can be owned and used as any other piece of property.

If the body is a machine, it can be owned and used. It becomes possible and perhaps even desirable to manipulate the body for one's own purposes. For example, the body can be the means of highs achieved through the use of alcohol or drugs. If the sexual organs are only machine parts, the owner of these machine parts has a right to use them for any purpose he wants. For example, if an individual wishes to use his sexual devices to achieve a sexual high, e.g., masturbation, it is his right as an owner to do so. Further, owners can alter machines at will. If the body is a machine which is owned, it can be changed. Thus, tubal ligations, vasectomies, and contraception are justifiable. The body, as a thing, i.e., as property, could be bought and sold. The owner could sell the body for any purpose whatsoever, e.g., pornography or prostitution. There would be no difficulty in renting a womb or any other part of the body. The womb is a machine part and if the individual owns that part, she can choose to rent it to someone else. Surrogate motherhood would thus be justifiable.

If all bodies are machines, then any individual can own any body. Parents would own children. Slavery, the owning of another's body, a machine, makes perfect sense. The owner could use that body for any purpose whatsoever. It should be noted that age makes no difference. A child's body is as much a machine as an adult's body. Anyone, e.g., pimps, would have a perfect right to buy, rent, or sell any bodily machines including those of women and children.

The production of new machines should be in the hands of the owner(s). New biological machines, i.e., babies, could be made in any feasible way, including reproduction in test tubes. Babies, as new machines, would be owned by the parents. In this (false) view, these new machines are the property of their owners, their parents, and if these new machines were manufactured unnecessarily or by mistake, they could be destroyed, i.e., aborted.

Further, if the body is a machine, then in any physical contact between two human bodies two machines touch, not two persons. The bodily union of a husband and a wife would be indistinguishable from the contact of two robots with one another. It would also be indistinguishable from the touching of two cars in a crash. It could easily be argued that physical abuse of a child or a spouse really does not injure any person. It is only the machine, the body, which is damaged. Such damage can be repaired (as a damaged clock might be) without much *personal* involvement. Further, when a doctor treats a patient or a surgeon operates, he would be a technician (a machine, i.e., a robot) making adjustments on another malfunctioning machine. Clearly, with this understanding of the body, in heart surgery it would not be an individual's, that is, a person's, heart healed by surgery but rather a machine part adjusted by another machine.

In medical circles it is not uncommon for a surgeon to compare a specific part of the human body to a part of a machine, e.g., the heart to a motor. Transplants have intensified this system of reference. The body can easily be seen as a resource for spare parts or a collection of aging parts needing replacement (depending on whether one is the donor or the recipient).

Of course, it is sometimes important for doctors, especially for surgeons, to abstract from the mystery of the human person so that they can help their patients. The human body does have parts and they must function in a certain way if health is to be maintained. In a certain sense, there is a machinelike quality to the body. Clearly, many surgical operations are simply mechanical procedures which must be executed in each case in exactly the same way with great efficiency and often with great speed. Surgeons operating must concentrate on the details of how each part of the body does function. However, their abstraction from the order of existence for the sake of their patients' health does not necessarily mean that they would accept the body as merely a collection of parts working together. In fact, knowing from their own experiences that each human body reacts differently, they might be the first to admit that each body expresses a unique, individual person who is different from all others.

Since doctors seem to have the power of life and death, they are often imitated. There is almost a cult of doctors and of medicine. Many nonmedical organizations have internships. Any number of companies and institutions have staff meetings and even consultations. These imitations of medical practices lend a certain aura of science to nonscientific areas. Many times the imitation of medical customs is useful and beneficial.

Unfortunately, physicians' references to the human body are also often imitated. Sometimes those outside the medical profession begin to talk of the body as a machine. Finally, those who voice such thoughts come to believe what they are saying. Unlike the doctors, they do not see the reactions of different people to the same medical procedures. They have no reminder that they have abstracted from one of the essential mysteries of the human person, i.e., that the body is the expression of the person. In their view, the body becomes a machine which is inhabited. What is absolutely necessary for doctors becomes positively dangerous for many others.

Of course, the body is not a machine. It cannot be treated as a thing, i.e., as something to be owned, manipulated, used, bought, or sold. The body is part of the gift of life from God. It is given to us so that we might express ourselves, our persons, in the physical world. Any attack on the body offends God and is a vicious act against humanity.

There are a number of people who would object that this view of the body subjects man to biology. According to their argument, the human person should not be a slave to his biological processes. As a person made in the image of God with a mind and a will, a man or a woman is a spiritual being who can only find his or her fulfillment in the spiritual realm. The superiority of spiritual values over bodily ones must be established and applied in every life if the individual is to fulfill himself. If a conflict arises between spiritual values, e.g., love and companionship, and the demands of our biological structure, the spiritual must take precedence. The human person, using his intellect and subjugating all of creation to himself, should obtain freedom from encumbering and enslaving biological determinants.

For these critics of Pope John Paul II, the Church's teaching against contraception is an outrage. To them, the Church is denying the very thing it constantly claims to profess: that human beings are superior to the rest of creation. The Church denies the human person's superiority over all of creation by insisting that men and women must be enslaved to their biology, e.g., to conception. In their view, the supremacy of the spiritual values of love and companionship must be restored. Every human being must have the freedom to change and alter his body to achieve a greater spiritual good. For the critics, certain human biological potentialities, e.g., fertility, can, if not altered, destroy infinitely more precious spiritual goods.

In 1960, eight years before Pope Paul VI's famous encyclical on birth control *Humanae Vitae* (*On Human Life*) was written and long before the foregoing argument against the Church's teaching was widely proposed, Karol Wojtyla had refuted it. In his book *Love and Responsibility*, Wojtyla wrote, "The habit of confusing the order of existence with the biological order, or rather, of allowing the second to obscure the first, is part of that generalized empiricism which seems to weigh so heavily on the mind of modern man . . . and makes it particularly difficult [for him] . . . to understand the principles on which

Catholic sexual morality is based."[18] For Wojtyla, there is an order of existence and an order of biology. The two are related, but quite distinct.

The order of existence, or nature, has its origin in the Creator, almighty God, and cannot be altered or changed by us. To change or alter the order of existence is a prerogative of the Divinity. Thus, when Christ calmed the storm, the apostles concluded that he must be divine. Only God, the Creator who held authority over the very existence of all things, could demand obedience from the weather and the sea.

On the other hand, the biological order is a creation of our intellect. It is an abstraction from the order of nature. "The 'biological order', as a product of the human intellect which abstracts its elements from a larger reality, has man for its immediate author."[19] Since man is the author and arbiter of the biological order and it is an abstraction from the order of nature, it can easily (but only falsely) seem that man is also the author and arbiter of nature, i.e., that he has authority over the order of nature or existence. Of course, this is to put human beings in the position of the Creator. In the proper view, our authority is only valid within the abstracted biological realm. We may never extend our autonomous authority beyond the boundaries of our abstraction. In other words, biology, an abstraction (when the human body is its subject) from the human person, may never be employed to alter or harm the person.

Scientists study human biology in order to understand the human body. Since the body exists to reveal the mystery of the human person, the more scientists know about the body, the more they (and we) know about the human person. The study of human biology is an attempt to understand the mystery of the human person through an examination of the body. Thus, biologists contribute to our knowledge of ourselves. Secondly, biology is studied to enhance the expressive function

[18] See LR, p. 57.
[19] Ibid.

of the body. When disease or other disorders threaten the body, doctors, relying on those who have studied the bodily functions, are able to assist the individual so that his body will again express his person in the way God intended "from the beginning".

As part of our lives, our bodies belong to the order of existence. When the body is perceived only as a biological machine, there exists a confusion of the biological order with the order of existence. However, when the body is examined within the biological realm, it may seem to be just a biological machine. But, this picture is incomplete. It is an abstraction from reality, from the order of existence. Through those apparently understandable biological functions (understandable in the abstracted realm of biology) is expressed (in the real world) the mystery of the human person. Although biologists can come to understand certain bodily aspects, the body remains, as all life, fundamentally a mystery.

Far from enslaving man to his biology, the Church's position frees mankind from the meddling of human scientists who might wish to recreate the human race in their own images. There is always the specter of the irresponsible scientist shaping everyone into his own image. It seems far preferable to be in God's image. Further, the Church's position defines and thereby protects true science. The Church gives to biologists a noble task: to penetrate the mysteries of the human person by examining his outward expression in and through the body. With this understanding of science, scientists can be sure of their conclusions because these results will always lie within their own discipline. In addition, the human race can put full trust and credence in scientific conclusions. However, when there is a confusion of the order of existence and the order of biology, scientists can no longer be sure of their own results and humanity cannot trust either the scientific professionals or their conclusions.

None of us bought our bodies as we might buy a machine, e.g., a car. The body was given to us as part of the gift of life. We received the body when we were given life by God through the cooperation of our parents. Our life, in every aspect, including the body, ultimately belongs to God. We do not own our bodies any more than we own our life. We dare not think of our bodies as machines which we own. As part of the gift of life, we are obligated to guard and protect our bodies. We may not harm them. To alter a healthy, functioning part of the body is to assume the prerogatives of the Creator and to attack oneself.

John Paul's understanding of the human body rests on the principle that the body is given to us to manifest our persons. For John Paul, the body is not merely a biological machine. We are not ghosts imprisoned in machinelike shells. Despite all the medical and technical advances (and all the "tinkering" now possible with our bodies) our bodies are still ourselves. They are not machines or appendages which we carry around with us. When the body is injured, the person will say, "I hurt myself"; not, "I have damaged my exterior"! We must affirm the truth about the body-person unity and then seek some way to recover from the devastating effect of original sin: the loss of integration.

D. The Redemption of the Body: Presentation

For Pope John Paul II, it is absolutely impossible for those tainted with original sin, i.e., the entire human race with the sole exception of the Blessed Mother, to act according to the original will of the Creator. Our bodies no longer express our persons as they were created to do. Our bodies are no longer subject to our minds and wills. As Saint Paul wrote, "I do not do what I want, but I do the very thing I hate."[20] But if we are not integrated, if our bodies no longer adequately

[20] See Rom 7:15.

express our persons, our very humanity is threatened. To be human means to be a person manifested in and through a body. As persons, beings endowed with minds and wills, we are made in God's image. But, as we have seen, it is not merely man's interior structure which is made in God's image. The human body, when it is subject to the mind and will, is a physical image not only of our own persons, but also of the divine Persons. When a human person acts in accordance with God's will and this act is expressed through the body, the body becomes a physical sign, a sacrament, not only of the person who acts, but also of God. However, when our bodies are not subject to our minds and wills, then they do not express our own persons and are not a reflection of God. But we are made to be and to act in the likeness of God, both in our spiritual and physical structures. It is clear then that original sin attacked our very humanity. After original sin, we are the most pathetic of creatures. We are created for one purpose and we are unable to fulfill it because of a tragic flaw, which we willingly inflicted on ourselves. Of course, God's purpose also seems frustrated.

To be human, to fulfill our very purpose, we must find a way to restore our original integrity. However, this seems impossible. Every offense is measured not only by what is done, but also by the one offended. The greater the honor owed to an individual, the more serious is an offense against that person. With the sin of our first parents, God is offended. But God is infinite and almighty, worthy of every praise and gratitude. Thus, the offense of this sin (and, for that matter, any sin) is infinite.

Man and woman could not make up for this offense because they are finite creatures. God in his infinite mercy and justice sent his only-begotten Son, the God-man, who as God could offer the infinite sacrifice in reparation for sin, and, as man, could act for the entire human race. In the supreme sacrifice on the Cross of Calvary, he made a recompense for all of us and he accomplished the "redemption of the body".[21] It was in his human flesh that he died. It was because he possessed a body that he could die, that his body and soul could be separated. It was in his flesh that he won for us again the possibility of functioning the way we were created to do as images of God both in our interior structures and in our bodies. In his body, he accomplished the redemption of our bodies.

It is possible for us to bridge the gap of original sin, to return to a life according to the original will of the Creator through Christ. However, it is absolutely impossible for us to return to the *state* of original innocence. But it is possible for us to live in accordance with God's will provided we have the strength of Christ in us. We have this strength of Christ when we participate in the divine life he won for us on the Cross, i.e., grace.

Grace, God's own life, has two functions for us, human persons tainted with original sin. As in Adam and Eve, it is the promise of future glory. It makes us children of God. With grace, we are not merely creatures, but adopted sons and daughters with the expectation of a heavenly inheritance. This function of God's grace is the same in us as it was in Adam and Eve. However, in us grace has a second function. It makes it again possible for us to live as God intended "from the beginning". For Adam and Eve before the fall, it would have been easy for them to express their persons through their bodies. For us, it is almost impossible without grace. Grace makes integration possible, but it is still a struggle. God did not restore the *state* of original innocence because it is fitting that we should bear the marks of our revolt against God as a constant reminder of the terrible offense that sin is. However, in his infinite mercy, God did not leave us frustrated beings. Now, if only man and woman will make an effort of the will, they can become what they are made to be: enfleshed persons who

---

[21] See TB, no. 49.

manifest their persons through their bodies. To the inevitable question we put to Christ, "How can we possibly live according to your commandments when we suffer from the effects of original sin?" the answer is the same for all ages: "My grace is sufficient for you."[22]

Christ is calling each man and each woman back to the integrated life which Adam and Eve led in the Garden of Eden. He asks that human beings act in accordance with the original will of the Creator. The Lord wishes, to use the papal terms, that the body express the person. In other words, Christ is asking all of us to be human, to act as Adam and Eve did when he first created them. It must be remembered that this challenge is addressed to historical man, the man tainted with sin who on his own can never return to the integrated life. It is only in and through the redemption that man can act as he should. But this redemption, accomplished once and for all on Calvary, must be applied to each one of us. Our participation in the redemption occurs through our sharing in the divine life, God's grace, dispensed through the sacraments of the Church. It is clear that for us to function as human beings (without even considering our hope for eternal life in heaven), it is absolutely essential that we remain close to the sacraments and in the state of grace. Grace makes us whole and gives us the possibility of living as we should. God's mercy has restored our humanity to us after we almost destroyed it through the self-inflicted fault of original sin. How could anyone reject this infinite mercy of God: our re-creation through the redemption? The alternative is to remain in the most pathetic of states: a creature with a tainted nature unable to fulfill its own destiny.

Of course, even with grace we are not perfect. Sin and shame still exist in us because we have not been restored to the *state* of original innocence, but only to the possibility of self-control (integration). We are subject to the temptations of the flesh, e.g., lust, and sometimes we yield to these temptations and sin.

[22] See 2 Cor 12:9.

After such an act, or even during it, we are ashamed because, for us just as for our first parents, shame is the direct result of sin. Shame exists when we choose a bodily action that is contrary to our own values. As such, shame leads to an attempt to overcome the discord within us. When we experience shame, provided there is no psychological disorder or imbalance, we know the need for self-control.

Privacy is essential to self-control. Our first parents sewed fig leaves on themselves because they experienced lust. Those first clothes hid their lust from one another. They wished to keep their desires private and within themselves so that they could more easily control and overcome them. Thus, shame gives rise to the need for privacy.

With God's grace, it is possible for historical man to preserve his body as the expression of his person but only if shame and the need for privacy resulting from shame are protected. But when the body in its God-given beauty becomes a subject for art, there is a danger that the right to privacy will be violated. In art, the body can only be reproduced as an expression of a person when the artist respects shame and personal privacy.

The artist must also understand and respect the human body as the means of a personal gift of one person to another. According to the Holy Father, this proves extraordinarily difficult because "the artistic objectivation of the human body in its male and female nakedness . . . is always to a certain extent a going outside of this original, and, for the body, its specific configuration of interpersonal donation."[23] The body is the means of expressing the gift of oneself to another. This gift is threatened when the body is reproduced in art because "the element of the gift is, so to speak, suspended in the dimension of an unknown reception and an unforeseen response."[24] In art, there is great danger that shame, privacy, and the element of personal gift expressed through the body would be violated.

[23] See TB, no. 61.
[24] Ibid., no. 62.

When any one of these is not respected as it should be, the body is not preserved in the art form as an expression of the person.

However, the person whose body is represented in art "can be violated only in the intentional order".[25] It is what the artist intends in representing the naked body that is the controlling factor. If he intends to respect the body as the expression of a personal gift of one person to another together with the values of shame and privacy, his work does not offend either the subject or those who enjoy the art. If the artist is talented, his intent to preserve the values inherent in the meaning of the body sometimes results in an artistic masterpiece. Such work is distinguishable from the work of an artist who fails to intend the preservation of these values.

> There are works of art whose subject is the human body in its nakedness, and the contemplation of which makes it possible to concentrate, in a way, on the whole truth of man, on the dignity and the beauty—also the "suprasensual" beauty—of masculinity and femininity. These works bear within them, almost hidden, an element of sublimation, which leads the viewer, through the body, to the whole personal mystery of man. In contact with these works, where we do not feel drawn by their content to "looking lustfully," about which the Sermon on the Mount speaks, we learn in a way that nuptial meaning of the body which corresponds to, and is the measure of, "purity of heart."[26]

Thus, an artistic reproduction of the human body, if it is to be true art, must reflect "the whole truth of man". If the artist intends anything less, his work will not be worthy of the art he is employing and, more importantly, he will have violated the dignity of the human person.

[25] Ibid.
[26] Ibid., no. 63.

E. The Redemption of
the Body: Possible Difficulties

There are objections which even some Christians might raise to the foregoing view of the redemption of the body. It might appear to some that Christ when he commands us not to look lustfully is condemning the body. However, in reality Christ radically affirms the good of the body. It is precisely because the body is called to be a physical manifestation of the human person and of the divine Persons, that we are called to master the body. This was such an important value that the God-man gave his life in part so that it might be retained. "The appeal to master the lust of the flesh springs precisely from the affirmation of the personal dignity of the body and of sex and serves only this dignity."[27]

Secondly, there are some who would see a similarity between Christ and modern philosophers, e.g., Marx, Freud, and Nietzsche. They seem "to judge and accuse man's 'heart'" as Christ does.[28] But unlike these men, Christ does not merely accuse man, he also makes an appeal to him. Furthermore, there is not only an appeal (the challenge to self-mastery), there is also a means given to achieve it: God's grace. The difference between Christ and these other philosophers is that Christ offers us a way out of our dilemma while the others do not because they cannot. Christ offers optimism with his grace. Marx, Freud, and Nietzsche, in the last analysis, can only throw up their hands with a cry of frustration.

A third objection turns on the supposed distinction between eros (erotic) and ethos (ethic). In rejecting lust, some might argue that no sexual delight is licit and that only dreary duty remains. In the view of these critics, the Pope has eliminated the erotic from all love. But since Christ affirms the love of a married couple expressed in and through their bodies as a

[27] Ibid., no. 45.
[28] Ibid., no. 46.

reflection of the Trinity, the God-given bodily and spiritual joys of this union are also affirmed. Eros is the attraction of the human person toward the good and that is exactly what Christ teaches in the ethic of the gospel, i.e., that we should be attracted to the good. Lust and (false) eroticism is the attraction of man and woman toward a partial good, sexual pleasure. True eroticism, which is identical with the ethic of Christ, is the attraction of one person to the total value of another person. If anything, eroticism is enlivened by the ethic of the gospel because one sees and appreciates the entire person in all of his dignity as made in the image of God. Thus, the eros of the gospel is greater than the eros of these critics and is identical with ethos. If there is a division in one's own experience between these two phenomena, the difficulty lies in the individual's attraction to only a partial good of another person. Of course, true eroticism, in the sense of the gospel, lies exclusively in integration and self-mastery.

Finally, there are those who would argue vehemently against the papal position because it, they claim, destroys spontaneity. Self-mastery means self-control and control means that not every spontaneous impulse may be acted upon. The Holy Father responds that "there cannot be . . . spontaneity in all the movements and impulses that arise from mere carnal lust, devoid as it is of a choice and of an adequate hierarchy. It is precisely at the price of self-control that man reaches that deeper and more mature spontaneity."[29] Spontaneity refers to a voluntary, free act. If a person is compelled within himself by passions, e.g., lust, the resulting act is neither voluntary nor free. In speaking of bodily activity, an act is only free, i.e., spontaneous, when it is chosen by the will and then expressed in and through the body. Although it may seem paradoxical, it is only through self-control that spontaneity exists. The drunk who cannot refrain from drink is not a free person. No one would describe him as free. Only when he is capable of refusing the drink will he be

[29] Ibid., no. 48.

free. The person who cannot say "no" is the person whose "yes" does not mean anything. Self-control gives us this freedom. True spontaneity springs from self-mastery.

Christ has announced a new ethical norm which "does not invite man to return to the state of original innocence because humanity has irrevocably left it behind", but to take up again "the original ethos of creation". This effort of the will shall be successful "to the extent to which the ethos of the redemption of the body dominates the lust of the flesh and the whole man of lust".[30] The task therefore is to achieve integration through God's grace.

Saint Paul wrote, "The desires of the flesh are against the Spirit, and the desires of the Spirit are against the flesh."[31] "It is not a question here only of the body (matter) and of the spirit (the soul) . . . but that disposition of forces formed in man with original sin, in which every 'historical man' participates."[32] There is, then, a struggle in man, a warring. If the ethos of the redemption is to win, it will overcome the flesh by "an effort of the will, the fruit of the human spirit permeated by the Spirit of God". "In this struggle between good and evil, man proves himself stronger, thanks to the power of the Holy Spirit."[33] Nevertheless, the struggle goes on in the human heart.

Integration, achieved through God's grace, involves self-control, but it is also, as we have seen, the source of freedom. Christ challenges us to rediscover the original state of man and woman, and to choose our acts without any impairment of our freedom, either internally or externally. Christ makes it possible for us to live according to our full dignity. With God's grace, in our interior acts of mind and will and in our outward acts, we can again function as God made us. We can be fully human because we are able to express our own persons in and through

---

[30] Ibid., no. 49.
[31] See Gal 5:17.
[32] See TB, no. 51.
[33] Ibid., no. 50.

our bodies. With this capability, we are also able to reflect God interiorly and outwardly through our bodies. We truly fulfill our unique calling to be images of God. Without grace, historical man is not integrated. Without integration, man is not what he was made to be. He is not fully human. Grace is essential if we, tainted with original sin, are to be human, i.e., to be images of God.

The struggle for integration is not an end in itself. Rather, it becomes the means for us to fulfill our vocation to do what God does. God loves. We are called to love, as he loves, through a self-donation. When we love others as he loves, we reflect the Holy Trinity. The primary reflection of the trinitarian love should be found in the family. A secondary reflection of trinitarian love should exist in the workplace. The two are interrelated. We cannot understand ourselves and our calling to be images of God (subjective turn) without an examination of the love which should exist in the family and in the workplace.

The Family and Sexuality

A. Man and Woman (Images of God) and Love

After twenty-five years of thought and reflection on marriage and the family, Karol Wojtyla was called to the chair of Saint Peter. As a theologian in his own right, he developed a new understanding of the moral precepts of Christ. This development can already be seen in his early work, *Love and Responsibility.* Later, as archbishop of Cracow and as a participant in the Second Vatican Council, he proposed his new moral theology to the other conciliar fathers. His new understanding was received by the Council and became part of its teaching in the *Pastoral Constitution on the Church in the Modern World.* Now, as the Vicar of Christ, John Paul II has offered the world his fully matured moral theology in his papal addresses entitled *Theology of the Body* and in his apostolic exhortation, *The Role of the Christian Family in the Modern World.* Since this new development is found in the conciliar documents, John Paul II is teaching us what the Second Vatican Council intended.

The central idea in the new theology of John Paul II is the subjective turn founded on the revelation in Genesis that we are made in God's image. Endowed with a likeness to God, we have been created to act as he does, i.e., to love, to give ourselves as he does within the Holy Trinity. Our dignity lies in our similarity to God. When we fail to act as he does, we destroy ourselves and our dignity. As John Paul wrote in his first encyclical, "Man cannot live without love. He remains a being that is incomprehensible for himself, his life is senseless."[1]

[1] See RH, no. 10.

Continuing the same theme in his document on family life, the Pope says, "Love is therefore the fundamental and innate vocation of every human being."[2] Thus, the Holy Father insists that we must love. This necessity flows from within ourselves. God does not compel us to love. Rather, the obligation to love is derived from the kind of creatures we are, i.e., persons made in the image of God.

However, God must show us how to love because love is primarily a divine activity in which we, through God's creative act, are called to share. (Thus, Christ, the God-man, is absolutely central to each and every human being. Only in him can we see how God loves, i.e., how we should love.) We know from revelation, i.e., from the Old Testament and most perfectly from Christ, that God loves through a complete self-donation of himself. This love is perfectly present in the Holy Trinity where each divine Person totally surrenders himself to the others. This total self-gift of each Person within the Trinity, while preserving the distinct features of each Person (Father, Son, Holy Spirit) establishes a complete union. The love of each divine Person is a personal choice, a will-act, made by each based on knowledge of the truth. The self-donation of each divine Person to the others unites all three in a *communion of Persons*. In effect, there is an attitude, a choice, to act as one. This is what love is: an act of the will to do what another wills.

God's self-gift of himself is extended to us and made known to us in the creation and most especially in the redemption. In creation, God shared himself with us and all creation because he shared what he is: existence. He gave himself to what he created. Of course, in a unique way, he gave himself to man and woman when he created Adam and Eve in his own image. But his creative act, as much of a self-surrender as it was, is infinitely less precious than the total abnegation of self that is manifested in the Incarnation. As Saint Paul wrote, "Though he was in the form of God, [Jesus] did not count equality with God a

---

[2] See FC, no. 11.

thing to be grasped, but emptied himself, taking the form of a servant being born in the likeness of men."[3] The Incarnation, God taking the nature of one of his creatures, shows us how God loves. But even the assumption of a human nature did not completely reveal the full extent of God's love. Only on the Cross do we see how far the self-surrender of God extends. He gave himself for our sakes that we might have life. He gave until he had nothing more to give and he did it totally for us. This is love! Since we are made in God's likeness, we are made to love as he did and does: an all-encompassing self-surrender for the sake of others. Only when we mirror the love of the Trinity in our love do we fulfill ourselves as God created us. Only then is life meaningful.

Wojtyla points out that the vocation to give ourselves in love is a call given to us because we are persons: creatures endowed with minds and wills. In other words, as personal beings, we can know the truth and we can choose to give ourselves to another person or persons. Thus, like the Trinity, we have the capability of entering a communion of persons. We are first called to enter a communion of persons with God and then with other human beings. Failure to form a communion of persons is an attack, an aggression, against our very persons. We must love. It is a subjective need which every human being has.

Of course, a communion of persons, a relationship of love, cannot be established unless there are at least two persons who individually choose through a personal will-act to give themselves to each other. Thus, we cannot, properly speaking, love a thing or even an animal. These beings do not have wills; they do not have the ability to give themselves to others. They cannot love and since love is a reciprocal gift of at least two persons, we cannot love them.

Love is an activity proper to persons. Love is also the *only* way to relate to persons. In one of his early works on love,

[3] See Phil 2:6–7.

John Paul teaches that a "person is a good toward which the only proper adequate attitude is love". "This [personalistic] norm, in its negative aspect, states that the person is a kind of good which does not admit of use and cannot be treated as an object of use and as such the means to an end."[4] The dignity of persons as created in God's image makes them superior to the remainder of creation. That superiority gives them a right to be treasured for their own sakes, not as means to an end. We must, then, relate to other persons only through love, i.e., in and through a communion of persons. The dignity of other persons and our own dignity require such a stance. Should one person treat another as a means to an end, as someone to be used, the second becomes, for the first, less than a personal being. The first person is reducing the second to a thing. Of necessity, because the first person is equal to the second, the first is also reducing himself to a thing. The dignity of persons, our own and that of others, requires that the personalistic norm always be observed.

As human persons, we are not merely spirits. We have bodies and they, as we have seen, are given to us by God as part of the gift of life so that our persons might be expressed in a physical way. Of all the persons in the universe, the three Persons in God, the angels, and humans, only human persons have bodies. Of all the bodily creatures in the world, only we are persons. Thus, we are unique. Only we can express in the physical world how a person loves. Only we can manifest a communion of persons in a physical way. The body is the means by which our love is expressed. But it is also a means by which the love of others may be received. As such, it can only be viewed as an object of love. The body is not an appendage which a person carries around with him. To treat the body as a thing is to treat the person as a thing. The body is the expression of the person and it should be loved as the person should be loved. The personalistic norm is not limited to the spiritual aspects

_____
[4] See LR, p. 41.

of persons. It includes the bodies of persons. We may never exclude the body from the dignity proper to personal beings. Many different practices traditionally taboo in most societies could be justified if the body were divorced from the person. But we dare not permit such an opinion to gain acceptance because it would irreparably harm human dignity.

B. The Family as a Communion of Persons

In his creative act, God specified two particular communions which should exist for us when he said to Adam and Eve, "Be fruitful and multiply, and fill the earth and subdue it."[5] We are called, by creation and "from the beginning", to enter into a communion of persons so that we may increase and multiply and to enter into a communion so that the earth might be subdued. Of course, the first communion is the family. The second is that found in the workplace. In both communions, the activity of man and woman reflects the acts of God, not only in the self-gift which establishes the communions, but also in the effects of the self-gift. When God loves, it is life-giving. When man and woman love within the family, new life is brought forth. When people work, they dominate creation. They are acting in a way analogous to God, who, as the Creator, has total dominion over the world. Still, the first communion is the more fundamental. It is the one which reflects God's trinitarian life more closely because it is a total self-surrender of one person to another. In the workplace, we do not give ourselves completely to one another. Second, the communion of persons of the family is life-giving whereas that of the workplace is not. The love of a man and a woman is usually fertile as God's love is fertile. Thus, in this way, the communion of persons which is the family reflects God's love more closely. It is appropriate to consider the family as the first and most important communion

[5] See Gen 1:28.

of persons and then to examine the relationships which should exist in the workplace.

"Male and female he created them."[6] If we are called to love one another, as God loves, i.e., to surrender ourselves completely to one another, and if our bodies are to express our persons, it is most appropriate that there be bodily differences which allow us to express our love for one another. By God's holy will, there are such differences: God created us as men and women (although both male and female bodies equally express the human person). The physical gift of a man and a woman to each other is the outward sign, the sacrament, of the familial communion of persons. The body, then, is the means and the sign of the gift of the male-person to the female-person. The Holy Father calls this capacity of the body to express the total self-surrender of one person to another the nuptial meaning of the body. In this total physical surrender based on the communion of persons, the married couple becomes, physically, an image of God. When a married couple acts in accordance with their vows and God's will, they are a sign (a sacrament), a physical manifestation, of the love of persons. They are an image of God in their bodily gift to one another.

The Pope also stresses that the communion of two persons expressed through their bodies is a mutual giving and acceptance. The gift of each spouse mirrors God's gift of himself in creation. Spouses give themselves as the Creator did when he created the world. They give themselves for the sake of the other. Similarly, the acceptance of the other's gift on the part of each spouse is an act of gratitude to the Creator for the gift. The entire physical creation participates in the gratitude of the man and the woman to the Creator for the gift each has received. The married couple gives as God gives and each responds with gratitude and in that response, all creation responds to the Creator thanking him for the gift of being. At

[6] Ibid., 1:27.

one and the same time, the couple is an image of God and a sign of creation's response to the Creator.

In his *Theology of the Body* series, the Holy Father defended the ancient biblical terminology for the sexual union of a man and a woman: to know. Of course, since we gain self-knowledge through our acts, the self-gift of a husband and a wife to one another does reveal to each of them more about themselves. But the knowledge gleaned from the gift of a husband and a wife to one another transcends the truth they know about themselves from their other acts because this act of self-surrender is more Godlike. The gift of love, acting as God does, expressed through the body, touches the central mystery of the human person in a way in which most of our other acts do not. Therefore, the verb, to know, is most accurate for the self-gift of a man and a woman to one another.

The knowledge gleaned from this act may be specified in three areas. First, there is the knowledge of oneself and the other in the mutual communion of persons. In this mutual giving, one experiences and knows oneself as well as the other in a much fuller way than would otherwise be possible. Second, the hidden treasures of humanity are revealed in motherhood and fatherhood. The woman, whose femininity is hidden, is revealed to herself and to others (especially to her husband) in motherhood. Similarly, the new relationship of the male to the child, fatherhood, reveals to the husband and to others (especially to his wife) an aspect of humanity not previously experienced. Third, in the child, both the man and the woman see and know themselves.

Of course, true love, the surrender of oneself to another, is a freely chosen act of a person. Acts of human persons have (or should have) their origins in the faculties of mind and will. The physical union of a man and a woman is not simply an act of their bodies. It is founded on their marriage vows. These vows are choices or will-acts grounded in the dignity of the beloved by which an irrevocable union—a communion of persons—is established. This communion can then be expressed in the physical order through their bodies because God gave their bodies a nuptial meaning when he created them male and female.

Marriage vows, then, are freely chosen will-acts. In the vows, the spouses promise to give themselves to each other. These vows are not (or should not be) exchanged solely on the basis of sensuality or sentiment. Rather, they should be exchanged because the spouses, perceiving the dignity which God gave the beloved in his creative act, wish to give themselves to each other. Unlike some sensual or sentimental feelings, marriage vows are always under the control of the ones making them. The spouses promise to love each other forever, i.e., to give themselves to each other until death. The spouses can always be faithful to their promises, can always give themselves to each other, no matter what feelings they have or what the other does. Good feelings might cease, but marriage must be founded on a firmer basis than transient emotions. If marriage were only constituted by the feelings of each spouse, there would be a violation of the personalistic norm. In this case, implicitly, men and women would marry because their spouses make them feel good. If that good feeling should cease, the marriage would end. In other words, the spouse would have been there to make the other feel good. With such a union, there would be no assurance for either spouse that the marriage would endure. The spouses could not be sure that they would feel good in two months, five years, let alone forty or fifty years. It is quite clear that a union founded on a selfish desire to achieve an emotional high through the spouse is directly contrary to the commitment of marriage, which is based on a Godlike self-donation of each spouse to the other. Marriage, if it is to be a communion of persons, must originate in the will, must be rooted in the personalistic norm, and must be an imitation of the Trinity. Sensuality and sentiment will then accompany the marital communion instead of determining it.

Marriage reflects God's love within the Trinity and his love for us, because marriage is constituted by the irrevocable choice in the wills of the spouses. In the Trinity and in creation, love is a choice in the will of the divine Persons. The familial communion of persons reflects the trinitarian communion of Persons because the irrevocable will-acts of the married partners, establishing a mutual self-surrender, mirror the unbreakable fidelity of God to himself (within the Trinity) and to those whom he loves (us) outside the Trinity. He never will cease loving himself or us because he has chosen to do so and his will-acts are, as those of married partners ought to be, irrevocable.

An act of the will is within the control of the one who makes it. Neither the spouse, nor even the angels, including the devil, can cause us to alter our own choices. It is within the power of the fallen angels to tempt, i.e., to suggest possible choices contrary to God's will, but they can never actually make us choose what we do not choose ourselves. Only God has such power and he will never choose for us. If he were to do that, it would destroy us because we would be reduced to the status of animals, lacking free will. Of course, through lack of cooperation, sickness, or a variety of other causes, the expression of the mutual self-donation in marriage may be hampered. However, that does not alter the gift itself.

Since the love of a husband and a wife should be a communion of persons based on the truth of the infinite dignity with which the Creator endowed both of them, it is not offensive, as sacred Scripture has it, to ask wives to be obedient to their husbands. Nor is it too demanding to ask husbands to be willing to die for their wives as Christ died for the Church. In the exchange of marital vows, both the man and the woman give themselves completely to each other. They each promise, "Not my will, but thine be done."[7] To ask obedience of wives is simply to remind wives of what they have already promised. Obedience, if it is a human act based on a relationship between persons, must be an act of love (personalistic norm). Otherwise, the demand for obedience would be an act of tyranny and the

---

[7] See Lk 22:42.

one who is obedient would be acting as a slave. Obedience is
the willing cooperation of one with the other because both are
united through their freely chosen will-acts. Of course, wives
should obey their husbands, i.e., they should be united with
them in their wills. That is what was promised on the marriage
day through the vows. Similarly, when Saint Paul asks husbands
to be ready to die for their wives, he is only reminding them of
what they promised. They, in the vows, promised everything
they had to their wives: a total self-surrender. In that total gift,
they function as creatures made in the image of God. They
act as Christ acted. If necessary, husbands must be ready to
do what Christ did, surrender everything for the sake of the
other. What Saint Paul affirmed of husbands is equally true of
wives and what he said of wives is equally true of husbands.
Husbands and wives have promised obedience, i.e., a union of
wills, to one another. They have voluntarily given themselves
totally to one another and each should be ready to die for the
other. Seen in the light of John Paul's personalism, Saint Paul's
teaching is not sexist. It is the obvious corollary to the total
union which husbands and wives are called to form with one
another.

The gift of a man and a woman to one another in marriage
must be indissoluble as long as both live. They surrender
themselves to each other and receive the gift of the other in
return. Once given, the gift may never be withdrawn. Once
received, the gift of the other may never be rejected. As *The
Role of the Christian Family in the Modern World* argues, "The
indissolubility of marriage . . . [is] a sign and a requirement of
the absolutely faithful love that God has for man and that the
Lord Jesus has for the Church."[8] In other words, God's love is
always characterized by perfect fidelity. Human love, since it is
to be a reflection of God's love, must also be faithful forever.
God is always faithful in his love because anything less would
not be a total self-surrender. A gift, if it is total, is not bounded

[8] See FC, no. 20.

in degree or in time! To give oneself only for a period of time and not forever (at least, for as long as marriage is possible, i.e., until the death of one of the spouses) is to limit the gift. But anything less than a total surrender of oneself for the other is, as we have seen, a violation of the requirement of love, a violation of the personalistic norm. It is, in effect, to use someone rather than to love him.

Someone who has divorced a spouse and remarried has treated the first spouse as a thing. When the offended spouse ceased to please, that spouse was rejected. One may treat cars, boats, and even animals as objects to be used, but never may a human person be so humiliated (personalistic norm). Since the offended spouse was presumably sincere in the total self-surrender at the time of the vows, that spouse cannot help but feel totally devastated. First, the offended spouse, believing in the gift of the other party, fell victim to a broken covenant (which is, in itself, devastating) and, as a result, unwittingly became an object of use, a "thing". Second, and even more humiliating, the offended spouse is now rejected even as a "thing" to be used! Objects are at least useful, but the abandoned spouse is not even considered to have a use! No wonder there are such psychological difficulties for those who have been set aside by their spouses! The Pope continually stresses that marriage should be an affirmation of the value of the person. However, when it is no longer indissoluble, it not only ceases to confirm the personal dignity of the individual spouses, it actually has the potential of destroying the sense of self-worth and dignity in the offended spouse. Once that awareness of one's own value is destroyed, it is most difficult to recover it. Spouses rejected in this way have been used as things and may believe themselves to be just that: things (perhaps even worthless things).

The indissolubility of marriage is not harmed either by separation of the spouses without remarriage or by the death of one of the spouses and a subsequent second marriage by the surviving spouse. Separation (in practice in the United States, civil divorce without a second marriage) is an evil, but it is sometimes justified. As John Paul says so descriptively, one or both spouses "may cease to feel that there is any subjective justification for this union, and gradually fall into a state of mind which is psychologically or both psychologically and physiologically incompatible with it. Such a condition warrants separation from 'bed and table', but cannot annul the fact that they are objectively united, and united in wedlock."[9] Even living apart, they are wedded and bound to one another. Their separation, as all other decisions, should be mutually agreeable. But, even if one unilaterally separates, i.e., moves out, that does not change the union in which the spouses are joined. In separation, the self-surrender of both parties remains intact, but it is not expressed. A second marriage after the death of the spouse does not prejudice the self-surrender in marriage because marriage is both a spiritual and a bodily reality. When one of the spouses dies, i.e., when the body and soul separate, the marital union ceases. A widow or widower is free to remarry.

It should be clear that the conclusions of the foregoing discussion regarding the indissolubility of marriage are founded on the principle that marriage is a total communion of persons established by the will-acts of the spouses. Once the self-gift of the man and the woman is made in the marriage vows, it is irrevocable. Even if both cease to feel any stirrings of sensuality or sentiment in the presence of the other, they are still united as husband and wife. They chose one another forever.

C. Revisionist Sexual Morality: An Attack on the Family

The familial communion of persons was established by God in Genesis. Through this union of love, man and woman were to fulfill their calling to love as God loves. However, original sin

[9] See LR, p. 215.

intervened and prevented Adam and Eve from surrendering themselves to each other as God had planned "from the beginning". Indicating that our first parents, by sinning, tottered on the precipice of total self-destruction, the Pope teaches that with the loss of God's grace and the concomitant loss of the dominion of the mind and will over the body, there was a "constitutive break within the human person, almost a rupture of man's original spiritual and somatic unity".[10] Further, there was an "ending of the capacity of a full mutual communion".[11] It is "as if the body, in its masculinity and femininity, no longer constituted the 'trustworthy' substratum of the communion of persons".[12] After sin the other (usually of the opposite sex) is often looked upon not for his own sake, but for selfish reasons: What can he do for me? How can he satisfy my selfish desires and inclinations? But, "man indeed, as a person is 'the only creature on earth that God has willed for its own sake' and, at the same time, he is the one who can fully discover his true self only in a sincere giving of himself."[13] Thus, original sin attacked man in his most essential activity, his sincere giving.

Offenses against the sincere giving in the family, i.e., against the first and primary communion of persons established by God in his creative act, have been committed by men and women since the fall. For example, in divorce and remarriage, as we have seen, the offended spouse is treated as an object. This is a violation of the familial communion of persons caused by selfishness. Selfishness also attacks the family in many other ways, e.g., premarital intercourse, polygamy, adultery and lust, abortion, contraception and artificial conception (test-tube babies), and homosexuality. In our age, most of these practices are not only commonplace (as they have been in past ages), but they are even defended. Many would like to justify these acts and cease making an effort to resist them.

[10] See TB, no. 28.
[11] Ibid., no. 29.
[12] Ibid.
[13] Ibid., no. 32

Four different positions are often advanced in favor of this revisionist morality. The first is proposed by those who misunderstand freedom. They mistakenly equate it with a selfish independence, precluding all forms of self-donation. But this attitude, as well as the actions flowing from it, destroys true freedom because only in an unselfish gift of love is our freedom realized. God made us to love and he also made us free. The two are not in conflict and cannot be because we are made in God's image. Just as God loves and is at the same time perfectly free, when we love unselfishly we are perfectly free. Furthermore, failure to love unselfishly destroys us and consequently our freedom. This is the experience of people who have accepted the "do your own thing" attitude. They ruin themselves, leading miserable lives, because they fail to love, the "fundamental and innate vocation of every human being".[14]

Others would justify these selfish violations of the familial communion of persons by divorcing the body from the human person. This is a fundamental misunderstanding of how God made us. They would argue that if the body is meant to express the person, then the individual should be able to choose how his body should express his person. In their eyes, the Christian sexual ethic makes people slaves to the biological functions of their bodies. If we are to be the masters of nature, why can we not govern our own bodies, freely choosing to express whatever we want through them?

But the human person is not the arbiter of nature! The order of nature is the same as the order of existence and depends upon God, the first cause. On the other hand, the biological order is a scientific abstraction from nature. Showing incredible insight, Karol Wojtyla stated twenty-five years ago that our sexuality "owes its objective importance to its connection with the divine work of creation. . . . and this importance vanishes almost completely if our way of thinking is inspired only by the biological order of nature" which "as a product of the human

---

[14] See FC, no. 11.

intellect . . . abstracts its elements from a larger reality".[15] The Holy Father insists that the body expresses the person as it is because God made the body as well as the soul. In other words, people do not govern their bodies absolutely because their bodies belong by God's creative act to the order of nature, not only to the biological order. There is an integral view of the human person in John Paul's thought, i.e., the body, in all of its functions, is a gift from God just as life itself. As we may not tamper with our lives, so we may not tamper with our bodies.

Still others might argue that since the Christian norms are ideals which can never be attained, God would not ask us to live by them. They might point to the seeming unnatural demands made by the Christian ethic on men and women. Therefore, in their view, acts contrary to these teachings are not sins, i.e., subhuman, but rather are normal (read: permissible) for us. Of course, the commandments are impossible for fallen man without God's grace. With God's grace, however, anything is possible. What is natural for man and woman is the state of original innocence where lust and selfishness were not a problem. In a sense, then, our present state is unnatural. Christ calls us to return to our original state. In response to the questions the Pharisees asked him about divorce, he taught, "Have you not read that he who made them from the beginning made them male and female, and said, 'For this reason a man shall leave his father and mother and be joined to his wife, and the two shall become one'?"[16] The phrase, "the beginning", is a clear reference to the first words in Genesis, to the time before the fall. In other words, Christ told the Pharisees that married people must live the way Adam and Eve did before the fall in a total communion of persons without any tinge of selfishness. This is clearly impossible for fallen man left to his own devices. But Christ would never ask us to do the impossible. His victory

[15] See LR, p. 57.
[16] See Mt 19.4–5.

on the Cross makes God's grace available to us and with that it is possible to live as Adam and Eve did.

A fourth objection to the moral teachings of the Church begins with the same premise as the third one: the Christian moral life is comprised of ideals impossible for us to reach. Since we often fall short of these ideals while striving through our best efforts to live by them, some would argue that we must not be burdened with the full force of the moral ideals, but rather congratulated for what we have attained. Thus, they claim there are differences in the application of the law to individuals, what the Pope calls a gradualness of the law.

However, the Holy Father teaches, as we have seen, that the Christian life is possible with God's grace. It is always attainable. Therefore, we are always bound by the moral teachings. But it is quite clear that we find it easier to do things we have done before. As we practice the Christian life, we grow accustomed to it. There is a growth in virtue. The moral precepts always bind, but they become easier for us to practice. This is not a gradualness in the application of the law to an individual. Rather, it is a gradual perfection of the person in his practice of the Christian life (or as John Paul labels it, the law of gradualness in human behavior).

The Church is *for* man. It has the optimistic view of man. The Church repeats to each human person the message of Christ, "Yes, you can live as God's image!" Those who wish to justify acts opposed to the teachings of the Church and the nature of man and woman see the difficulties and hardships many people have in living according to Christian norms. Although those opposed to Church teaching seem to be motivated by compassion, in effect they are pessimistic about our possibility of ever overcoming the effects of sin. If their position were to be accepted, we would be reduced to a level beneath that planned for us "from the beginning". The Pope counters the arguments of the critics by an insistence that true compassion is that shown by Christ on Calvary. Through the blood of his Cross, we can live as Adam and Eve before the fall, if only we are willing to cooperate with God's grace. As the Pope teaches, "to diminish in no way the saving teaching of Christ constitutes an eminent form of charity for souls".[17] There is no compassion without the truth. Let us always offer the truth compassionately.

D. Violations of the Familial Communion of Persons

1. PREMARITAL SEX

The physical union of a man and a woman before they are married (premarital sex) is an attempt to express with their bodies a union which is not as yet present in their minds and wills. If the body is the expression of the person and if a person is characterized by a mind and a will, then nothing can be expressed with the body which is not in some way known and chosen through the mind and the will. In premarital intercourse, the marital union is not yet present, but the man and the woman are uniting as though they were married. Such is less than a personal act for each because their wills have not yet chosen the union. The self-surrender has not been made, but their bodies are (as though they were independent) surrendering themselves.

Of course, putting the case this way begs the question. As those engaged in premarital sexual contact will argue, the union is present. "I do love her; I do love him. Why must we wait for the symbolic [read: empty and meaningless] marriage vows?" The union of a man and a woman in marriage is, as we have seen, a total self-surrender of each spouse to the other. Marriage is reciprocal. There is no communion of persons without at least two persons. the gift of each spouse is dependent on the other. No one may risk such a total donation without knowing with

[17] See FC, no. 33.

as much certainty as is possible that the other is truly making the same self-donation.

It is not possible to know with certainty that the other intends to make a lasting irrevocable self-donation unless it is a public act. Marriage is a reciprocal self-donation. Private promises are hardly sufficient for each to be sure of the other's self-donation. Even in the lesser self-gift which constitutes employment agreements, most would not trust a private, and therefore, nonbinding agreement. How much more, then, when it is one's total self which is being surrendered, is it necessary to know with certainty that the other is truly making a self-donation.

The public act makes the community the witness and the guarantor of the mutual agreement. Society is willing to secure the marital union because without such an assurance for the spouses, the dignity of its members who enter marriage is at great risk. Further, society is necessarily concerned about its future members, i.e., the children of marital unions who are also put at great risk if the marriage is not surrounded with safeguards. With the public as witness, both spouses are quite aware of the seriousness of the commitment. With that knowledge, each may be reasonably certain of the intention of the other. They both will have given their decisions more careful consideration than they would a nonbinding private act.

Of course, the preceding comments prescind from the marriage of baptized Christians. when two baptized people marry, a sacrament of union is brought into existence. Through the sacrament, the two spouses are united in Christ, not only in a communion of persons between themselves. Christ seals their love, i.e., their self-gift, and unites them in himself. It is as though Christ writes the name of each person on the soul of the other. Christ elevates the spousal communion of persons to a union in the Trinity. If the communion of persons of the nonbaptized requires a public act, how much more should the sacrament of matrimony, an act of the Church, require a public act before a priest or, by special dispensation, before another official. Obviously, Christians cannot express this union before it is present. Premarital sex is thus gravely wrong because it is a violation of the sacramental union as well as a violation of the call given by God in his creative act to form a familial communion of persons.

2. POLYGAMY

In *Familiaris Consortio, The Role of the Christian Family in the Modern World*, the Holy Father writes that the familial communion of persons "is radically contradicted by polygamy: this, in fact, directly negates the plan of God which was revealed from the beginning, because it is contrary to the equal personal dignity of men and women, who, in matrimony, give themselves with a love that is total and therefore unique and exclusive."[18] Polygamy, the union of one man with more than one woman is contrary to the personalistic norm because the one individual divides himself among many (does not give himself totally to any one woman. Polyandry, the union of one woman with more than one man is contrary to the personalistic norm because the one individual divides herself among many (does not give herself totally to any one man). When one man has several wives, each of them may surrender herself to him, but he does not give himself totally to each of them. "Polygamy . . . is in practice conducive to the treatment of women by men as objects of enjoyment and so at once degrades women and lowers the level of morality amongst men. . . . The abolition of polygamy, and the re-establishment of monogamy and the indissolubility of marriage are necessary consequences of the command to love."[19] The same is true with regard to the abolition of polyandry. Few in our society would quarrel with these conclusions.

---

[18] Ibid., no. 19.
[19] See LR, p. 213.

3. ADULTERY AND LUST

Adultery, a married person giving himself physically to someone who is not his spouse, is a betrayal of the familial communion of persons. Just as with divorce and remarriage, the husband or wife guilty of adultery offends his spouse in two ways. First, the married adulterous man or woman presumes to offer what is no longer his to give. A married person has already surrendered himself to his spouse. It is impossible for a husband or a wife to take back this gift from the spouse and bestow it on another because the gift of love must be forever. Second, the adulterous spouse rejects the self-donation of the legitimate spouse. Not only do adulterers presume to take back their own self-gifts, but they also scorn the self-donations of their legitimate spouses. By presuming to take back their own gifts and by rejecting the self-gifts of their spouses, the adulterers treat their spouses as things. It is also clear that adulterers treat their present sexual partners as things. But the sexual partners are at least useful things whereas the legitimate spouses are treated as useless and worthless things.

Adultery has always been one of the gravest sins not only because of the terrible wound to the dignity of the offended spouse which it causes, but also because it is a falsification of the familial communion of persons, which should be a reflection of the trinitarian communion of persons. In the familial communion the spouses have pledged themselves until death. Their love should be faithful as God's love is faithful. Adultery is directly contrary to such a union. Adultery is also a grave sin because, as all sin, it is self-destructive. Through this sin, the adulterers fail to act as God acts, as the images of God which they are. Adultery offends the spouse, the familial communion, and the adulterer.

Christ extends the definition of adultery to a lustful look. Christ teaches, "You have heard that it was said, 'You shall not commit adultery.' But I say to you that every one who looks at a woman lustfully has already committed adultery with her in his heart."[20] Commenting on the words of Christ, the Pope says that a lustful look is an "interior act of the heart", but "a look expresses, I would say, the man within".[21] In this look, the other person is reduced to an object which is viewed as a means to one's own personal gratification. The men or women who look lustfully wish to gratify their physical desires without the sincere giving of themselves that would be present in a true communion of persons. There are, however, further problems with this behavior. The lustful look violates the dignity of the one who looks and the one who is desired. The one who is desired becomes an object, a thing. But those who look lustfully are, at the same time, reducing themselves to things. If people seek to unite themselves with things, then how are they superior to them? The look violates the infinite dignity of both persons.

Of course, Christ's expansion of adultery to include an interior act of one's heart indicates that even two spouses may commit "adultery" with one another. Adultery is the reduction of another human being to a thing. When a married person thinks of the other as an object (lustful look) or uses the spouse in an act, e.g., forced intercourse, that person is committing "adultery". If the dignity of both spouses is preserved, neither may use the spouse in these ways. In other words, the personalistic norm must be observed or adultery is committed.

Lust also "entails the loss of the interior freedom of the gift".[22] Since a gift ceases to be a gift when it is the result of compulsion, lust makes the self-surrender, the gift of one spouse to the other, impossible. When lust dominates one of the spouses, the mutual, selfless, free giving necessary to the expression of the communion of persons is missing. Only God's grace allows the spouses to gain control over themselves and

[20] See Mt 5:27–28.
[21] See TB, no. 39.
[22] Ibid., no. 32.

makes it possible for them to give themselves to each other freely without any tinge of selfishness stemming from lust or any other cause.

It is important to note the difference between a lustful look and an admiration of God's beauty as manifested in the human body and in art. "There are works of art whose subject is the human body in its nakedness, and the contemplation of which makes it possible to concentrate, in a way, on the whole truth of man, on the dignity and the beauty—also the 'suprasensual' beauty—of his masculinity and femininity. These works bear within them, almost hidden, an element of sublimation, which leads the viewer, through the body, to the whole personal mystery of man."[23] In the hands of great artists, the naked human body is painted, sculpted, or otherwise depicted truly as the expression of the person. Thus, in Michelangelo's works we are not led to lustful looking. With *Playboy*, the purpose is quite different. The same principles apply to our own admiration of the physical beauty of another. Providing we are focusing on the whole mystery of man, the full truth about the other, then we will not be led to adultery in the heart.

4. ABORTION

The familial communion of persons is founded on the self-donation of each spouse and in this way is an imitation of the Holy Trinity. When God loves, it is life-giving. He loved us in creation and gave us life. In the redemption, he surrendered himself totally for us and this love brought forth life, divine life, in us. Since we are made in his image, our love, the love of persons, is also life-giving. In the familial communion of persons, the gift of a man and a woman to each other in their bodies does serve life, new life. This is plainly stated by John Paul when he writes, "Thus, the couple, while giving themselves to one another, give not just themselves but also the reality of children,

[23] Ibid., no. 63.

who are a living reflection of their love, a permanent sign of conjugal unity."[24] "A relationship between spirits which begets a new embodied spirit is something unknown in the natural order."[25] Procreation is the most profound blessing which can be bestowed on the love of a couple. They have cooperated with God in giving life to a person, a spiritual being. With this gift, there are responsibilities. Married love, the willingness to bear burdens for the sake of the spouse and children, makes these responsibilities a joy.

Abortion, the killing of a yet unborn child, is evidence of a deep-rooted selfishness. If, in the physical union of a man and a woman, one or both are seeking their own desires, one or both will not hesitate to use the other's body as a thing to achieve some other end. If the other's body is treated and used as a thing, it is a small (but logical) step, when pleasure is the goal, to regard the child as merely so much tissue, a product of conception. Paralleling the attitude toward the other, the selfish man or woman views the child as just a thing, a biological growth, which may be cut out or manipulated (e.g., fetal experimentation) in any way. The removal of this growth through abortion might seem to be especially appropriate if the self-centered man or woman does not like it because the child is handicapped or even because the child's gender is not the one desired. The possibility (or so someone with such an attitude might think) of new growths which may be preferable is always present. Unborn children then become things (like the sexual partner) which persons rooted in selfishness can make and use to suit themselves. This is selfishness carried to an extreme. With such an attitude, the human race cannot survive because God made us to love, to give, not to be selfish.

Abortion, as an extreme manifestation of selfishness, is a radical contradiction in the familial communion of persons. Moreover, in the premarital or adulterous union, abortion

<hr />

[24] See FC, no. 14.
[25] See LR, p. 55.

is an even more extreme indication of selfishness than the relationship itself. In all cases, abortion is a sign of the total rejection of the child's mother or father. When the partners in marriage truly make a self-donation to one another, i.e., when they love one another, they are open to life. A rejection of life is a rejection of love. On the other hand, the giving and acceptance of new life is the most profound realization of the familial communion of persons. But even outside of marriage, a baby is always flesh of the parents. To reject that person, a new life and the fruit of love, is to reject the sexual partner. Thus, abortion is not only destructive to children (undoubtedly the most terrible aspect of the war on the unborn), it also destroys mothers and fathers. Short of the murder of the spouse or of one's sexual partner, abortion, the taking of life, is the greatest possible rejection of another.

5. CONTRACEPTION AND ARTIFICIAL CONCEPTION

As we have seen, the personalistic norm is violated by divorce and remarriage, premarital intercourse, polygamy, adultery and lust, as well as abortion. Contraception also attacks the total gift of a man and a woman to one another. Husbands and wives cannot give themselves to each other completely when they refuse to surrender themselves at least potentially as mothers and fathers. In one of the clearest and most forceful statements on contraception, Wojtyla writes that couples who practice contraception " 'manipulate' and degrade human sexuality— and with it themselves and their married partner—by altering its value of 'total' self-giving. Thus, the innate language that expresses the total reciprocal self-giving of husband and wife is overlaid, through contraception, by an objectively contradictory language, namely, that of not giving oneself totally to the other."[26]

[26] See FC, no. 32.

Human persons, created in God's image with bodies and souls, should reflect God, i.e., they should love by giving themselves unreservedly to others. Since we are embodied spirits and the body is the expression of the person, it is appropriate that there be a bodily means of giving ourselves to one another, i.e., of loving one another. The bodily differences between a man and a woman are the physical means by which the unselfish donation in love is made. The sexual act should be the total physical surrender of each spouse to the other. As such, it should be a sign and expression of the fundamental union the spouses enjoy in the familial communion of persons established through the marriage vows. Since we are made in the divine image, it is fitting that our love be fruitful as God's love is fruitful. Thus, the self-donation of a man and a woman to one another includes the possibility of procreating new life. Contraception alters the sexual act and makes it something other than a self-surrender. For the contracepting couple, the sexual act is a lie because the spouses refuse to give themselves to one another as potential mothers and fathers. They engage in what is only an apparent act of self-surrender. In other words, since the sexual union is no longer the expression of a total gift, it does not mirror the spousal communion of persons.

But even for the premarital or adulterous couple, contraception cannot be defended. Adultery and premarital intercourse are offenses against the familial communion of persons because in such acts the man and the woman attempt to surrender themselves to each other without having properly chosen each other in their wills. In effect, they presume to divorce their bodies from their persons and still to give themselves to each other in a bodily way. However, in contracepting, they even refuse to give themselves fully to each other in their flesh. Even the bodily union is not a gift. It is only an apparent gift, i.e., a lie.

In an act of love, husband and wife should give themselves to each other and should be open to the transmission of life. The denial of either good, conjugal love or procreation constitutes a falsification of the act. With conjugal love or procreation denied, the act no longer reflects God's fruitful love. Most would grant that a husband seeking only children from his wife without any thought of her welfare is using her. Such a man denies the value of conjugal love. However, the husband who denies the possibility of procreation also is using his wife. (The wife, of course, would be using her husband if she denies either conjugal love or the procreation of children.) For God, life and love are not separated and thus, for us, as images of God, life and love should not be separated, i.e., conjugal love and life should always be united.

Contraception and the other abuses against the familial communion of persons are violations of the personalistic norm and therefore aggressions against human dignity. They occur because of original sin and its effects, especially selfishness as manifested in lust. But other forms of selfishness, in addition to lust, are equally damaging to the communion of persons and human dignity. For example, some couples may selfishly wish to have a large number of children although they cannot care for all of them. Such children can become mere objects possessed by their parents. This is a grave violation of human dignity. Another form of selfishness is apparent in some couples who experience difficulties in conceiving a child. They desire children more than any other gift God could give them. Desperately seeking to conceive a child, they might turn to their physician for advice. The doctor may suggest that they visit one of the clinics where babies are conceived in test tubes.

This practice, however, cannot be tolerated. The couple's selfish desire for children leads them to violate their own dignity by manipulating and using their bodies. The practice of artificial conception reduces procreation to a merely biological, laboratory act when it must be, by God's will, the fruit of a covenant, a communion of persons, as expressed in the conjugal embrace of a man and a woman joined in marriage. A new spirit, a baby, must be conceived within a union of spirits, i.e., the spousal union. Artificial conception is a manipulation because it divorces the life-giving potential of the body from the person.

Similar to the contracepting couple, the test-tube baby couple refuses to accept God's will in their own lives and claims total control over their bodies. But the body is not a machine and it is contrary to human dignity to manipulate it.

When a couple contracepts or conceives artificially (or when these practices are defended by others), sexuality is reduced to a merely biological function. With this understanding of sexuality in place, there is no reason to object to surrogate mothers, artificial insemination, and many other serious abuses which are now proposed and even practiced. Such a view destroys both love as it is expressed physically, and life as the fruit of the love of spirits, i.e., persons. The widespread acceptance of artificial conception and these other abuses shows how the contraceptive mentality has accustomed us to view our bodies as machines. If human dignity is to be preserved, we must abandon this false understanding of ourselves.

6. HOMOSEXUALITY

The bodily differences between a man and a woman given by God in his creative act are the physical means of expressing a familial communion of persons. Further, the bodily expression of love serves life, new life, because God willed that our love be fruitful as his love is fruitful. Homosexual activity can never be a physical expression of familial love. Familial love is precisely the union of a man and a woman in a total self-donation, which is physically expressed through their masculine and feminine bodies. Since it is impossible for two men (or two women) to give themselves physically to one another, any attempted union between them ceases to be a gift. It becomes a using of each other, or, at least, a using of each other's bodies. Again, such use is a violation of the personalistic norm and not an expression of the familial communion of persons. A further indication that homosexual acts cannot be the expression of a true self-donation of each to the other is that such acts are always and in every case sterile. They do not serve life. Two men (or two women) can never form a familial communion of persons.

Still, if both homosexual and heterosexual orientations are transmitted by genes, neither is consciously chosen. Even if homosexual tendencies are learned or acquired in some other way, they are not usually the result of a free personal choice. The person with a homosexual orientation has not chosen to violate the vocation to love. But, of course, a homosexual act is the result of a choice in the will. When a homosexual chooses to act on his tendencies, he chooses to use himself and others. Therefore, specific homosexual acts are contrary to our call to love. On the other hand, the homosexual orientation, even though it may make a true self-donation to a person of the opposite sex difficult, does not directly contradict our vocation to imitate God's love.

The less difficult road is the one of least resistance: to surrender to selfishness and then to justify the actions. In the present era many have followed this path. Not only have some people used other people, but they have also justified such actions. The false ideas employed to justify such abuses have established thought patterns for our entire society. Thus, they are even more destructive than individual lapses against human dignity. Those who wish to reject the abuses and the arguments favoring them have difficulty because they, in doing so, are rejecting their own culture. They are acting counter-culturally, which is always most difficult.

It is clear that many who attack human dignity either in their behavior or, more seriously by justifying selfish acts, misunderstand human dignity or believe the Christian norms to be impossible ideals. The Pope teaches that our dignity rests on the divine image in each one of us. Knowing the destruction which the false concepts of human dignity have caused, how can we refuse to accept the truth of the papal understanding of ourselves? The Pope insists that our lustful and other selfish inclinations are gravely harmful to human dignity and that they can be overcome in Christ. Christ calls each and every one of us "to the beginning", to live as Adam and Eve did, despite original sin and its effects, and he makes this possible through his grace won for us by the blood of his Cross. Christ desires every human person to share his life, his grace with him. Therefore, he makes himself present to us in the sacraments. However, even blessed with grace we may fail in our effort to act as we were made "in the beginning", but his forgiving love, available in the sacrament of penance, restores us and allows us to make the effort again. Nonetheless, this optimistic view of the human person rests on the acceptance of the papal view of our dignity and the equally important principle that the effort to live in accordance with that dignity is worthwhile. We must acknowledge that the alternatives to the Christian norms are gravely injurious to our dignity, i.e., to our very selves.

F. Natural Family Planning

The Holy Father proposes that natural family planning be the means for teaching the world to observe the personalistic norm. This mandate from John Paul II is extraordinary. He advocates knowledge of the fertility cycle for everyone, even those not yet married. In *The Role of the Christian Family in the Modern World*, the Pope writes, "The necessary conditions [for marriage] also include knowledge of the bodily aspect and body's rhythms of fertility. Accordingly, every effort must be made to render such knowledge accessible to all married people and also to young adults before marriage, through clear, timely and serious instruction and education given by married couples, doctors, and experts."[27] Obviously, the Pope sees that the understanding of one's fertility, as taught in natural family planning courses, is essential to married life and even to one's life before marriage.

Natural family planning is a tool for understanding and examining human fertility. Through this tool, both married and

[27] Ibid., no. 33.

unmarried adults learn about their fertility. Then they make
use of this knowledge depending, of course, upon their state
of life. Many have identified the knowledge of fertility with the
decision of couples to avoid or to have children. However, the
distinction between the knowledge of fertility and the application of that knowledge within the sexual act is vital. Natural
family planning is used here to mean the tool for understanding human fertility. But the tool is distinct from how a couple
applies it in their sexual relationship. In other words, natural
family planning is a method. As a method for understanding
one's own fertility, it is universally approved.

In applying the method of natural family planning in marriage, couples are to exercise responsible parenthood. This
means that husband and wife are to have a definite family and
procreative attitude. They are to be *for* children because their
love should reflect God's love which is always life-giving. In
the normal situation, a married couple must decide each month
whether to seek a pregnancy or not. They must have sufficient
reasons for either decision. If "there exist reasonable grounds
for spacing births, arising from physical or psychological condition of husband or wife, or from external circumstances",[28]
then a couple may have recourse to periods of infertility and
may abstain from the sexual embrace during their fertile times.
Outside of marriage, young adults apply the knowledge of their
fertility responsibly when they exercise chastity.

The underlying reason why young adults, engaged couples,
and married couples should know natural family planning is
that this method teaches them that the body, as God made it,
is the expression of the person. For example, when husband
and wife accept the natural cycle of fertility and infertility as a
gift from God, not subject to artificial manipulation, they usually assent to the principle that the body is the expression of the

---

[28] See Karol Wojtyla (Pope John Paul II), "A Discipline That Ennobles Human
Love", *L'Osservatore Romano* (English edition), vol. 17, no. 36 (September 3,
1984), p. 6.

person. They experience themselves as spirits endowed with a body and they know that those who would divorce the body from the person misunderstand human beings.

An unmarried female might begin to observe the signs of the fertility and infertility of her own body and thus come to a greater appreciation of the mystery and wonder of herself as a woman. This greater appreciation of her dignity, gained through natural family planning, would foster in her the virtue of chastity because she in no way would want to compromise her dignity.

Pope John Paul has issued a universal and unrestricted call for all men and women to learn natural family planning, i.e., to know their own fertility. In John Paul's view, natural family planning is a means to counteract the entire sexually permissive mentality which encourages a manipulation of the body and a contempt of self-mastery. It is a means to teach the theology of the body. Natural family planning is thus the means by which many men and women learn to affirm human dignity by observing the personalistic norm.

F. Virginity

It is possible that the papal emphasis on the familial communion of persons could obscure the equally important principle that virginity and celibacy are treasured gifts from God as well. Those who have voluntarily remained unmarried for the sake of the Kingdom of God have entered a communion of persons (the Church), albeit not a familial one (in the usual sense, at least), which is expressed through their bodies. "In virginity or celibacy, the human being . . . in a bodily way . . . anticipates in his or her flesh the new world of the future resurrection."[29] Bodily this communion is expressed in the celibate's self-mastery,

[29] See FC, no. 16.

not unlike that expected of married couples. Further, the celibate or virgin does not view sexuality as something worthless. "When human sexuality is not regarded as a great value given by the Creator, the renunciation of it for the sake of the Kingdom of Heaven loses its meaning."[30] If love (a communion of persons founded on a total self-donation of one person to another) is not valued in marriage, it will not be held in high esteem in its other expression, celibacy and virginity.

G. Conclusion

"*The future of humanity passes by way of the family*"[31] because it is in the family that the incomparable dignity of each human person is first affirmed. Each family member should make a self-donation to the others. There can be no greater affirmation of one's own dignity than receiving the infinitely precious gift of other human persons. The self-donation, certainly on the part of the husband and the wife, must be total and it must be given as a response to the dignity of each family member. The children then learn to love from their parents, who are the teachers in this school of love called the family.

However, it is equally true that no institution can do more harm to individuals than the family. For, if the dignity of each is not affirmed because one or more (but, again, especially the husband or the wife) are acting for selfish reasons, the results are devastating to the members of the family.

[30] Ibid.
[31] Ibid., no. 86.

The Family and Work

A. Work: The Human Person
Shares in the Creative Act

In his third encyclical, *Laborem Exercens, On Human Work*, John Paul II proclaimed that "In the first place, work is 'for man' and not man 'for work.' . . . In the final analysis, it is always man who is the purpose of work." Man works and "these actions must serve to realize his humanity, to fulfill the calling to be a person that is his by reason of his very humanity."[1] In this teaching, Pope John Paul is echoing the *Pastoral Constitution on the Church in the Modern World*: "Human activity proceeds from man: it is also ordered to him. When he works, not only does he transform matter and society, but he fulfills himself."[2]

God created us in his own likeness and then invited us to participate in the divine activities: "God blessed them and God said to them . . . 'Fill the earth and subdue it.' "[3] The command to subdue and dominate the earth is a corollary to our creation in the image of God. In applying ourselves to the goods of creation, we subdue the earth. Through the tasks performed (the objective purpose of work), we achieve dominion over creation. Thus, it is through work that we participate, as God intended from the very dawn of the world, in the divine dominion over the world. This dominion is proper to us as images of God because it is a reflection of the dominion God has over the world. Therefore, through the objective purpose

[1] See LE, no. 6.
[2] See GS, no. 35.
[3] See Gen 1:28.

of work, the more important subjective purpose of work is achieved: we become what we are, i.e., images of God.

By the same token, when one fails to act as God does, i.e., does not work, he violates himself. The human person is made to participate in God's creative act and to realize his own humanity through work. When human beings refuse this august invitation from God, they fail to participate in God's dominion and they fail to realize themselves as images of God. They act in a way destructive to their dignity and even to their humanity. Both our dignity and humanity rest on our creation in God's image, which is realized partly through work. The application of the subjective turn to work clearly yields a new understanding.

John Paul teaches that "Man has to subdue the earth and dominate it because as the 'image of God' he is a person, that is to say, a subjective being capable of acting in a planned and rational way, capable of deciding about himself and with a tendency to self-realization."[4] One who works engages in a freely chosen rational activity. A worker must possess an intellect to understand the purposes of work. Secondly, a worker must possess free will to choose both the subjective and the objective purposes of work. Since only persons have minds and wills, personhood is a prerequisite for work. It is clear that of all God's earthly creatures only human beings, persons made in the image of God, can work. Animals and other nonpersons do not work. Lacking intellect and will, they are incapable of work (even though we sometimes speak of a machine or a farm animal "working").

Since human beings are not merely spiritual entities (as the angels are), but possess bodies which express their persons, it is fitting that the human body participate in work. The first tasks (objective purpose of work) entrusted to human beings involved physical labor, e.g., farming and hunting. God asked man to subdue the earth and this is what farmers do. "Have

---

[4] See LE, no. 6.

dominion" over the animals seems initially connected with hunting. Therefore, in the first place, human work refers to a bodily activity which is known by the intellect and chosen by the will. Even intellectual work has a bodily aspect. Our minds operate through sense impressions gathered through our bodily senses.

Since work is *for* man, it is also *for* the body, which shares in the dignity proper to every human person. In the first tasks given to human beings in Genesis, the gathering of food through farming and hunting, the work done was not directly *for* man in the subjective sense (i.e., in working man fulfilled himself by sharing in God's creative act), it was also *for* man in the objective sense (i.e., in the results of the work). The result of the work was food *for* man (i.e., for the body). When the objective purpose of work is directly related to the most basic necessities, it is most unlikely that a conflict will arise between the subjective aspect of work and its objective results. In this case the two aspects of work converge. However, in more complicated and advanced societies human work is often not as directly related to the worker's needs as in primitive societies. There can then be an emphasis on the results of work (the transitive aspect) to the exclusion of the primary purpose of work, i.e., that the worker fulfill himself by sharing in God's creative act. It was to point out such risks and possible solutions to them that Pope John Paul II wrote his encyclical *On Human Work*.

B. *Worker Solidarity: A Communion of Persons*

In working, people engage in an endeavor with one another. In working, people develop relationships from which social life, culture, and even political associations take shape. But in working with others, the personalistic norm must always be observed. Human persons may never be reduced to objects of use. "The person is a good toward which the only proper adequate attitude is love."[5] Love is primarily a union of wills of two or more persons. It was perfectly expressed by Christ in the agony in the garden when he prayed, "Not my will, but thine be done."[6] Workers acting together for a common purpose must unite their wills with one another and establish a communion of persons. They should know and will the same common goals. In their common effort, even if the product or result be insignificant in terms of society or economic gain, they are subduing the earth and, more importantly, fulfilling themselves as beings made in God's image and called to share in his activities. If an individual does not know or choose both the objective and subjective purposes of his work, it is difficult to understand how he would be acting in a way befitting a person. He would be little better than a machine functioning according to the will of the owner, e.g., the employer.

Work unites more than the few who are engaged in an individual project. It unites all people. The object of work, the natural resources of the earth, was given by God to everyone in his creative act. All people are entrusted with these resources and are invited to participate in the divine creative act by subduing and dominating them. Since work is an activity proper to all human persons and since its object is what all men and women possess as their birthright, work is a common project entrusted to all people. Work "embraces all human beings, every generation, every phase of economic and cultural development".[7] Work, since it is a universal phenomenon and since its object is what all hold in common, should unify everyone, the entire human race. In a sense, the specific objective purposes of work are merely part of the whole objective purpose of work, i.e., to dominate the earth. Each minute project is part of the larger whole. The worker, then, should will not only the individual task on which he is working, but also should will, together

[5] See LR, p. 41.
[6] See Lk 22:42.
[7] See LE, no. 4.

with the entire human race, the broader objective purpose of work. As his act of assent to the more particular task unites the worker with those engaged with him in the project, so his consent to the broader and universal objective purpose of work unites him with all people everywhere. Even when work is done alone, e.g., a scientist in a laboratory, or an author at a desk, the worker is still working with others in the sense that he wills his own work to be part of the general, objective purpose of all work. Not only do all workers participate in God's creative act through their work, but they also should have a common share in the fruits of their labor.

However, more importantly, the individual worker must not only know and choose the objective purpose of work, he must also will his own perfection in and through the work done. Further, just as he unites himself with others in knowing and choosing the objective purpose of his particular job and he joins with all workers in knowing and choosing the broad universal objective purpose of work, so must he unite himself with others in knowing and choosing the subjective purpose of work for all workers, i.e., that through work everyone would fulfill himself as an image of God. If everyone knew and chose the objective and the subjective purposes of work, no person would be viewed as a means for work. Rather work everywhere would indeed be *for* mankind.

In the final analysis, the individual work which each worker performs is less important than the subjective goal of all work, the fulfillment of each individual person. Of course, a worker cannot fulfill himself through work unless he is united with others. To work selfishly without a union of wills with others is not to work in the sense of Genesis. Worker solidarity flows from the subjective aspect of work. This also makes sense in terms of the most important activity of the human person: love. Human beings are made to love as God loves. When we love, we become more Godlike. If work also makes us Godlike, it must involve love. Therefore, we only fulfill ourselves through work if we love, i.e., if there is a communion of persons established in and through work. As the *Pastoral Constitution on the Church in the Modern World* teaches: "When he [man] works . . . he transcends himself."[8]

Work then becomes endowed with a dignity beyond compare, for through it the individual participates in a divine activity and becomes more perfectly an image of God. In addition, work becomes a unifying principle for all people. All workers, i.e., all human beings, are joined in a communion of persons because all will the primary (subjective) purpose of work (the perfection of each and every human being), as well as the broad and general (objective) purpose of work (the subduing of the earth). With a rightful and just share in the fruits of labor for all (implied by the union of wills, i.e., love, and the common ownership of the natural resources of the earth given by God in creation), this concept of worker solidarity is a program for peace for the entire world. It is important to note that this program of peace and solidarity rests on God's mandate in his creative act. It holds for all people because it is what we all must do to be true to our very selves as created in the divine likeness.

Since work is *for* man, work is a good thing. Of course, work, when it is forced upon people, can be the means of an attack on human dignity. Such is the situation in concentration camps where the prisoners suffer profound degradation, partially through work forced upon them without their willing consent or their knowledge of the objective purpose of the work. (Often, in fact, the work is useless, which degrades the inmates even further since in this case they are even less than an instrument or a thing.) The assault against human dignity through work occurs precisely because the human person is treated as a machine incapable of knowing and loving. As machines, the prisoners exist for work and not work *for* them. Through the denial of their personhood, their powers of knowing and choosing, they are robbed of their dignity and they no

[8] See GS, no. 35.

longer work as images of God who have been invited to participate in God's creative act. To impose work on another is to attack the human person, who is the very purpose of all work.[9] It is a particularly vicious attack against God and humanity and it should never be perpetrated by one against another.

Only when we act in accordance with our dignity as persons made in the image of God are we fulfilling ourselves in and through work. In working then, we must always function as beings endowed with minds and wills. With our minds we know that we are the purpose of all work, and with our wills we join ourselves in love for the common effort of fulfilling ourselves. If we are not to be reduced to the level of machines, we must know and love work as our share in the creative act of God. "Man develops through love for work."[10] Man

> wishes that within the production process provision be made for him to be able to know that in his work, even on something that is owned in common, he is working 'for himself.' This awareness is extinguished within him in a system of excessive bureaucratic centralization, which makes the worker feel that he is just a cog in a huge machine moved from above, that he is . . . a mere production instrument rather than a true subject of work with an initiative of his own.[11]

The subjective turn as applied to the working person clearly reveals that work is subordinate to the one working. The worker has a right to act as a person, i.e., to know and to love, in his work. Only with these rights guaranteed is his dignity as a person preserved and only in this way does he fulfill himself in work.

[9] See LE, no. 6.
[10] Ibid., no. 11.
[11] Ibid., no. 15.

C. Work: For Man and for the Family

I. THE RELATIONSHIP OF THE TWO
COMMUNIONS, WORK AND FAMILY

Pope John Paul II teaches that "Work constitutes a foundation for the formation of family life."[12] Although work is *for* man, it is also true that human persons are *for* the family. Human beings are *for* the family in the sense that they are called to give themselves in familial love, if not as a spouse, certainly as a child. (Even those who remain unmarried still are bound to give themselves in love within the families which gave them life.) If work is *for* man and man is *for* the family, then the communion of persons in the workplace is *for* the family. Through work, a worldwide communion of persons is established. But this is not the primary communion of persons. The first and foremost communion of persons (aside from our share, through God's grace, in the trinitarian communion of Persons) is the family. The familial bond was established by God prior to the invitation to share in his creative act through work. Further, the family is more closely associated with God since it is in the family that new life is brought forth. Just as God gives life when he loves, so his images, human persons, share the same privilege in the family. But the love among workers does not bring forth new life. Moreover, only in the family is there a complete and total self-surrender of one individual to another forever. Workers do not love each other in this way.

Work serves us as individuals and as members of a familial communion of persons. Therefore, there should be no conflict between family and work. This relationship is quite clear in the farm community. All family members join together in work to produce food and the other necessities of life for the family. The familial communion of persons becomes the communion of persons of the workplace. Although engaged in a specific

[12] Ibid., no. 10.

project, i.e., obtaining the necessities of life, the familial communion of persons at work is joined to all other workers in solidarity across the globe in the common project of subduing the earth. It is important to note that the familial bond is the *raison d'être* of the second bond. Thus, work should nourish the family and not destroy it.

2. THE TWO-CAREER FAMILY

The neglect of the subjective aspect of work has given rise to certain modern difficulties in the relationship between work and the family. Ignoring work as the fulfillment of the divine image in us, there is an emphasis on what is produced or on one's own material success in work. The object of work becomes more important than the worker. Things, which the worker should dominate, become more important than him. With such an attitude, the individual becomes an object for work. But work should always be *for* man.

The loss of the primary importance of work in the subjective sense has divorced the communion of persons in the workplace from the communion of persons in the family. If the human person is *for* the family and also for work, there is quite naturally a tension between these two demands on his time. Instead of the one serving the other, there is a genuine competition between two (seemingly) equally important vocations. The family usually suffers more than work because the loss of the subjective importance of work occurs precisely because workers value things, creation, more than themselves. With this value judgment in place, the family will always lose the competition because the family is composed of persons and the workplace (in this view) is concerned with things. Quite naturally and logically then, the family is less and less important to many workers.

Although the subjective sense of work is sometimes lost in our society, certain elements of it are almost always retained. For example, it is generally believed that everyone, men and women,

has a right to work. In past decades it was thought proper for men
to work in the marketplace and for women to tend the home.
Now, this practice is viewed as almost a degradation of women.
Of course, women, created in the image of God, have as their
birthright a vocation to work. But when this valid, subjective
sense of work is coupled with the contemporary (false) belief
that the worker exists *for* work, the family is gravely threatened.
With this view in place, it would be possible for both husband
and wife, perhaps even the children, to insist on working outside
the home. Work would then become more important than the
family (because work concerns things which in this view are
more highly valued than people). Each family member would
not only neglect essential tasks within the home, but would even
neglect the other members of the family for the sake of work.
Caring for each other, especially in difficult situations, e.g.,
sickness, would involve tasks considered unworthy of a human
being because such "work" does not produce anything tangible
or enhance one's career! Constant fighting would develop over
whose work (outside the home) would be more important
and the familial communion of persons would be threatened.
The problem does not lie in the insistence that women have a
vocation to work. The difficulty is founded on a fundamental
misunderstanding about work itself.

The Holy Father's new emphasis on the subjective aspect
of work corrects this false view and offers a solution to the
familial difficulties arising from it. Through his reference to
the two mandates God gave to Adam and Eve in Genesis,
John Paul clearly demonstrates that the vocation to the familial
communion of persons is primary. Both parents and children
must care for (love) each other in the family first. It is as wrong
for the father to ignore the family in favor of work as it is
for the mother. In fact, the first "work" we are called to do
is the "work" of love in the family. To place this "work" in
a secondary role is offensive not only to those in our family
but also to our own selves because it is a failure to love as we
should. Secondly, the restored subjective emphasis also indicates

that it matters little what the object of one's work is so long as the family has the necessities of life. The results of work, the object of work or its transitive aspect, cannot be valued more highly than persons and the familial communion. Decisions, then, about employment for *all* family members must be made on the basis of whether or not a particular occupation interferes with the obligations of that family member within the family and whether or not it provides the means to obtain the necessities of life.

3. WOMEN AND WORK

There is a further consideration regarding the employment of family members. Work, as we have seen, is connected closely with the body. God made human beings male and female, and their bodily differences are *for* the family. These differences exist so that there is a bodily way of expressing the familial communion of persons. Since work is *for* the individual and the family, it may never place physical demands on a person which would be destructive to his body or would interfere with his capacity to express conjugal love and care for children. Work may never threaten the familial communion of persons by competing with the family or by making physical demands on family members which harm the nuptial meaning of the body.

A mother's role in the family is very much a physical and emotional one, i.e., a bodily one. It is she, in an extraordinary way because of her motherhood—a bodily as well as a spiritual reality—who lavishes love, affection, and care on her children. By nature, she is suited for this. A father's love is not expressed in nearly such an intense physical, i.e., bodily way. It is necessary then for the mother to be with the children in a physical way and to be physically capable of caring for the children. This, of course, implies not only health, but freedom from physical and emotional exhaustion. A mother's role is not only crucial to the family, but also to society. However, this seems to contradict the principle that all men and women have as their birthright the vocation to work in the marketplace, i.e., to subdue and dominate the earth. How can a mother fulfill her own vocation to work in the marketplace?

First, as the Pope reminds us in a moving passage, "Toil is something that is universally known, for it is universally experienced. . . . It is familiar to women who sometimes without recognition on the part of society and even of their own families bear the daily burden and responsibility for their homes and the upbringing of their children."[13] A mother's vocation in the family is work! Primarily it is the "work" of love in the familial communion of persons. (Fathers have an obligation in this regard as well as mothers.) A mother's work in the home is also work in the sense of the marketplace. She "subdues and dominates" the things of the home for the sake of her family. She brings order to the part of creation around her. Further, this work is of the noblest kind for it is directly concerned with people. Thus, her vocation to work and her vocation as a mother are synonymous.

The Holy Father also clearly affirms the right of women, even mothers, to work outside the home. He writes that women

> should be able to fulfill their tasks in accordance with their own nature, without being discriminated against and without being excluded from jobs for which they are capable, but also without lack for their family aspirations. . . . The true advancement of women requires that labor should be structured in such a way that women do not have to pay for their advancement by abandoning what is specific to them and at the expense of the family, in which women as mothers have an irreplaceable role.[14]

Women, like men, have a call to work, first in the familial communion of persons, and then *for* the family in the marketplace. No mother should be compelled to work outside the home. If she does so, the work, just as with a man's work, should never interfere with her family obligations. Of course, these

13 Ibid., no. 9.
14 Ibid., no. 19.

conclusions are self-evident if the subjective aspect of work is understood.

4. THE ECONOMIC AND
SOCIAL RIGHTS OF THE FAMILY

John Paul challenges society to restore the superiority of the family and the individual over work. He suggests "a social re-evaluation of the mother's role, of the toil connected with it and of the need that children have for care".[15] He also proposes that there be "grants to mothers devoting themselves exclusively to their families".[16] Society, short of risking its own demise, cannot allow anything to harm its members or its families. Of course, a false understanding of work in the marketplace threatens individuals and families. If work is more highly valued than the worker, mothers and fathers, even children, become machines who exist for work, not *for* their families. The papal proposals, if implemented, would eliminate some of the modern threats to family life in two ways. First, very practically, they would make it possible for families to live as families. Mothers, for example, would be more likely to fulfill their familial obligations. Second, more theoretically, the papal proposals directly conflict with the principle that the human person is for work. Since this (false) idea provides the foundation for many modern threats to family life, John Paul's suggestions would at least weaken the theoretical base for some modern attacks on family life. For example, if the papal proposals were put into practice, the dignity of a mother's work in the home would be affirmed. In other words, the Pope's suggestions would teach everyone that work is *for* man.

Beyond this restoration of the subjective aspect of work as it relates to families, society must organize to do everything possible to ensure employment for at least one member of the

[15] Ibid.
[16] Ibid.

family. All have a right to work, but, when the scourge of unemployment attacks a society, preference must be given to the primary workers in each family. Families need a decent income and thus at least one family member must be employed. It does not seem reasonable to offer employment to members of families which already have an income if there are other families without anyone employed. A second worker in the family, provided the family is already receiving an adequate income from the first worker, is a luxury. But *an* income is necessary to each family. In an ideal situation, there would be jobs for all, and if there were not, those families which had a second income would offer jobs to other families which had none. Such would be the only responsible course because it is not in accord with human dignity that one family should have an abundance while another family lacks the basic necessities. The goods of the world and the fruits of human labor belong to all workers, i.e., the entire human race. The employer has some obligation to offer employment to those in real need.

John Paul also affirms that "just remuneration for the work of an adult who is responsible for a family means remuneration which will suffice for establishing and properly maintaining a family and for providing security for its future."[17] Just because a man or a woman is working in the family, this does not deprive that person of the right to share in the fruits of labor. Rather, he should be given some of the goods of the earth and the fruit of labor through the family member who does earn a salary in the marketplace. Wages must be measured against the worker and his needs as an individual and as a member of a family, the primary vocation of all. There must be a family wage.

Wages, then, cannot depend solely on the work done. Wages must be determined by the needs of the worker as an individual and, even more importantly, as a member of a family. Neither men nor women should be paid on the basis of what is produced —that would be to measure the infinite dignity of a human

[17] Ibid.

person by mere things. Wages must be determined by needs. There could be a minimum salary which all heads of households with dependents would receive. It might also be that those who do not have familial responsibilities would not receive this same minimum, even for the same task. They would not be doing the familial "work"! Thus, the motto equal pay for equal work would need some modification. Once the minimum is guaranteed and the needs of individuals and families are met, it is certainly proper to offer incentives and salary increases for more difficult tasks and for better work. But the first responsibility of society is to ensure that the needs of individuals and families are satisfied. Of course, as mentioned earlier, there are possibilities other than a family wage, e.g., grants to mothers who stay at home. Such grants would provide them with their share in the goods of the earth and fruits of labor, and it would recognize in a public way the contribution of their work to society.

The Holy Father teaches that

> Besides wages, various social benefits intended to ensure the life and health of workers and their families play a part here. The expenses involved in health care, especially in the case of accidents at work, demand that medical assistance should be easily available for workers and that as far as possible it should be cheap or even free of charge. Another sector regarding benefits is the sector associated with the right to rest. In the first place this involves a regular weekly rest comprising at least Sunday and also a longer period of rest, namely the holiday or vacation taken once a year or possibly in several shorter periods during the year. A third sector concerns the right to a pension and to insurance for old age and in case of accidents at work.[18]

[18] Ibid.

D. Materialism: The Corruption of Work and the Family

The communion of persons in the workplace, what the Holy Father indicates by the word solidarity, joins all workers, i.e., the entire human race, in love, a self-surrender to each other. The specific task that engages each worker is less important than the fulfillment of one's own humanity and the assistance given to others to fulfill their humanity. But if this is the common purpose shared by all men and women, no one would deprive another of the rights which he possesses as made in God's image. Such an act would be directly contrary to the common goal. Worker solidarity as proposed by John Paul II ensures that the rights and privileges of each individual will be respected and granted to him.

One of the most fundamental human rights is the right to develop one's humanity, i.e., to share in God's creative act through work. But if human persons are reduced to producers of goods and are used as mere machines in the production line, they are deprived of this right. A machine has no rights. Such workers, at least in the eyes of those who own them, have lost the rights that God gave them. It is hardly surprising, then, when those workers are also deprived of lesser rights, even the ones necessary to a decent human life. It is obvious that those owning these machines will try to wring from them the highest production capacity with the least possible maintenance.

In other words, if a person is seen as an object for work, then it becomes quite clear that he has been deprived of all rights and he will be granted merely what is necessary to keep production up. But this is not only a denial of the spiritual rights of all human beings, but also of the material rights of everyone, i.e., the right to share in the goods of the earth and the fruit of human labor. The fundamental error and the source of the difficulty is an emphasis on the objective or the transitive aspect of work. With this view in place, workers are for work. Since they are reduced to mere machines, it is possible to deny them even the most basic necessities. Any time human dignity is violated through a denial of human rights, material or spiritual, war is on the horizon. Men and women will demand their fundamental rights by force, if necessary. The Pope's new subjective emphasis restores the worker to center stage and corrects the mistake. If work is *for* man, it is impossible to deny anyone his basic rights. Thus, the communion of persons in the workplace, i.e., worker solidarity, is a program of peace for the entire world.

All of us, flawed by original sin, crave material wealth in differing degrees. This selfishness or greed is the primary motive for treating workers as tools of production, thus depriving them of rights and therefore causing wars.[19] But even if everyone in the world had all the necessities of life and was treated in accord with his dignity, the new materialism, the emphasis on material wealth, would inevitably lead to wars. As the Holy Father has written, "Material goods by their very nature provoke conditionings and divisions, the struggle to obtain these goods becomes inevitable in the history of humanity. If we cultivate this one-sided subordination of man to material goods alone, we shall be incapable of overcoming this state of need."[20] In other words, material goods are finite and limited. The more we emphasize these, the more everyone will want them. People will be measured by the extent of their material wealth. Since we all wish to be highly successful, more and more people will struggle for more and more goods, which will be more and more limited as people possess and use them up. Even those with vast material wealth will still want more. People will never be satisfied and they will violate human rights, spiritual and material, to obtain more and more things.

The Holy Father proposes that we center on spiritual goods.

[19] See GS, no. 9.

[20] See Karol Wojtyla (Pope John Paul II), "Peace through Truth and Justice" (Address of His Holiness to the United Nations on October 2, 1979), *The Pope in America* (St. Paul: Wanderer Press, 1979), pp. 15–16.

Human persons should not be measured by what they have, but by what they are, i.e., whether they have fulfilled themselves through love in the family, in the workplace, and, of course, in the Church (love of God). Unlike the desire for material goods, the desire for spiritual goods does "not divide people, but puts them into communication with each other".[21] The accent on material goods as opposed to spiritual ones, the emphasis on production rather than on the individual in the mystery of his human personhood, has led to two trends: (1) a constant struggle for the limited material goods and services available, and (2) the deprivation of even the most basic rights, both spiritual and material, for entire peoples and nations so that some might have more possessions. The only hope for humanity is a return to the essential truths about human beings: that the human person is not for work and that "it is what a man is, rather than what he has that counts".[22]

Discrimination and the lack of civil liberties often are also the fruit of greed. It is not unusual that one group of people would be denied certain rights so that another group would gain economically. Certainly, the wholesale violation of human dignity which has occurred in Soviet Russia and the Eastern-bloc nations was fundamentally motivated by economics, i.e., the entire system was predicated on the (false) principle that things are more important than people. With the restoration of the human person as the primary purpose of all work, the violation of the spiritual rights of human beings should cease.

Of course, greed is only one of the many factors which result in violations of human spiritual rights. Other motives, e.g., power, influence, fame, also may cause the denial of human rights and dignity. Nevertheless, the Pope believes that if the error of materialism is countered through a proper understanding of work, human persons will be seen in a different light. This new understanding of human beings in the sphere of work will

---

[21] Ibid., p. 16.
[22] See GS, no. 35.

carry over into other areas and will lessen the violation of human rights whatever the cause might be. The Holy Father is currently attacking the major reason for the violation of human rights in our time and he is counting on that teaching, once accepted, to have a beneficial effect on the other causes of the denial of human rights.

Pope John Paul II believes that work is the key to the entire social question. As he has written,

> The fundamental criterion for comparing social, economic, and political systems . . . must be the humanistic criterion, namely the measure in which each system is really capable of reducing, restraining, and eliminating as far as possible the various forms of exploitation of man and of ensuring for him, through work, not only the just distribution of the indispensable material goods, but also a participation, in keeping with his dignity, in the whole process of production.[23]

If every single worker is restored to his proper place, one of the substantial threats to peace in the world will have been eliminated. In the papal view, war is caused by the violation of the dignity of human beings which occurs when basic human rights are denied or restricted. The materialistic emphasis leads to violations of individuals and their dignity. A restoration of the human person as the primary purpose of work can counter the prevailing consumer mentality.

E. Christ: The Redemption of Work and the Family

But it is quite clear that the human race will never achieve peace on earth. Sin entered the world, and with sin disharmony and war. The history of the human race after the fall, as told in Genesis, graphically illustrates the results of sin: war, confusion, disharmony, and the concomitant violation of human rights.

[23] See Karol Wojtyla, "Peace through Truth and Justice", p. 16.

Still, Christ has come and strengthened us so that we are able
to overcome the effects of sin. With God's grace, we are able
to resist the selfish motives which sometimes encourage us to
hold others in subjugation to satisfy our own selfish desires, e.g.,
greed. At the same time, it is Catholic teaching that the gradual
extension of Christ's Kingdom through the sanctification of
souls will never reach fulfillment until his Second Coming. But
there will always be those who will reject Christ and his life-
giving grace even though the grace of Christ is the only hope for
humanity, the only hope we have to live as God intended "from
the beginning", and the only hope for peace. The mysteries of
sin, grace, and free will can be seen in this rejection of our
only hope for ourselves and our society. Of course, anyone
who has at one time rejected Christ may, touched by God's
hand, change his mind, i.e., experience a conversion. But the
point is that as long as anyone rejects God's grace, peace will
not be found in every human heart and in every corner of the
world. Further, even if everyone did "put on Christ",[24] there
still would not be perfect peace because we all commit some
sins. But, as the Pope reminds us, "Earthly progress must be
carefully distinguished from the growth of Christ's kingdom.
Nevertheless, to the extent that the former can contribute to
the better ordering of human society, it is of vital concern to
the kingdom of God."[25] Still, we can only expect perfect peace
and harmony when we are all one in Christ at the parousia.

John Paul reminds us that our Lord Jesus Christ worked. Jesus
taught a gospel of work not only in words, but above all in deeds.
"He who proclaimed it [the gospel of work] was himself a man of
work, a craftsman like Joseph of Nazareth."[26] Although original
sin changed the nature of work, it remains a blessing. But what
was once a total gift now is associated with difficulties and toil,
i.e., suffering. Still, work, even after sin, could not be something

---

[24] See Gal 3:27.
[25] See LE, no. 27, and GS, no. 39.
[26] See LE, no. 26.

unworthy of human persons since it was worthy of a divine Person, Christ! Even after sin, work remains a blessing. The sweat and toil of our work can be offered to God in union with Christ for the forgiveness of sins. The suffering occasioned by work would have been meaningless without Christ because it is impossible for us, a sinful race, to offer anything acceptable to God in reparation for sins. Now, however, we can offer our sweat and toil to God in union with Christ, the spotless victim whose offering is always acceptable to the Father. Our work through Christ's gift of grace is raised to a dignity beyond compare and becomes a means for making reparation for sin. In fact, in accepting the difficulties associated with work, we "fill up those things that are wanting in the sufferings of Christ".[27] As John Paul teaches, "By enduring the toil of work in union with Christ crucified for us, man in a way collaborates with the Son of God for the redemption of humanity. He shows himself a true disciple of Christ by carrying the cross in his turn every day in the activity that he is called upon to perform."[28] The effects of sin, the toil of work, far from remaining a terrible evil, become a means of establishing a close union with God, a union with Christ, God the Son, in his redemptive work. In the very act of redeeming us, he allows us to share in that work. As he overcame sin with death, an effect of sin, so we share in his victory by offering to God another effect of sin, the suffering of work, transforming it into a means of grace. Sin is conquered through itself. This is an indication of God's mercy, the drawing of good from evil, *par excellence*.

[27] See Col 1:24.
[28] See LE, no. 27.

Christ and the Family

A. Christ, the Perfect Image of God

"Man cannot live without love. He remains a being that is incomprehensible for himself, his life is senseless, if love is not revealed to him, if he does not encounter love."[1] As we have seen, the human person is made in the image of God and is called to do what God does, i.e., love in a communion of persons in imitation of the Trinity. However, although he is called by God's creative act to establish a communion of persons in the family and in the workplace, this proves impossible unless he knows how God loves. Christ shows us God and reveals his love. Further, it is impossible for us to give ourselves in love without knowing ourselves. When a gift is given, the one giving should know the value of the gift given. Unless we know ourselves, we cannot love. Since Christ "fully reveals man to himself",[2] to know ourselves, we have to know who Christ is. Therefore, a knowledge of Christ is vital to every human being if he is ever to function according to his humanity. We are never able to leave unanswered the question of who Christ is.

"And Jesus went on with his disciples, to the villages of Caesarea Philippi; and on the way he asked his disciples, 'Who do men say that I am?' And they told him, 'John the Baptist; and others say, Elijah; and others one of the prophets.' And he asked them, 'But who do you say that I am?' "[3] Our Lord Jesus Christ first put this question to his disciples, the apostles.

[1] See RH, no. 10.
[2] See GS, no. 22.
[3] See Mk 8:27–29.

125

However, through them, he is addressing this same question to every man, woman, and child who has had the gospel preached to them. This question "never ceases to be asked in one form or another"[4] because, for each of us, to ask who Christ is, is to seek one's own identity. In asking the apostles who he was, Christ was giving voice to a question each person asks in the recesses of his own heart: Who am I? In this question and its answer lies the entire mystery of the human person.

All of us, because we are persons, have a consciousness of ourselves knowing, willing, and expressing ourselves through our bodies. This consciousness or awareness is one of the most important characteristics distinguishing persons from the remainder of God's creation. However, this consciousness of ourselves leads us, from the very beginning, to ask questions of ourselves. Adam was the first to experience these primordial questions common to all mankind. In the solitary experience of naming the animals, Adam discovered that only he was a person with a consciousness and with a body which expressed his person.[5] In that first moment when Adam experienced himself acting in naming the animals, he also began to ask the questions all too familiar to us: Who am I? Where did I come from? Where am I going? and the most difficult one, Why am I here?

The fathers of the Second Vatican Council taught that everyone has these questions about himself. As the *Pastoral Constitution on the Church in the Modern World* notes, "Every man remains a question to himself, one that is dimly perceived and left unanswered. For there are times, especially in the major events of life, when no man can altogether escape from such self-questioning."[6] At these moments in life, everyone will attempt to formulate answers or to push aside these disturbing questions. But the answers, depending on whether they are

[4] See SC, p. 107.
[5] See TB, no. 7.
[6] See GS, no. 21.

based on truth (reality) or on falsehood, will either lead each of us to a true and genuine hope or to a bottomless pit of despair. If we try to ignore them entirely, we will not know who we are and thus will despair in much the same manner as if we had arrived at the wrong answers.

Thus, a consciousness of ourselves as acting persons leads us to an agonizing experience of self-questioning. Adam experienced this and so does everyone who has come into the world. The only answers are found in the revelation of God. We do not have the answers within ourselves. If we did, we would not be as we are today. In the present situation, man puts "forward, and continues to put forward, many views about himself, views that are divergent and even contradictory. Often he sets himself up as the absolute measure of all things, or debases himself to the point of despair."[7] Most of the problems in the world can be traced to one of these two points of view: to two false answers to the eternal questions, especially to the question, Who am I?

The only true answer to this question is given in the Sacred Scriptures, especially in Genesis where we learn that we are endowed with an incomparable dignity because we are created in God's own image and likeness. We are persons like the three Persons in God. If we are created in God's image, then we must function like God. God loves, that is, he gives himself totally to others. Since we are in his image, we should function in the same way. The answer to the question, "Who am I?" is: I am a creature made by God in his own image. Where did I come from? God created me out of love. Where am I going? If I am like God, I am called to share eternity with him in heaven. Why did God make me? God made me to love, to give myself to others as he did when he created me. I will love first in this world and then more fully and completely in the next when I will be associated with the Holy Trinity as closely as is possible for a human being. At the same time that we experience the Scriptures, the Scriptures reveal to us the meaning of our own

[7] Ibid., no. 12.

experiences. The sacred pages reveal who we are. They teach us who God is, but because we are in his image, they teach us who we are! They truthfully answer the questions that we have about ourselves.

Of course, Christ is the fullness of revelation. The entire Old Testament, including Genesis, points to Christ and is a preparation for him. In the Old Testament God gradually revealed himself, but in Christ he showed us himself. The second Person of the Blessed Trinity, God the Son, assumed to himself a human nature, body and soul. Thereby he, God the Son, expressed his divine Person through his human body. In other words, in the God-man, the human body actually became the expression of a Divine Person. Thus, Christ not only told us about God, as had the Holy Spirit through the Old Testament, he *showed* us God. Knowing how God acts (through the Old Testament) is not as good as seeing how God acts (through Christ and the New Testament). God became man not only to tell us about himself, but also to allow us to see how God acts. If knowing about God clarifies human experience, how much more does seeing how God acts "reveal man to himself"![8] Thus, in Christ, we see ourselves. We, made in the image and likeness of God, learn how to act in and through Christ. "Christ the Redeemer of the world, is one who penetrated in a unique and unrepeatable way into the mystery of man and entered his 'heart.'"[9] He enters our heart because he, and he alone, is the God-man who, in showing us God and how God acts, reveals man to himself. Of course, revelation ended with the death of the last apostle because God, beyond showing himself to us, could not reveal himself any further. What more could he have told us about himself after he had allowed us to see the body which expressed his divine Person?

Thus, when we ask ourselves, as everyone at some point in his life does, "Who am I?" God responds in Genesis: you

[8] Ibid., no. 22.
[9] See RH, no. 8.

are made in my image. But this answer is incomplete. The full response comes in Christ. Therefore, to ask who Christ is, is to ask who each one of us is. The answer to the question posed by Christ to the apostles, "Who do men say that I am", is the answer to the internal subjective question of identity found in every human heart. Christ is the one who enters into the subjective experience of everyone, revealing to him the true answers to his most fundamental questions about life. Christ is therefore *for* everyone. This subjective turn in regard to Christ is an instance of the theological revolution begun in the Council, especially in the *Pastoral Constitution on the Church in the Modern World* under the influence of the Lublin/Cracow school, and continued in and through the new theological synthesis of Pope John Paul II.

It is clear, then, that the answer to Christ's question becomes absolutely crucial to every single human being. Saint Peter gave the first answer, "You are the Christ."[10] But the content of Peter's answer must be repeated for each age in a language appropriate to that era. Therefore, every pope since Saint Peter has answered the question of every human heart voiced by Christ to the first Pope. The popes have confirmed who Christ is and thereby they have confirmed who we are. They do this as a service to humanity as Peter did it in service to the apostles and the early Church.

John Paul's answer, which takes a form appropriate for our age, was given in the first words of his first encyclical, *Redemptor Hominis*: "The Redeemer of man, Jesus Christ, is the center of the universe and of history."[11] From our reflections, it is clear why Jesus Christ is the center of history. History concerns human persons and their activities. Everyone finds himself in Christ. Therefore, all history (i.e., all people and each of their individual decisions) finds its focal point in Christ. Without Christ, no one would be comprehensible to himself or to those

---

[10] See Mk 8:29.
[11] See RH, no. 1.

around him. He and his personal history (and therefore the personal histories of everyone, i.e., all of history) would be senseless. The tragic Macbeth would be right when Shakespeare has him say, "Life's but a walking shadow, a poor player that struts and frets his hour upon the stage and then is heard no more: it is a tale told by an idiot, full of sound and fury, signifying nothing."[12] Of course, this is a false answer to who we are. But it is the alternative to Christ as the center of history! Few would accept Macbeth's version with its rampant pessimism. Therefore it is necessary to examine with precision the content of John Paul's assertion that Christ is the center of history. Only with this knowledge will we know ourselves and make sense of our lives and deeds.

Christ first reveals our incomparable dignity. "Human nature, by the very fact that it was assumed, not absorbed, in him, has been raised also in us to a dignity beyond compare."[13] In creation, we were made a "little less than God",[14] because we were created in God's image. This likeness to God was tarnished and disfigured by original sin. We lost the possibility of integration. There was a "constitutive break within the human person".[15] No longer did we function as we should as creatures made in the image of God. Rather, the body and its demands imposed themselves on the will, the opposite of what God had intended. We lost the dignity with which we had been created. Christ not only restores that dignity, he also raises us to an even greater dignity. Since he shares our humanity and he is God, every human act, except sin, becomes worthy of God. He thought as we do. He experienced what we experience. He shared our frustrations. He felt every human emotion. He played as we do. He studied in schools. He worked as we do. He suffered in an even more profound way than we do. Every

---

[12] See William Shakespeare, *Macbeth*, Act V, Scene V.
[13] See RH, no. 8, and GS, no. 22.
[14] See RH, no. 9, and Ps 8:6.
[15] See TB, no. 28.

single human act through him takes on a dignity worthy of God himself because Christ, the God-man, shared it.

Intimately connected with our dignity as beings made in the image of God and redeemed by Christ is our proper activity: love. As we have seen, love is the only way for us. "Man cannot live without love. He remains a being that is incomprehensible for himself, his life is senseless, if love is not revealed to him, if he does not encounter love."[16] God made us in a certain way, and we either recognize that truth and act accordingly, or we remain miserable. Of course, we have a choice. But who, knowing the alternatives, would choose to be miserable?

Original sin not only tarnished our dignity, but also made our proper activity, love, the total gift of oneself, difficult, if not impossible. Further, as the Pope teaches in the quote from *The Redeemer of Man*, love must be revealed to us, because since the fall, we do not know our proper activity. Our minds and wills no longer perceive and choose as God intended they should. Christ then comes and reveals our dignity and how we are to act, i.e., how we are to love, and then makes that possible through grace.

B. The Cross of Christ: The School of Love

God, in and through Christ, and in every other instance, loves us in a merciful way. From one (false) point of view, mercy is a patronizing gesture manifested by a superior to an inferior. Thus, we could argue that God has mercy on us because we are the creatures and he is the Creator. However, from this standpoint, God would not really love us because love is a relationship between equals. (In reality, God does love us and his love enables us to love him because we become his children.) But if God were truly acting in a condescending way,

[16] See RH, no. 10.

he would render us incapable of loving him, the activity for which we were made. Thus, through his mercy (so understood) God would be violating his own creative act. Pope John Paul II rejects this understanding of mercy.[17]

For the Holy Father, mercy is the ability to draw good from evil. Evil entered the world through original sin; and yet from this horrendous act came the Incarnation, the most wonderful manifestation of God the world has ever known. God, in the Incarnation, loved us in a merciful way. From the evil arising from original sin, God drew the infinite good of the Incarnation. In the *Exsultet*, the Church's Easter song, the joy of all people at the Incarnation is expressed. In that musical prayer of praise, the Church refers to original sin, the primordial sin, as a happy fault (*felix culpa*). Of course, God's merciful love is expressed perfectly and preeminently in Christ's Passion and death. The unjustified death of the innocent God-man is an even greater evil than original sin. Still, from this infinite evil, there emerged the greatest good ever to grace the world: the redemption of the human race. We are called to love God and to love our neighbors in the same way, i.e., we are called to be merciful, to draw good from evil.

God allows us to love him with mercy. On the Cross, it is not only God who shows mercy to us, we are also allowed to show mercy to the suffering God-man. Christ, dying a shameful and miserable death, allows us to love him the way he loves us. He permits us to show mercy to him, to draw good from the evil of the Cross. Who does not feel compassion for Christ when Pilate presents him to the crowd crowned with thorns and bloodied from the scourging? Who does not feel a tenderness toward him while contemplating the terrible journey to Golgotha with the heavy cross weighing against his body dripping with blood and sweat? Finally, who can gaze upon the crucified one, transfixed between heaven and earth, and not want to ease the pain?

But our sins put him there. Our sins are the reason why he

---

[17] See DM, no. 6.

suffers. Our compassion and tenderness toward our suffering Redeemer find expression in the avoidance of sin. We do not wish to sin because we do not want to be the cause of more pain for him. Even though we have caused him to suffer in the past, we resolve not to inflict any further suffering upon him. We gaze on the Cross and draw good (resisting sin) from this shameful death. Thus, avoiding temptations and sins becomes an expression of our merciful love of the Redeemer. As the Holy Father once wrote, "For many people the scourging of the Lord became the decisive reason for their determination to break the bonds of sin, the reason for mortifying the concupiscence of the flesh, for turning their desires toward the noble and the holy."[18] (Of course, this point has immense significance for the sacrament of penance.)

God "*invites man to have 'mercy' on his only Son, the crucified one*". "Could man's dignity be more highly respected and ennobled, for, in obtaining mercy, he is in a sense the one who at the same time 'shows mercy'?"[19] We are called to love as God loves. In the total revelation of that merciful love, the Cross, God not only shows us his own inner life of love, but he draws us into it so that, beginning with that moment, we could love him as he loves us. We show mercy to the Redeemer, to the God-man. This is why the Cross stands at the center of our proper activity given to us in God's creative act: love. Creation and redemption are inseparable because in the redemption, creation is restored. Each one of us is created in God's image and is called to love God as God loves. All this is made possible, even after original sin, through Christ's death on the Cross.

There is a further important point emerging from the exchange of love found through the Cross. We often pray to God asking for this or that and especially asking that God relieve us of some suffering or burden afflicting us. But on the Cross, God is subject to the most abject and terrible suffering imaginable.

[18] See SC, p. 75.
[19] See DM, no. 8.

He accepts it as a helpless victim. His nobility consists not in asking his Father to remove it from him, but in his acceptance of it according to the will of the Father. John Paul suggests that this attitude is appropriate for all Christians, but especially for the many, found everywhere in the world today, who suffer for their entire lives. God has not abandoned them. Rather, he has given them a share in Christ's task, and their nobility, or dignity, consists in emulating Christ. After all, Christ's acceptance of his Cross led to the ultimate manifestation of God's mercy: the Resurrection. In the Resurrection, evil was finally overcome. From the evil of suffering, God drew good. If we bear our crosses, we will experience that same glorious mercy of God.

The merciful love of God is revealed further through the parable of the Prodigal Son. The Holy Father analyzes this story to exemplify more fully the characteristics of God's merciful love for us. Of course, since we are called to love as God loves, the characteristics of God's love for us should form and shape our expression of love toward God and our neighbor. The parable is familiar. The son of a wealthy landowner asks for his inheritance and he receives it from his father. The son travels to a foreign country and squanders his inheritance in loose living. A famine comes upon that land and the son, forced by hunger, takes a demeaning job where he lacks the most basic necessities. He realizes that even the hired servants at his father's ranch are treated better than he is. He returns to his home saying to his father that he is not worthy of his own sonship. He wishes only to be treated as a servant. The father welcomes him, kisses him, puts a ring on his finger, and has a joyous party for the son who was lost and now is found.

In the Holy Father's view, the son "in a certain sense is the man of every period. . . . The parable indirectly touches upon every breach of the covenant of love, every loss of grace, every sin".[20] When the son senses a need, it is a material need.

---

[20] Ibid., no. 5.

He is hungry and wants food, and so he returns home. "He measures himself by the standard of the goods that he has lost, that he no longer 'possesses.' "[21] Of course, to subject oneself to a yardstick of things is to offend one's own dignity. The prodigal was created by God for his own sake, as we all were. However, in measuring himself by material things, he made them superior to his own being, to the one created in God's likeness. Thus, the prodigal son offends his own dignity. But this attack on himself is only the result of his first attack on his own dignity: when he left his father's house, he denied his own sonship, i.e., he denied himself. The prodigal squandered his dignity when he left his home and now this loss is manifested by his false measurement of his own worth, i.e., by his judgment that things are more important than he himself is. The prodigal son is forced to acknowledge the truth that he is not worthy of his own sonship because he lacks material goods. This moment of truth is the beginning of the son's rehabilitation.

When the son returns to the father, the father, offended though he is by his son's actions, has compassion. Through the son's return, "*his* [the son's] *humanity is saved*".[22] The son's dignity can be restored because the son, in returning, admits the truth that he has squandered his own humanity, i.e., his dignity. However, the son's dignity can be restored only by the love (mercy) of the father, who, rather than taking offense, has compassion. Good is drawn from evil. Of course, the love of the father in the parable is the love of God for each of us. "This love is able to reach down to every prodigal son, to every human misery, and above all to every moral misery, to sin. When this happens the person who is the object of mercy does not feel humiliated but rather found again and 'restored to value.' "[23] Thus, Christ "reveals man to himself"[24] by restoring

[21] Ibid.
[22] Ibid., no. 6.
[23] Ibid.
[24] See GS, no. 22.

human dignity after sin and by teaching us how to love, to love in God's way.

The sacrament of penance is the moment when Christ meets each and every one of us as prodigal sons. He is, in this sacrament, the loving (merciful) father and we are the sons who have lost our dignity by squandering the inheritance of grace. But Christ, as the father in the parable, wishes to save the good of our humanity, made in God's image and destined to reign forever with him in heaven. As long as we come to the same truthful realization that the son did, i.e., that we acknowledge to ourselves and then to the father (to Christ in the sacrament of penance) that we have lost our dignity, Christ can and will help us. He will restore our humanity to us.

Christ came to restore creation. In the sacrament of penance, Christ restores us. Sin tarnishes and disfigures our dignity making it impossible for us to love as God loves. But through his grace, won for us on the Cross, Christ returns our dignity to us and again allows us to love as God loves. "He who is forgiven little, loves little."[25] Thus, those who have been forgiven sins love more, i.e., they fulfill their humanity in an even greater way than would have been possible if they had not needed God's forgiving love. It is clear that in this sacrament, the mystery of the Cross is applied to every individual penitent. The Cross draws good from evil. In the sacrament, Christ draws love for himself from the sinful penitent. Christ loves us through this sacrament with a merciful love.

The most significant insight in this analysis of the sacrament of penance is that in the personal exchange between Christ and the penitent, it is the dignity of the penitent that is healed and restored through the gift of God's love. It is an interior affair of the heart, which occurs through a meeting with Christ. "How . . . could one desire to deny the human person, the individual human person of every faith, the right of a personal unique conversation with God, by means of the consecrated

[25] See Lk 7:47.

ministry?"[26] The individual confession of sin is necessary precisely so that, with the prodigal son, we too can come to the full realization of the truth that we have lost our dignity! Pope John Paul II has a profound understanding of the sacrament of penance. In the mystery of this unrepeatable meeting of man and God, the God-man shows us who we are!

C. *The Work of Christ*

Christ is, as John Paul wrote in his first encyclical, the center of history because he shows the human race the dignity each person possesses and the activity proper to that dignity: merciful love. However, to be ourselves as created in God's image, we must act like Christ, i.e., we must act like God. Therefore, it is not only important to know what is revealed, but also how Christ reveals it, i.e., how Christ acts. It is one thing to know what should be done. It is quite another to know how to do it.

In Christ God is revealed, but this revelation occurs through human nature. Since we are persons created in the image of God and since we possess human nature, we are able to imitate Christ. But we can only follow his example if we know how Christ's humanity became the vehicle for expressing the divine realities which we are called to share. Failure to imitate Christ means a failure to live according to our nature as created in the divine image. Of course, the imitation of Christ is only possible with the gift of God's grace. Christ is the one who shows us who we are and how we should act. He also makes it possible for us to act the way we should by his gift of grace.

In Christ "human testimony becomes the expression of the salvific mission of God" through "the threefold power of Christ as priest, prophet, and king".[27] Christ is a priest, a prophet, and

---

[26] See Karol Wojtyla (Pope John Paul II), "God Works through the Sacrament of Penance", *The Wanderer* (April 9, 1981), p. 9.

[27] See SR, p. 219.

a king because he is a man. It is in these three offices that he expresses the dignity of humanity and the merciful love to which we are called. The priest is the one who gives himself and all creation to God. "Man can fully discover his true self only in a sincere giving of himself."[28] We are called first to give ourselves to God because it is the only proper response to God's revelation. Further, we, as made in God's image, are the only creatures on earth who can render praise to the Creator on behalf of inanimate creation and the animal world. Thus, the priesthood, the power by which we give ourselves and all creation back to God, expresses the deepest aspirations in us. Christ is the one high priest. He is the one who possesses the fullness of the priesthood. He shares his priesthood with us in baptism. We should exercise our share in Christ's priesthood in imitation of him. We should give ourselves and all creation totally to God. It is Christ's priesthood that reveals and makes possible our proper activity, merciful love.

The priesthood of Christ was manifested most clearly in the sacrifice of the Cross when Christ the priest offered himself in a total gift to the Father. The Cross demonstrated how complete the sincere gift of oneself must be. Christ the priest confirmed his role when he said as he breathed his last, "Father, into thy hands I commit my spirit."[29] Even at that time his thoughts still were concentrated not on himself, but on the Father. Further, Christ, the one true priest, restored the original order of creation through his sacrifice on the Cross. We should be priests with Christ. We should surrender ourselves as he did. We should cooperate in the restoration of creation. Otherwise, we will not be true to ourselves. Of course, such a selfless priesthood is possible only in and through God's grace granted in baptism.

In his prophetic office, Christ reveals our incomparable dignity. He reveals God, in whose image we are created. After

[28] See GS, no. 24.
[29] See Lk 23:46.

the fall, we did not know God and thus, did not know our-selves. We had accepted a lie about God. Christ teaches what we should have known "from the beginning". He restores the truth about our dignity to us.

From the very first moment that sin entered the world, it was associated with a lie. "The truth about the God of the covenant, about the God who creates out of love, who in love offers humanity the covenant in Adam, who for love's sake puts to man requirements which have direct bearing on the truth of man's creaturely being [made in the image of God]— this is the truth that is destroyed in what Satan says."[30] Satan told Eve that the fruit of the forbidden tree would make her like God. Satan implied that God had forbidden Adam and Eve to eat that fruit in order to protect himself and his position from any competition. Satan, with his lie, destroys God as a loving Father in the eyes of Adam and Eve. God, after the acceptance of the lie by Adam and Eve, is seen as someone jealous of his own power and authority, as one imposing unreasonable rules and demands. Satan's lie also affects humanity. If we are made in God's image and God is distorted, then we do not know who we are.

Christ corrects Satan's lie and teaches us the truth about ourselves, i.e., he shows us our incomparable dignity by virtue of his prophetic office. In effect, he reveals much, much more than Adam, before sin, would have known about God. This revelation is as full as we can absorb. It ensures that Satan's lies will never again be accepted, at least not by humanity as a whole. "From the moment of the very first denial, Truth—the divine Truth—will always seek . . . to penetrate world history, to enter the minds and hearts of men."[31] Of course, the truth revealed in the prophetic office of Christ penetrates history and individuals in a way that no other revelation of God ever has or ever could.

---

[30] See SC, p. 30.

[31] Ibid., p. 48.

A damaging result of Satan's lie is the tendency to denigrate the goodness of God's creation. Many different (false) philosophical and theological traditions throughout history have held that creation is evil, e.g., Gnosticism, Manichaeism, Albigensianism, Puritanism, Dualism, and Jansenism. This opinion is contrary to Christ's prophetic witness. Genesis reveals clearly and repeatedly that God's creation is good. It seems, though, that many wish to blame God's creative work rather than themselves for the evil that exists in the world. (However, it is not God's creation which is the cause of evil. We, because of original sin, have a tendency to corrupt God's handiwork.) Christ stands squarely against this effect of the first lie. He reaffirmed the goodness of creation and demonstrated to us how we should act. Christ's entire life testified to the goodness of creation. By his carpentry trade, he showed the nobility of working with God's creative goods. He owned property, part of God's creation. He made one hundred and twenty gallons of wine for the wedding feast at Cana. He enjoyed a good meal. He, Truth incarnate, destroyed the basis for the disorder in creation by exposing the first lie.

In Christ's testimony before Pilate, we come to understand how far our own witness to the truth must extend. Facing a horrible death and the terrible cruelty of his executioners, Christ still truthfully answered Pilate's question: " 'Are you the king of the Jews?' Jesus answered, 'You say that I am a king.' "[32] For Christ to have denied his kingly office would have been to deny his very self. But it is exactly the same for every one of us. To deny the truth is to deny our very selves and the rest of creation. Only in the truth are we free, and only in freedom do we realize ourselves as made in God's image. Every lie is unworthy of us because it destroys our freedom, which can be found only in the truth. Is anything worth the rejection of our own dignity and the denigration of creation? Christ answers this question solemnly and movingly: No! Christ stands to lose

---

[32] See Jn 18:33, 37.

his life, his reputation, everything the world holds dear. But at no other moment does he give such testimony to the truth. It may not be surrendered for any reason. When he stands before the judgment seat of the Roman civil authority represented in the person of Pontius Pilate, Christ shows us how valuable the truth is and how we must treasure it and confess it. We can imitate Christ in confessing the truth because, through baptism, we share in his prophetic office. But do we love the truth sufficiently?

At that moment before Pilate, Christ confessed that he held the office of a king. The first person a king must govern is himself. He must have possession of himself and be in command of his person. In other words, to use terms now familiar, a king must be integrated.

Christ demonstrated this kingly self-rule primarily through his Passion and death. His humanity recoiled in fear from the tortures he was about to undergo. This fear is especially evident in the agony in the garden. However, he *willed* each and every stroke of the lash, each and every thorn on his head, and each and every labored breath on the Cross. He willed it because he loved his Father and his Father willed it. The union of wills is love. Pontius Pilate and the Roman soldiers did not take Christ's life. He, in perfect freedom, willed his own death out of love (union of wills) for his Father. (Of course, the Father willed Christ's death for the sake of our salvation and Christ shared this motive.)

Thus, Christ's death was not imposed on him by any human authority, nor by any internal compulsion. But did not the Father impose his will, i.e., that Christ should suffer and die, on him? The problem is often posed in the following way. Christ is God. God cannot sin. To violate the Father's will is to sin. Christ could not violate the Father's will. Therefore, he had to die. Since he had to die, we are not redeemed because his death was not a sacrifice, i.e., a free-will offering to God. On the other hand, we might argue that it was possible for Christ not to die. But, then, we admit that he could have sinned. The dilemma results, in part, from a false conception of freedom. The accent must be on love. Christ loved (gave himself to) the Father. He freely chose this gift of love. Thus, his death was not imposed on him. Rather, it was a freely chosen act of love. Through his love, his will and the Father's were united, and this union of wills was achieved in full freedom.

Freedom is fully present in God. God wills freedom for all persons. Thus, anything else that he wills regarding persons is willed in consonance with freedom. For it is impossible for God to be in conflict with himself. Therefore, freedom is not a choice between good and evil. It can only be a choice *for* God, i.e., *for* good. With the proper understanding of Christ's love for his Father and with a correct understanding of freedom, it is clear that Christ freely chose to give his life for us.

The primacy of the will over emotions is an absolute requirement of love, of a free gift. The will's dominion must never be surrendered no matter what the consequences are. Of course, Christ promises us his divine help and grace. He also offers us a means of acknowledging our failures when we do fall: the sacrament of penance. Through that sacrament, he restores our dignity to us. He can do this because in him that dignity was never tarnished even under the burden of the Cross! "Jesus came in order to reveal the kingliness of man. And here, visible to the whole of humanity, stands Jesus crowned with thorns! The price paid for dignity is the blood of the Son of God."[33] "No human investigation is capable of reconstructing the mystery of Jesus, who is dying on the cross. We stop still, in silence, on the threshold of all that is most holy in the history of the world."[34] There is no greater manifestation of the kingly transcendence in us, than in Christ on the Cross. To this kingly transcendence, all of us are called.

We should imitate Christ. We should cultivate a kingly self-rule by strengthening the dominance of the will within us. This

[33] See SC, p. 77.
[34] Ibid., p. 79.

necessity stems from our creation in God's own image. It is only in kingly self-rule that we are able to express love (priestly office) in accordance with the truth (prophetic office). It is Christ's kingly office which enables us to overcome the effect of original sin, the "constitutive break" within us.[35] It is kingly self-rule which enables us to achieve integration.

For Pope John Paul II, the greatest martyrs have shared this kingly testimony of Christ. As a son of Poland, the life and death of Saint Maximilian Kolbe comes often to the lips and the pen of the Pope. Father Kolbe was a prisoner in a Nazi concentration camp. When a group of men were chosen to die by starvation, Father Kolbe was not among them. However, he willingly offered to take the place of one of the men who was a husband and a father. Like Christ, Father Kolbe offered his life in full freedom. He was in no way compelled to die at that moment. "All the prisoners knew that he died of his own free choice. . . . And with that particular revelation there passed through that hell-upon-earth a breath of fearless and indestructible goodness, a kind of intimation of salvation."[36] Father Kolbe gave himself as he was created to do. He gave himself in truth with full consciousness of his own dignity and of his task. He gave himself with a kingly self-rule which guaranteed the freedom of the gift.

Christ's kingship was demonstrated in his kingly self-rule, but also in his dominion over creation. Humanity should govern the created order. This privilege was granted to the human race in God's creative act. But, through sin, we sometimes subject ourselves to the things of the world. Christ taught us through the exercise of his kingship in its second function, i.e., dominion over creation, that our dignity requires that we never be subject to the things of this world. Christ taught this principle through his work as a carpenter. His work was a preparation for his apostolate. It was *for* him. It was not work for the sake

[35] See TB, no. 28.
[36] See SC, p. 51.

of money (that would be to measure a man—in this case, the God-man—by something unworthy of him). He worked only for the advancement of the mission he had received from his Father. Further, Christ did not measure the people he met by the amount of goods or money they had accumulated. In fact, he taught us that we dare not do this.

Further, Christ enabled creation to fulfill its purpose, i.e., to be a means to lead us to God, when he took ordinary goods and made them the instruments of advancing our relationship with God. Oil, bread and wine, and water are humble items, but Christ made them the means of our union with God.

Our share in the kingship of Christ not only enables us to exercise kingly self-rule, but also to exercise that dominion over creation which God gave us in his creative act. Of all the creatures of God, only human beings were given dominion over the world and the command to subdue it. This kingly activity, marred by original sin, is restored through Christ's kingship. Self-rule is the first function of Christ's kingship. Our restored dominion over the world is the second function of Christ's kingly office.

We exercise Christ's kingship over creation when we live according to the norm taught by the conciliar fathers, "It is what a man is, rather than what he has, that counts."[37] "What a man is" has been revealed by God in Genesis: "Let us make man in our image."[38] But original sin altered the relationship between creation and humanity. Material things came to be valued more highly than the human person, e.g., man became someone (or even, *some thing*) for work instead of work existing *for* man. The purpose of creation was frustrated. It is *for* man, but no longer did we treat it as something subject to us. Rather we, at least in part, became subject to it. Obviously, we no longer acted as beings sharing in the creative act of God. "The man of today seems ever to be under threat from what he produces, that is to

[37] See GS, no. 35.
[38] See Gen 1:26.

say from the result of the work of his hands."[39] Thus, our own advancement, which, in the original plan of the Creator, was intended to occur through our kingly rule over the remainder of creation, did not or could not result. Needless to say, with the loss of our dominion over creation, creation ceased to be a means to lead us to God. Christ, by allowing us to participate in his kingship, makes it possible for us to dominate creation as we were made to do. Of course, this second function of Christ's kingship depends on its first function. We must first exercise kingly self-rule before attempting to dominate the remainder of creation.

Through his kingship, Christ ruled and governed himself and all of creation, restoring the things of creation to their original purpose. We are able to govern ourselves and all of creation because we participate in Christ's kingship. However, our share in Christ's kingship and his other offices occurs through the Church. The Church continues the work of Christ. The Church reveals men and women to themselves in their dignity and proper activity. Further, the Church, by dispensing God's grace in the sacraments, makes it possible for men and women to live as the images of God they are. Thus, if we are to know our God-given dignity and proper activity and if we are to act as we should, we must examine the continuation of Christ's work in and through the Church.

D. The Work of Christ Continued: The Church

"The Church looks at the world through the very eyes of Christ", proclaimed Pope John Paul II on October 2, 1979, during his homily at Yankee Stadium in New York City.[40]

[39] See RH, no. 15.

[40] See Karol Wojtyla (Pope John Paul II), "Jesus Christ, Living Peace and Living Justice" (Homily of His Holiness at the Mass in Yankee Stadium on October 2, 1979), *The Pope in America* (St. Paul: Wanderer Press, 1979), p. 25.

From one point of view, it is hardly astounding that a pope should claim that the Church has the eyes of Christ. Since the time of Saint Paul, the Church has called itself the Body of Christ. However, this bodily image of the Church has been used in recent times to explain what the Church is, its being and the bonds which tie all the members together. The members of the Church are joined to one another in a way similar to the physical union of the parts of a body. This Body, the Church, is recognizable, as all bodies are, from its Head, Christ. Thus, the Church is the mystical Body of Christ and it has the eyes of Christ. But in the above quotation, John Paul is not emphasizing the unity of the members of the Church in Christ. Rather, he is clearly accenting an activity of the Body, i.e., looking. For him, the Body of Christ, the Church, is acting. It is looking.

In other words, the Church is not only a body which exists, it also acts. Acts of looking clearly involve understanding. The Church looks at the world and understands it the way Christ understands it. The Church does not look as animals do without knowledge. It looks as people (persons) do, i.e., with a mind. But if the Church has the capability of seeing with understanding, with the mind of Christ, then the Church is more than just the Body of Christ. It is, in some sense, the person of Christ. A body alone could never act in any cognitive sense. But the Church does and therefore it is more than a body. It is a person, the person of Christ. Thus, the Church is not just an object of study as a body might be. It is also a subject who acts and thereby reveals itself. The self it manifests (or expresses, to use John Paul's term) is Christ. Therefore, when the Church acts, it is Christ who is acting. The Church acts in looking and in many other ways. On October 5, 1979, in an address to the American bishops in Chicago, the Pope remarked that "in our time, Jesus was consecrating anew his disciples by truth; and he was doing it by means of an ecumenical council."[41]

---

[41] See Karol Wojtyla (Pope John Paul II), "Remain Faithful to the Universal

The Council was an act of the Church and therefore an act of Christ.

The Pope's understanding of the Church as the person of Christ is remarkably faithful to Saint Paul's teaching that the Church is the Body of Christ. Following John Paul, there would be no difficulty in equating the body with the person. In John Paul's new synthesis, the human body is the expression of a person. The Church is the Body of Christ. But if a body is the expression of a person, it must be united to that person. Thus, if it is true that the Church is the Body of Christ, then it is also true that it is the person of Christ. The Church cannot be Christ's Body without being his person. Such would be a lifeless body without the animation which only a person can give to a human body. The Church has a body, a visible reality, which reveals its invisible reality, the divine person, Christ. Saint Paul has the same understanding of the Church. For the Apostle, just as for the Pope, the body does not denote only the physical body, but rather the entire being, i.e., the person. Pope John Paul II and Saint Paul are echoing the same truth. To speak of the body of Christ is also to speak of his person.

In First Corinthians, Saint Paul writes in the famous passage about charity, "If I deliver my body to be burned, but have not love, I gain nothing."[42] Obviously Paul does not use the word body here to mean only an attribute or an appendage of a person. Rather, body refers to the whole person. Earlier in the same epistle the Apostle writes, "The body is not meant for immorality, but for the Lord, and the Lord for the body. And God raised the Lord and will also raise us up by his power."[43] At first in this passage Saint Paul is speaking of the body, but then he switches to the personal pronoun us. When the body

---

Magisterium" (Address of His Holiness Delivered in Chicago to a Plenary Assembly of the Bishops of the United States on October 5, 1979), ibid., p. 54.

[42] See 1 Cor 13:3.

[43] Ibid., 6:13-14

is raised, it is we (us) who are raised. The body, for Paul, refers not just to a part, but to the whole, i.e., to the person. "It is obvious that here it is not just the body which is meant, but the whole 'I.' "[44] Generally, the Hebrews did not draw as sharp a distinction between the body and the person as Western thought does. For the Semites, a human being was one entity, body and soul, and either word could be employed to denote the whole. Thus, when Saint Paul referred to the Church as the Body of Christ, he certainly did not intend to exclude the image of the Church as the person of Christ, rather he was affirming the Church as the person of Christ.

In another passage of First Corinthians, Saint Paul identifies the Church with Christ. He is discussing the divisions in the church of Corinth and he asks his readers, "Is Christ divided?"[45] Clearly, for Saint Paul, when there are divisions in the Church, it is Christ who is rent apart. It is not merely Christ's body which is torn apart by these divisions because what happens to the body happens to the person. Thus, Paul identifies the Church with the person of Christ. In this approach, Paul is only following the Lord's own words. On the road to Damascus, Christ asked Paul, "Saul, Saul, why do you persecute me?" Paul answered, "Who are you, Lord?" Christ answered, "I am Jesus, whom you are persecuting."[46] Of course, Saint Paul was persecuting the Church, but Christ identified himself with the Church. Since it is impossible to persecute a mere body (it is always a person who is persecuted), the only possible conclusion is that the Church is the person of Christ.

The underlying concept for Saint Paul's ecclesiology is the corporate personality of the Old Testament. The Jews, many

---

[44] See Heribert Muehlen, *Una Mystica Persona: Die Kirche als das Mysterium der heilsgeschichtlichen Idenitaet des Heiligen Geistes in Christus und den Christen: Eine Person in vielen Personen*, 3d ed. (Paderborn: Ferdinand Schoeningh, 1968), p. 117. The original reads, "Es ist offensichtlich, dass hier . . . nicht der blosse koerper gemeint ist . . . sondern das ganze 'Ich.' "

[45] See 1 Cor 1:13.

[46] See Acts 9:4–5.

though they were, were joined together as one, as a corporate person. (However, this idea is not to be confused with a legal person, such as a modern corporation.) The corporate person has four characteristics. First, the corporate entity has a past, present, and future. Second, the group is a real entity, which is actualized in its members. Third, the name of the group can be applied either to an individual, to the head, or to the whole group. Finally, even when an individual is seemingly in the foreground, the corporate personality remains intact. What is said of one, can be said of the group.[47] In terms of Pope John Paul's new synthesis, it is apparent that a corporate personality is a communion of persons. There are three distinct levels of corporate personalities. The first is the grouping of all those who live and work in the same area (communion of persons in the workplace). The second is a union of people founded on a biological link (familial communion of persons). The third, and the strongest, is the religious corporate personality, e.g., the Israelites after the covenant with the Almighty.[48] The Israelites of old were formed into one people by the power of God. The communion of persons established by God transcends all purely human communions because it has as its foundation not merely the will-acts of human persons, but the will-act and the power of God.

The *communion of persons par excellence*, the Church, is brought together by Christ, who sends the Holy Spirit to each of its members. As recorded in Saint Matthew's Gospel, Saint Peter's confession of faith, made for himself and for the other apostles, was a response to Christ's question, "Who do men say that the Son of Man is?"[49] Christ is clearly referring to the Old Testament "son of man" found in Daniel. But in Daniel, the son of man is not merely an individual, but the representative

---

[47] See Muehlen, *Una Mystica Persona*, p. 77, and H. Wheeler Robinson, "The Hebrew Conception of Corporate Personality", *Beihefte zur Zeitschrift für die alttestamentliche Wissenschaft*, vol. 66 (1936), pp. 50–55.

[48] See Muehlen, *Una Mystica Persona*, pp. 81–84.

[49] See Mt 16:13.

of the corporate personality. "The human figure coming with the clouds of heaven is explicitly identified as the people of the saints of the most high. This means that their unity is so realistically conceived that it can be concentrated into a single representative figure."[50] Christ identified himself with a corporate personality and clearly indicated that he will be the new Son of Man, the builder of a new corporate personality, i.e., the Church.

Saint Paul, following the very words of Christ and the Jewish conceptions which they connote, conceives the Church as a new corporate personality or, better (because it avoids confusion and is familiar to us), a new communion of persons in Christ. In many passages, the Apostle speaks of the Church or members of the Church as being "in Christ".[51] This typical Pauline phrase expresses the reality of the union of persons forming one whole, i.e., Christ. This new communion is the person of Christ because, following the Old Testament and the principles of the corporate personality, the whole is identified with all its parts and the parts with the whole. In Galatians this view is confirmed when Saint Paul writes, "For as many of you as were baptized into Christ have put on Christ. . . . For you are all one in Christ Jesus."[52]

The corporate personality or communion of persons underlies all Pauline ecclesiology. In describing the Church as the Body of Christ, Saint Paul is attempting to explain the communion of persons in Christ through an image. The other image, the people of God, is another attempt to explain the same reality. The Church is a communion of persons in Christ whereby each person, through God's grace, is identified with the whole, the person of Christ, and the whole with its parts. The Church is Christ.

However, it is obviously impossible to identify the Church

[50] See Robinson, "The Hebrew Conception of Corporate Personality", p. 52, and Muehlen, *Una Mystica Persona*, pp. 89, 110.

[51] See, for example, 1 Cor 1:2; 1 Th 2:14; 2 Th 1:1.

[52] See Gal 3:27-28.

with the physical Christ. One difference between the Church and the physical Christ lies in the elements of the union. In the Incarnation, it is the second Person of the Blessed Trinity who unites in himself the divine and human natures. In the Church, it is the Holy Spirit who unites the baptized (persons) in Christ. Thus, the Incarnation is one Person (God the Son) in two natures, and the Church is one Person (God the Holy Spirit) who unites many persons in Christ. A second difference between the Church and the physical Christ lies in the mode of union. The union of the two natures in Christ is accomplished in his Person and the union in the Church is accomplished through sanctifying grace given to us by the Holy Spirit. A third difference between the Church and Christ lies in the differing resulting unions. In Christ, human nature is united to the divine Word (the hypostatic union). However, the members of the Church are not all united with the Logos, as though he were incarnate again in each of us. No, the union is not another hypostatic union. Nevertheless, the baptized are united with Christ in a mystical union. Thus, we refer to the Church as the mystical person of Christ to distinguish it from the physical Christ. The Church is a mysterious communion of persons (the baptized), which forms the mystical person of Christ by the grace of the Holy Spirit.

Some might still quarrel with this interpretation of Pauline ecclesiology. They could object that the image of the Church as the Bride of Christ[53] precludes an identification of the Church as the mystical person of Christ. There is no question that the Church, viewed as a collection of individuals, i.e., those who are to be united, is as a bride to the bridegroom. The members of the Church stand ready to receive the Holy Spirit sent by Christ. They are as brides waiting to receive the gift of their husbands. In this sense, then, the Church can be compared to a bride. However, viewed as the resulting union, after the gift has been received, the Church is the mystical person of Christ.

---

[53] See Eph 5:25-31.

Even the bride and the bridegroom, after they are united, are two in one flesh.[54] Flesh denotes not only the physical bodies, but the persons in all their potentialities.[55] The couple is joined in a communion of persons and acts as one. Thus, the bride and bridegroom, after they unite, are two in one, as the Church is one in Christ after it receives the gift of the Holy Spirit. Of course, each member of the Church, as an individual, may at any time be bridelike in that he is receiving the grace of God anew through the sacrament of penance. Further, those to be received into the Church, i.e., the unbaptized—either children or adults—are as brides. They await the grace of God, which unites them with Christ.

Saint Paul is able to compare the union of a man and a woman in a sacramental marriage to the union of Christ and the Church because they both are communions of persons founded on grace. They are comparable because the principle of union, grace, is the basis for both. Nevertheless, the Church is the greater mystery and the greater union. Thus, in Ephesians, when Saint Paul compares the two,[56] it is not the union of husband and wife that is the image of the Church. Rather, it is the relationship between the Church and Christ which is normative for the husband-wife union. It is not so much that the Church is like the bride, but that the bride is to be like the Church, i.e., to receive the gift of her husband in such a way that she is as closely united to her husband as the Church is to Christ. Of course, the husband is to be united to his wife as Christ is to the Church.

The Fathers of the Church, following the lead of Saint Paul, understood the Church as the person of Christ. Saint Augustine often referred to the Church as the person of Christ.[57] For Augustine, the images of the Church as the Body of Christ and the Bride of Christ are metaphors. The mystery of the Church

---

[54] See Eph 5:31, and Mt 19:5-6.

[55] See Muehlen, *Una Mystica Persona*, pp. 124-25.

[56] See Eph 5:25-31.

[57] See Muehlen, *Una Mystica Persona*, pp. 27-33.

is inadequately, but differently, expressed in both. The true elements of both images are found in the more accurate term for the Church: the person of Christ.[58] In this interpretation, Augustine is true to Saint Paul. For the Apostle and the bishop of Hippo, it is the communion of persons in Christ, the mystical person of Christ, which is the foundation for all the other images of the Church. Saint Gregory the Great taught that "Christ and the Church are one person."[59] According to a somewhat older, but valuable, work by John Gruden, there are many Fathers of the Church, most notably Saint John Chrysostom and Saint Gregory of Nyssa, who identified the Church with the person of Christ.[60] Thomas Aquinas accepted Augustine's formulation of the Church as the person of Christ using the phrase, *una persona*.[61] In another passage, Saint Thomas refers to the head and members of the Church as one mystical person (*una persona mystica*).[62]

The recovery of this long-standing tradition of the Church's understanding of itself began with Pope Pius XII and the publication of his encyclical *Mystici Corporis, The Mystical Body of Christ*. In that letter in 1943, Pope Pius wrote that "the unbroken tradition of the fathers from the earliest times teaches

[58] Ibid., p. 31. Muehlen expresses this thought when he writes in *Una Mystica Persona*, "Der Ausdruck, 'una quaedam persona,' ist die Summe und Fülle dessen, was in den beiden erwaehnten Metaphern (Braeutigam-Braut, Haupt-Leib) jeweils nur unter einem bestimmten Gesichtspunkt zur Aussage kommt."

[59] See *Patrologiae Latinae*, edited by J. P. Migne, vol. 76, col. 110.

[60] See John C. Gruden, *The Mystical Christ: Introduction to the Study of the Supernatural Character of the Church* (St. Louis: B. Herder, 1936). Gruden notes that John Chrysostom wrote that all Christians are "one person in Christ" (see p. 118). Further, he notes that Saint Gregory of Nyssa wrote that the "whole body of Christ [i.e., the Church] will surrender to the life-giving strength of God. The surrendering of this body is called the submission of the Son Himself" (see p. 116). In fact, Gruden's entire discussion of the mystical Christ in the writings of the Fathers is still very worthwhile; see pp. 103–33.

[61] See Thomas Aquinas, *Summa Theologiae*, III, q. 15, art. 1 ad 1, and Muehlen, *Una Mystica Persona*, p. 40.

[62] See Aquinas, *Summa Theologiae*, III, q. 49, art. 1, and Muehlen, *Una Mystica Persona*, pp. 40–41.

that the divine Redeemer and the society which is his body form but one mystical person."[63] It is the concept of the Church as the mystical person of Christ which is the guiding thread, the underlying foundation (as with Saint Paul and Saint Augustine), of the entire second section of the encyclical.[64] *Mystici Corporis* had a profound effect on ecclesiology and it shaped the thoughts of the fathers of the Second Vatican Council.

The Second Vatican Council was primarily concerned with the Church. Two of its four constitutions considered the Church. The Second Vatican Council began its work by presuming that the Church is the mystical person of Christ. The first question which the conciliar fathers posed for themselves was, "Church, what do you say of yourself?"[65] Of course, only a person can speak and have an understanding of himself. Therefore, the conciliar fathers, in expecting the Church to formulate an answer to their question, conceived the Church as a person. Undoubtedly, this rediscovery of the personhood of the Church (as taught in Saint Paul, the Fathers, and Saint Thomas Aquinas) can be traced to the impact and influence of Pius XII's encyclical.

Most interestingly, this first question posed by the bishops in council is reflexive. The Church, as a personal subject, is asked to reflect on itself. This is evidence of the influence of the phenomenological school on the Church's Magisterium, at least with regard to the mystery of the Church itself. Pius XII's encyclical *The Mystical Body of Christ* stimulated an examination of the rich tradition of the Church as the mystical person of Christ. At the same time, the new phenomenological revolution, especially as developed in Poland at Lublin/Cracow, was emphasizing that a person is a subject who acts. The recovery of the tradition of the mystical person came at precisely the moment that the Lublin/Cracow school through Karol

---

[63] See Pope Pius XII, *Mystici Corporis, The Mystical Body of Christ* (Washington: National Catholic Welfare Conference, 1943), no. 66.

[64] See Muehlen, *Una Mystica Persona*, pp. 44–45.

[65] See SR, pp. 35–36.

Wojtyla was prepared to teach the world the subjective turn. The conciliar teaching on the Church thus resulted from two separate strands of thought which met at the Council. The Second Vatican Council applied the new and revolutionary subjective turn to the old, but rediscovered concept of the Church as the mystical person of Christ. As in many other areas, the *J. P. II Revolution* has infused a classical teaching found in the holy Scriptures, the Fathers, Saint Augustine, and Saint Thomas Aquinas with a new subjective understanding. In the conciliar teaching, the Church is no longer simply an object of study! It is a personal subject, an acting person, possessing a consciousness, an awareness of its conscious acts.

The mission of the mystical person of Christ is identical to Christ's mission. Christ showed us who we are because he, the God-man, could show us the significance of our creation in the image of God. Those who saw Christ saw the Father. His human nature expressed his divine Person. The Second Vatican Council teaches in its *Pastoral Constitution on the Church in the Modern World* that "Christ . . . fully reveals man to himself."[66] In the very same document, the Council teaches that the "Church . . . opens to him [man] . . . the innermost truth about himself."[67] Of course, "to reveal man to himself" and "to open up the truth" to man about himself are the same thing. Thus, there can be no doubt that the Church has the same mission as Christ.

E. The Family as the Domestic Church

I. BAPTISM AND MATRIMONY

In the sacrament of baptism, the faithful "put on Christ", i.e., they are united with Christ in one mystical person, the Church.[68] Not only are they united with Christ they are also

---

[66] See GS, no. 22.
[67] Ibid., no. 41.
[68] See Gal 3:27.

united with all others who are united with Christ, i.e., with other baptized people. Of course, the union with Christ is more intimate than the union with other people.

In the sacrament of matrimony, a baptized man and woman join in a familial communion of persons in Christ. This intimate union is, in fact, a specification of the broader communion of persons which is the Church. In matrimony, the husband and wife are joined to each other in a union similar to each one's baptismal union with Christ. The matrimonial bond might be described as an intensification of the couple's baptismal union with each other.

The baptismal communion of persons, i.e., the Church, has its origin in the grace of the Holy Spirit. But the matrimonial, sacramental communion of persons also has its origins in the grace of the Holy Spirit. There is one Holy Spirit and one divine life given in both instances. Therefore, the two communions of persons are not radically different, but rather different aspects of the same reality. When Pope John Paul II in the apostolic exhortation, *Familiaris Consortio, The Role of the Christian Family in the Modern World*, calls the family a domestic church, he is not using a mere analogy, but is defining the family. In that document, he challenges families to "*become* what you *are*".[69] Since families are a domestic church, they ought to become a miniature church undertaking the same mission as the universal Church, the mission of Christ.

To fulfill the very purpose of family life, family members must first understand and then implement the mission of Christ. The mission of the God-man is to show us who we are through the triple offices of priest, prophet, and king. In assuming human nature, Christ revealed human dignity. Human nature was worthy of an intimate union with a Divine Person! Christ also showed us how to act as beings made in God's image. The Christian family accomplishes the mission of Christ, as the universal Church does, through its share in the triple offices of

[69] See FC, no. 17.

Christ: priest, prophet, and king. It is only through the exercise of these offices that the family becomes what it is, a miniature mystical person of Christ.

2. THE PRIESTLY OFFICE

A priest is one who offers sacrifices to God. Christ offered himself and through himself all people and all creation to the Father. Since all baptized Christians are priests with Christ, they can offer themselves to the Father and thus carry on the priestly mission of Christ in the world. Since man "can fully discover his true self only in a sincere giving of himself",[70] the sharing of Christ's priesthood, enabling and encouraging us to offer ourselves and creation to God, "denotes the simplest and most complete attitude"[71] derived from revelation. "The doctrine concerning Christ's priesthood and man's share in it is at the very center of the teaching of Vatican II and contains in a certain manner all that the Council wished to say about the Church, mankind, and the world."[72]

Human beings can only exist with love, i.e., by making a sincere gift of themselves. Revelation of the Trinity in and through Christ teaches that the most complete giving of self is found in the love of the three Divine Persons. The call to love, given in God's creative act, is elevated through the revelation of Christ to an invitation to enter into God's own life, to love as God loves in the Trinity. Those who respond to God's invitation express their sincere gift of self to God through the gift of Christ's priesthood, which enables them to love as God loves.

All the baptized are priests and all are called to offer themselves to God and to one another through their priesthood.

[70] See GS, no. 24.
[71] See SR, p. 224.
[72] Ibid., p. 225.

"However, the Lord also appointed certain men as ministers."[73] Those men ordained to the hierarchical priesthood have received a special power from Christ and they exercise it for the people of God. All the baptized are given the priesthood of Christ, but this baptismal office needs to be activated by the hierarchical priesthood so it may come to full visible expression. Clearly, the hierarchical priesthood differs "essentially and not only in degree"[74] from the common priesthood of the faithful because it is the active catalyst for the common priesthood.

Of course, it is especially in and through the holy Eucharist, "the source and summit of the Christian life",[75] that the ordained priest activates the priesthood of the baptized. It is only in the holy Eucharist that the sincere giving to God, the function of a priest, perfectly occurs because it is only in this sacrament that the one sacrifice of the Cross by the one priest, Jesus Christ, is re-presented. "Hence, the priesthood of ministers and that of the faithful are closely linked with the Eucharist."[76] In the Eucharist, the ordained priest together with the entire congregation expresses the priesthood of Christ.

However, the priesthood of the baptized is also activated through the other sacraments: confirmation, matrimony, holy orders, anointing of the sick, and most especially, penance. It is in penance that the merciful love of God is intensely experienced and known by each individual penitent. Merciful love draws good from evil. The penitent, after experiencing the forgiveness of God, usually loves God more. From the evil of sin, he develops a greater love of God, i.e., he is better able to exercise his share in the priesthood of Christ by giving himself more fully to God. Moreover, after experiencing the forgiving

[73] *Presbyterorum Ordinis, Decree on the Ministry and Life of Priests* (December 7, 1965), *Documents of Vatican II*, ed. Austin P. Flannery (Grand Rapids, Michigan: William B. Eerdmans, 1975), no. 2, p. 864.
[74] See LG, no. 10.
[75] Ibid., no. 11.
[76] See SR, p. 227.

love of God, the penitent is usually able to give himself to other human persons in forgiving, merciful love.

Activated as they are, the baptized are sent into the world to serve the Lord, i.e., to continue to sanctify themselves, their family, their friends, and their coworkers, by offering everyone and everything to God. Of course, their strength and power constantly need refreshment from Christ through the sacraments, especially through the sacraments of penance and holy Eucharist.

A baptized man and woman give themselves to each other in matrimony by virtue of their share in Christ's priesthood. In baptism, they were called to share in the divine trinitarian life. They were called to love as God loves in the mystical person of Christ. Now they are called to exercise their priesthood within the family, the miniature mystical person of Christ, which has as its foundation the very same trinitarian life as the universal Church. In other words, they are called to love each other in the very same way that the members of the Trinity love one another, that Christ loves the individual members of the Church, and that members of the Church are called to love God. This total self-gift in love is possible for us only through the gift of God's grace, which enables us to share in Christ's priesthood.

The union of two people in a total lifelong mutual self-donation is almost impossible for those tainted with sin. It is most difficult for us, who suffer the effects of original sin, to enter into a total donation of self. The mind and will no longer govern the body as they should. The loss of this control means that the body is not subject to the mind and will. The body does not respond to the decisions of the will. In marriage, the donation of self is radically hampered by the desires of the flesh. It is only through our share in Christ's priestly and kingly offices that marriage is possible for us.

Family members, activated by the hierarchical priesthood, exercise their priesthood by giving themselves within the family. This love is established first between the husband and the wife. When children are conceived and born, both the father and the mother give themselves to these new images of God who desperately need the love of their parents. Familial love must be a merciful love because spouses must forgive one another if the marriage is to remain healthy. The love for children is also a merciful love. How often is a parent called upon to forgive the children?

The common priesthood of the faithful is also exercised within the family in other ways. Family members "exercise that priesthood, too, by the reception of the sacraments, prayer and thanksgiving, the witness of a holy life, abnegation and active charity".[77] It is clear that prayer, charity, and a holy life are expressions of the priesthood of Christ. These acts are expressions of our self-donation to God. The reception of sacraments is also an active expression of the common priesthood because the faithful must dispose themselves properly for each sacrament and must actively seek to receive each sacrament. It is not only the hierarchical priesthood which functions in the reception of sacraments, it is also the common priesthood of the faithful. Clearly, when parents bring their children for the reception of the sacraments, e.g., first penance or first holy Communion, they are exercising their priesthood and teaching their children to exercise their baptismal priesthood.

The activation and exercise of the common priesthood of the faithful are essential if a family is to carry on its mission: to reveal human persons to themselves in their incomparable dignity and proper activity. It is the family's share in Christ's priesthood which enables the domestic church to demonstrate to all of us our proper activity, merciful love. The family's share in Christ's prophetic office enables it to reveal the incomparable dignity of the human person to each one of us.

[77] See LG, no. 10.

3. THE PROPHETIC OFFICE

Through baptism, each member of the people of God also shares in the prophetic office of Christ. As images of God, we were created to know the truth. However, unaided by grace, the human mind is incapable of knowing many truths about God. Our share in Christ's prophetic office, an effect of grace, is thus a fulfillment of God's creative act. As prophets with Christ, we are able to know Truth, i.e., God. Further, with original sin, our intellects were clouded and even those truths which we could know by the power of our own intellects became difficult to grasp. Christ's prophetic office makes it easier for us to embrace these truths as well.

The prophetic office endows each baptized member of the Church with a "sense of responsibility toward the gift of truth contained in revelation".[78] Through baptism, the intellects of the baptized are disposed toward revelation as a dry sponge is disposed toward liquid. The sponge is activated by water; the intellects of the baptized are activated by the proclamation of the gospel. Through our baptismal share in Christ's prophetic office, we each have a care and concern for revelation.

Since Christ is the fullness of revelation, the prophetic office, which gives us a responsibility to truth, gives us a responsibility to Christ. This office is the source of our fidelity to the Church and the *sensus fidelium*. "The obedience of each and every disciple of Christ to the supreme magisterium of the Church is the expression of responsibility to the word of God and to the gift of truth embodied in revelation."[79] When the Magisterium teaches, we should receive such teaching as a gift because it enriches our own knowledge of ourselves as other Christs. When the Church speaks to its members, Christ, in a certain sense, is speaking to himself. Our share in Christ's prophetic office enables us, other Christs, to accept the truths revealed in Scripture and Tradition as taught and interpreted by the

[78] See SR, p. 245.
[79] Ibid., p. 253.

mystical person of Christ, the Church. The Church does not impose its teachings on its members through coercive force. Rather, the faithful's acceptance of the truths taught by the Church flows from their own free choice, made in baptism, to join themselves to Christ. By their own free act, they wished to be united with Christ. Indeed, they wished to "put on Christ".[80] They united themselves in mind and will to Christ and to his mystical person. They have in their baptism accepted the truths taught by Christ and his mystical person.

As with the priesthood of the faithful, our baptismal share in Christ's prophetic office must be activated. We must hear the truth before we can have a sense of responsibility toward it. It is the task of the bishops in union with the Holy Father to proclaim the truth of revelation to the whole world. The Pope and bishops are the voice of Christ. They activate the prophetic office in the baptized. They serve the people of God by proclaiming God's word authoritatively. Of course, the Pope and the bishops share Christ's prophetic office in a different way from the laity, the deacons, and the priests. Theirs is the greater responsibility. But, through their episcopal ordination, God gave them the means of shouldering this responsibility. When they teach the truths of faith, they teach without error. Obviously, the mystical person of Christ cannot speak falsehood. The prophetic office is thus the foundation for the doctrine of infallibility.

The family, as a miniature mystical person of Christ, must fulfill the prophetic mission of Christ. Each member of the family, but especially the husband and the wife, must have a sense of responsibility toward the truths of revelation. Each must cultivate a faithful adherence to the teachings of the Church. The family must also teach the truths of the Faith to others. Particularly, the parents have the very serious prophetic obligation of teaching the Faith to their children, i.e., to evangelize their children.

---

[80] See Gal 3:27.

Family members must exercise Christ's prophetic office if the mission of Christ is to be accomplished in the domestic church. The mission of Christ is to show us who we are in our infinite dignity and our proper activity, love. The devotion to truth, which is the fruit of the prophetic office, teaches the family members, especially the children, that each and every human being is worthy of the truth, especially the Truth, i.e., God, which is, simultaneously, the truth about human dignity. In fact, God deemed us so worthy of the Truth that his Son became man to reveal God to us. Human dignity could not have been more wonderfully shown to us.

The priestly office enables us to give ourselves to God. If we sincerely surrender ourselves to God, we will what he wills. Among other things, we will choose to know him, the Truth. Thus, the priestly office stimulates our exercise of the prophetic office. However, it is equally true that love cannot exist in the absence of truth. Therefore, the prophetic office, which allows us to know Truth, i.e., God, stimulates the sincere giving of the priestly office.

Christ fulfilled his mission to show us who we are through the triple offices of priest, prophet, and king. In his priestly office, Christ revealed our proper activity. In his prophetic office, Christ revealed our incomparable dignity. If the family is to continue Christ's mission, it must exercise these two offices with Christ. But it must also exercise Christ's kingly office, which contributed in its own way to the fulfillment of Christ's mission.

4. THE KINGLY OFFICE

A king rules. Since we share in Christ's kingship, we are called to govern. A king must be able to exercise self-rule if he is to govern others. Therefore, as kings, the baptized are first called to govern themselves. A person governs himself when he freely chooses his acts. When we are free from internal and external compulsion, we are in control. We are able to express our persons in and through our bodies. It is our share in Christ's kingship which enables us to overcome, at least partially, the "constitutive break within the human person" which was caused by original sin.[81] It is kingly self-rule which allows the body to express the person even for historical man, the man tainted with original sin and its effects. It is our participation in Christ's kingship which enables the body again to be a physical image of the Divine Persons. Thus, it is our share in Christ's kingship which enables us to live integrated lives. Kingly self-rule facilitates the sincere giving which is the fruit of our creation and our share in Christ's priestly office.

A second aspect of our share in Christ's kingship also involves governance. We are to subdue the earth because all creation is *for* man.[82] This dominion over creation is the right of every human being. It pertains to the dignity of the human person that he is above mere material creation. The baptized should constantly strive to ensure that no person lacks the necessities of life when others have an abundance. We are able to struggle against such offenses to human dignity in virtue of our share in the kingly office of the Lord. In this aspect, our participation in Christ's kingly office makes it possible for us in practical ways to acknowledge the dignity of every human being. Thus, by ensuring that all have the necessities of life, our participation in Christ's kingship enables the sincere giving of the priestly office and the recognition of human dignity by the prophetic office.

As with the priestly and prophetic offices, the kingly office of the baptized needs to be activated through the hierarchical priesthood. This is the particular task of the ordained deacon. The first deacons were chosen to care for the widows. They, together with others who would follow their lead, were to provide the necessities of life for those who could not provide

[81] See TB, no. 28.
[82] See Gen 1:28.

for themselves. In this way, the first deacons activated the second aspect of Christ's kingship in the baptized.

However, the Acts of the Apostles makes it quite clear that the deacons were to be holy men.[83] They were to be characterized by kingly self-rule. Shortly after the seven deacons were chosen, Stephen gave witness to his kingly self-rule before the Jewish authorities. He gave witness to Christ, teaching the Faith even when he knew it would lead to his death. Even more, he showed his self-rule while praying for his persecutors, including Saul (later Paul), as he was stoned to death. As Stephen, deacons are called to witness to the Faith even under the most difficult conditions. Their example activates the first aspect of Christ's kingship in the baptized, self-rule or integration.

The deacon activates Christ's kingly office in the baptized. However, if the deacon is not a priest or bishop, he, as a baptized Christian, shares in Christ's priestly and prophetic offices as all the baptized do. The baptismal priesthood of the ordained deacon is activated by a priest or bishop. The baptismal prophetic office of the ordained deacon is activated by a bishop. Moreover, it should be noted that every priest is a deacon. Consequently, the priest activates both the kingly and priestly roles in the baptized. However, for the priest who is not a bishop, the bishop activates the priest's baptismal share in Christ's prophetic office. The bishop has the fullness of Christ's priesthood because he and he, alone, as deacon, priest, and bishop, activates the kingly, priestly, and the prophetic offices of Christ in the baptized.

The exercise of Christ's kingship is absolutely essential to family life. It is only through kingly self-rule that the husband and wife are able to give themselves to one another in and through their bodies. The family is called to be a physical image, a sacrament, of God's trinitarian love. The family becomes an image of the triune God only when the family actively participates in Christ's kingly office because love involves sacrifice.

---

[83] See Acts 6:1–7.

Without kingly self-control families would not be able to make the sacrifices love demands. For example, the exercise of responsible fertility encourages the mutual, total self-donation essential to all marriages, but it often demands kingly self-rule.

The exercise of Christ's kingship in its second aspect is also essential to family life. The parents must provide the necessities of life for each other and for the children. These obligations often impose enormous sacrifices on the parents. There are some mothers, who, while preferring to work in the marketplace, instead remain in the home, perhaps giving up careers for the sake of their children. Other wives might prefer to stay home with their children, but must work outside the home to provide for their families. Fathers often work in unpleasant or unfulfilling jobs for the sake of their children and their wives. Widows and widowers are often especially burdened in trying to provide for their families.

F. Conclusion

The subjective turn as applied to Christ results in the rather startling conclusion already found in the *Pastoral Constitution on the Church in the Modern World* that Christ "reveals man to himself".[84] As applied to the Church, and especially to the Church as the mystical person of Christ, the subjective turn yields an understanding of the Church as an acting person, as a personal subject with an intellect and a will. In turn, this understanding of the Church reveals a profound and important view of the domestic church, the miniature mystical person of Christ, i.e., the family. Without the new view of Christ and the Church resulting from the new presentation of the Faith, John Paul II's view of the family would be incomprehensible.

[84] See GS, no. 22.

APPENDIX TO PART ONE

Definitions of Key Terms
in the Thought of John Paul II

IMAGE OF GOD. In the Book of Genesis, God reveals that human persons are made in God's own likeness. Among all
the earthly creatures and inanimate things God created,
only the human being is like God. Only human persons
have minds and wills, the capacities of thinking and choosing. If we are in God's image, we are not only like him, but
we are created to act like him. Our creation in the divine
likeness is a constant theme of Pope John Paul II. It is a
pivotal concept in his theology.

PERSON. A person is a living being endowed with a mind and a
will, the capacities of thinking and choosing. Preeminently
this term belongs to the three Persons in one God and
then to the angels and human persons. A human being
is a person because he is made in the divine image. The
animals, plants, and other things in God's creation are not
persons. However, the human person is different from all
other persons because he has a body. The angels are persons
without bodies and the three Persons in God are without
bodies insofar as each is God. (The second Person has a
body because he became man.)

BODY. The body of a human being expresses his person. In
other words, our bodies are given to us by God so that the

acts of our minds and wills might be expressed in a physical way. Since we are persons in the image of God, we are made to act as God acts. Therefore, the body should be a physical manifestation of how God acts. In and through it, a person, a divine image of God, is made visible. Further, the body is not ours absolutely. The body is part of the gift of life from God and it expresses our persons as it is.

DIGNITY. Each and every human being is endowed with an infinite worth and value by God. Only we, of all God's creation in this world, are made in his own image. We are made for our own sakes and all else is made for us. But our dignity was enhanced even further through the Incarnation when God assumed a human nature and raised it to a dignity beyond compare. By creation, we were made a little less than God, but by the Incarnation, every human act, except sin, became worthy of God himself and therefore of incomparable value. We may never offend our own dignity or anyone else's by treating ourselves or anyone else as things to be used.

PERSONALISTIC NORM. "This norm, in its negative aspect, states that the person is a kind of good which does not admit of use and cannot be treated as an object of use and as such the means to an end."[1] Persons must be treasured for their own sakes. We must then relate to others only through love.

LOVE. Love is the act of God. This divine act is found perfectly and completely in the Trinity. Each Divine Person surrenders himself completely and totally to the other two and receives their gift of themselves in return. God's love is manifested to the world in the act of creation and especially in the Incarnation. In creation, God shared himself, being or existence, with the world. In the Incarnation, and most especially on the Cross, God "humbled himself and

[1] See LR, p. 41.

became obedient unto death, even death on a cross!"[2] Love is a selfless surrender of everything one is (and has) for the sake of another. There is the expectation in this selfless gift that the other or others will make a similar gift in return. Human beings love because they are made in God's own image. Without love, human existence is senseless.

CONSCIOUSNESS. Consciousness is the awareness which a person has of himself as a subject who knows, wills, and acts. Consciousness is a kind of inner image which a person has of his conscious (known and willed) acts. In other words, a person's consciousness mirrors every conscious action he does. Every deliberate act of a person is present in his consciousness. Human consciousness "contains" everything that a person consciously does within himself (i.e., conscious acts of thinking and willing) and outside of himself through his body. Consciousness is a characteristic of persons. This concept is critical in John Paul's understanding of the human person and of knowledge.

EFFICACY. Human persons experience efficacy when they know and freely choose a particular action. When a human being consciously chooses to act, he acts efficaciously. John Paul contrasts efficacious acts with other occurrences in each of us which we do not cause, e.g., one's heart beating.

FREEDOM. Freedom is the capacity to choose for oneself. A person is characterized by free will because he is an image of God and only acts as a person when he exercises his free will.

TRANSCENDENCE. Transcendence means exceeding a certain boundary. When a human person increases his knowledge of the truth, he crosses the boundary of his former knowledge of the truth. Since God is Truth, when we know the

---

[2] See Phil 2:8.

truth, we know God more fully. This is horizontal transcendence. Transcendence also applies to the will. Since we are images of God, we should act as God acts. When we will a Godlike action, we are stepping beyond the boundary of our natural physical processes. In this way, we decide not to be bound by our physical nature as animals are. This is vertical transcendence.

TRUTH. Truth is the way things are. Truth signifies reality. First and foremost, it refers to the reality of God. Second, it signifies all the things God has created. This truth, reality (God and all of creation), can be known by the intellect, but it does not depend on one's knowledge for existence. However, in us there must be a will to the truth. This necessity would seem to hamper human freedom. But freedom and truth cannot conflict. Freedom is a perfection of the human person, but so is truth a perfection of the human person, i.e., a perfection of the intellect. Human perfection is an integral whole and thus the perfection of the will (with freedom) cannot be opposed to the perfection of the intellect (with truth). Only when we choose the truth are we free.

INTEGRATION. Integration is the gathering into unity of the diverse dimensions of one's life, sense impressions, feelings, and emotions, under the governance of the mind and will so that a freely chosen good act (which reflects God) might be outwardly expressed through the body. When a vertically transcendent act is perfectly expressed in and through the body, the individual experiences integration. For historical man tainted with sin, grace makes integration possible.

VALUE. A value is something which is good or important in and of itself, as opposed to something that is merely subjectively satisfying or subjectively important. Thus, a value motivates a person's will and affective responses because of what it is in itself, not because of what it means to the person.

RESPONSIBILITY. Responsibility is the ability to respond. Responsibility for John Paul denotes the ability of a person to know the goods (truth and value) in all of God's creation and to choose (will) the proper response to those goods, e.g., the only proper response to another human being is love. Failing to respond properly to a good, one acts irresponsibly.

ATTITUDE. "An attitude is an active relationship, but not yet an action. It follows upon cognition and enriched awareness, but is something new and different from these. It involves 'taking up a position' and being ready to act in accordance with it."[3] It is a will-act, a choice, which is not yet expressed in action.

DIALOGUE. Dialogue is an exchange of ideas founded on the truth. "Men share with each other the truth they have discovered, or think they have discovered, in such a way that they help one another in the search for truth."[4] Dialogue is an exchange among men and women who are seeking the truth. Before dialogue can begin there must be an attitude of pursuing the truth, a will to truth. One cannot dialogue with those who reject truth, value, and good out of hand. Still, it is possible for people to disagree as to truth because it is possible for men and women to err, not because truth is divided. Dialogue is only possible among men and women of good will. This term is central to many of John Paul's writings and addresses.

COMMUNION OF PERSONS. A communion of persons is the effect of the gift of love among two or more persons. The

---

[3] See SR, p. 205.

[4] Ibid., p. 27. See also *Dignitatis Humanae, Declaration on Religious Liberty* (December 7, 1965), *Documents of Vatican II*, ed. Austin P. Flannery (Grand Rapids, Michigan: William B. Eerdmans, 1975), no. 3, p. 801.

perfect communion of persons is the Trinity. A human person is made in God's image and is called to love as God loves. God loves, i.e., gives himself in a total self-surrender, within the Trinity. This love is manifested to the world in the creation and especially in the Incarnation. By his creative act, God invites all people to enter into two communions of persons with other human beings: in the family and in the workplace. Further, in Christ and through the activity of the Holy Spirit, God invites everyone to enter a communion of persons with him and all those joined to him through his grace. We call this communion of persons the Church. A human person enters a communion of persons by recognizing in his mind the value of others (especially of God) and by choosing that value in his will. In a communion of persons, each person loves all the other members of the communion in accordance with the personalistic norm. A communion of persons results from responsible love and is the highest human calling. It is always an imitation of the Holy Trinity. The Trinity is the most perfect communion of persons. We are invited by God to share in this trinitarian communion through the gift of grace.

OBEDIENCE. Obedience is one of the effects of the communion of persons, a union of wills in the truth. It is most perfectly realized in the Trinity, which was wonderfully revealed to us in the prayer of Christ in the agony in the garden, "Not my will, but thine be done."[5] Obedience can only be the act of a mature adult who is joined willingly and freely in a bond of love. Thus, to ask spouses to obey each other is simply to ask them to fulfill the communion of persons, which they entered on their wedding day. Obedience is not the sign of immaturity, but rather of a mature love, a self-surrender in the will.

[5] See Lk 22:42.

GRACE. Grace is our share in God's own life. It was won for us by Christ's Passion, death, and Resurrection. Grace makes the body capable of expressing the person even for historical man, the man tainted by sin. More importantly, it is the seed of glory, the promise of eternal life. It is communicated to us through a personal meeting with Christ in the sacraments.

SUBJECTIVE TURN. The subjective turn is the new focus in the theology of John Paul II on the individual human person and his experience. It is the result of the union of phenomenology and the gospel. The philosopher who uses the phenomenological method seeks to know the truth about people through a study of human experiences. The gospel reveals the full truth about the human person as is especially clear in the text from Genesis, "Let us make man in our image."[6] Therefore, the truth about humanity found in revelation furthers the insights of phenomenology. At the same time, however, the subjective language and ideas of phenomenology becomes a means of persuading people of the truth about themselves revealed in the gospel. The subjective turn is the key and revolutionary aspect of John Paul's thought.

[6] See Gen 1:26.

PART TWO

A Commentary on
the Apostolic Exhortation,

Familiaris Consortio

"The Role of the Christian
Family in the Modern World"

The Document:
Context and Outline

The apostolic exhortation, *Familiaris Consortio, The Role of the Christian Family in the Modern World*, was promulgated by Pope John Paul II at Saint Peter's in Rome on the feast of Christ the King, November 22, 1981. This document is the Pope's response to a request of the bishops who attended the synod of the family which met in Rome from September 26 to October 25 in 1980. The fathers of the synod asked the Holy Father "to be a spokesman before humanity of the Church's lively care for the family".[1] In fulfilling the synodal request, John Paul wrote the most significant document the Holy See has ever issued on the family.

Still, the Holy Father is not a spokesman in the sense that he is merely "mouthing" the lines given to him by the bishops gathered in synod. Rather he is the author who has sought advice on certain points and received that advice critically. In fact, as is clear from his first talk in the *Theology of the Body* series, he was preparing for the synod on the family a full year before it met by teaching the world his understanding of the body and sexuality. His vision of the human body and human sexuality is the fruit of the application of the new synthesis of faith and reason with its subjective turn to these topics.[2] In other words, even before the synod had met, he had a framework regarding

[1] See FC, no. 2.
[2] See TB, no. 1, where he states that he began that series as a "preparation for the synod from afar".

human sexuality in place and he had presented it to the world. In fact, he continued his *Theology of the Body* series even after the synod had finished its deliberations.

While the theology of the body is essential to the theology of the family, the exhortation on the family does not merely repeat the points the Holy Father made in his *Theology of the Body* series. Rather, the exhortation summarizes, sometimes quite succinctly, the theology of the body and builds a theology of the family. In other words, in this apostolic exhortation on the family, John Paul does for the family what he did for the body in his Wednesday audiences.

It is important to note that John Paul's vision of the family was already developed before the synod met. The topic of family life has interested the present Holy Father since his early years as a priest. In his book, *Love and Responsibility*, published over thirty years ago, John Paul began to present his view of family life, but *Love and Responsibility* represents an earlier stage of Wojtyla's thought. The family as a communion of persons is the fruit of the subjective turn found in the new presentation of the gospel developed in Poland in the years before and after the council. However, unlike the theology of the body, the theology of the family had not been presented systematically to the world in its fully developed form before this exhortation. The exhortation on the family clearly represents a significant development as compared with the earlier work, *Love and Responsibility*.

Of course, the fathers of the synod on the family contributed to the exhortation. Their thoughts and ideas were incorporated into the document at the appropriate points. Still, the framework and the thrust of the document obviously bear the unmistakable mark of the Holy Father. The contributions of the synodal fathers could be incorporated because the scope of John Paul's vision is broad and because both the bishops and the Pope were seeking the truth. The truth does not contradict itself and, therefore, many of the comments of the bishops corresponded to John Paul II's existing framework.

The new theology of the family begins with the now familiar point that the human person is made in the image and likeness of God. The family, as a union of persons, should reflect the trinitarian communion of persons. The Christian family is in a very special way called to live the divine life as the Church does. In fact, the Christian family is, as the Pope teaches in his exhortation, a miniature church, a specification of the ecclesial communion of persons. Human dignity requires that family life be lived as God intended "from the beginning" and as Christ restored it.

The Church does not impose morality with its authority. Rather, it teaches with the authority of Christ how God has made us and what family life is as established by God at the dawn of the world. Of course, some may choose to live in a way which contradicts the very existence of human persons and family life. However, choosing this course of action, the individual is violating himself and his own family. He is destroying himself and his family. The Church teaches authoritatively for the sake of humanity so that all people might live in accordance with their dignity and their invitation to mirror God himself.

Not only does the theology of the family as presented in this exhortation begin with the concept that human beings are created in the image of God, it also is remarkably similar to John Paul's study of the Church. Since the family is a domestic church, a miniature mystical person of Christ, it should have the characteristics of the Church. Thus, in Part Three, the Holy Father suggests that the family should attain self-knowledge and self-realization, i.e., through its consciousness of its own proper acts it should realize itself (become what it is) and it should know itself. Self-knowledge and self-realization were the tasks which the Holy Father outlined for the Church in his study *Sources of Renewal*. Of course, the family will only achieve these tasks if it engages in its proper activity, its mission, which is identical to the mission of the Church. Part Three of the exhortation thus defines the mission of the family and it corresponds to the second part of *Sources of Renewal* where the Holy Father discusses the attitudes of the Church. In these sections of both works, the Pope discusses the mystical person of Christ as a personal subject.

Familiaris Consortio should not be viewed as a highly theoretical and theological document. The Holy Father does present new and important theological arguments, but these lend credence to some very practical conclusions. Among the most significant developments are the new arguments from the theology of the body and the theology of the family which support the Church's position on contraception.

Among the many very practical developments, three are especially noteworthy. First, John Paul II raises natural family planning to the level of an apostolate. Even young unmarried people are encouraged to become aware of their fertility. As they know more about themselves, they will come to know their own truth and value and act responsibly, i.e., with virtue. For John Paul, natural family planning encourages virtue and therefore it should be widely studied. Second, the Pope divides marriage preparation into remote, proximate, and immediate and asks that the Church do everything possible to ensure that most couples are prepared in all three stages. Marriage preparation has not often been understood as a program beginning with early childhood! Finally, the Pope assures those living in difficult situations, especially the divorced and remarried, that if they persevere in prayer, penance, and charity, God will grant them the grace of conversion. This is an extraordinary promise from the Vicar of Christ!

The Role of the Christian Family in the Modern World, is organized in four parts with an introduction and a conclusion. The introduction, conclusion, and each of the four parts are organized into articles. There are a total of eighty-six articles in the entire document. The introduction has three articles. Part One has seven articles. Part Two has six articles. Part Three has forty-eight articles. Part Four has twenty-one articles and the conclusion has one article. Part Three and Part Four both have four divisions. Although Part Two is the largest of the four parts, Part Two is the most significant section of the document. Article eleven in Part Two is perhaps the most brilliant summary of the theology of the body the Holy Father has ever written.

In reading the following commentary, the reader should have a copy of the document available. The commentary follows the document exactly and takes up the various points article by article. Further, while reading the commentary, it is well to keep in mind the broad outline of the document and especially the organization of the particular part which is being discussed. Even though John Paul has given his exhortation a rigorous organization and is always consistent, sometimes, in the details, the major points can be forgotten. In addition, the commentary relies heavily on the points made in the first part of this volume and therefore, the authors recommend that the reader examine the first part of this work before reading the commentary. It is well to read the commentary from beginning to end, since, within itself, it relies on points previously made. In this regard, the commentary is very similar to the document itself. Quotations from *Familiaris Consortio* are noted only when they are from a previous or subsequent article. When the quotations are taken from the particular article under discussion, we have not cited the reference. When we quote the document and it is quoting from another source, e.g., the Scriptures, we indicate that there is a quote within a quote, but we do not cite the reference. The reference can be found in the document itself.

Outline of the Document

INTRODUCTION

   A. *Familiaris Consortio* is addressed to families.

      1. Who know what marriage is.

      2. Who are searching for the truth.

      3. Who are not free to live as families.

   B. The occasion for issuing this document is the 1980 synod of bishops, which considered the family.

   C. The family exists to announce the gospel.

   D. The family also exists to discern vocations.

   E. The Church has a profound interest in the family.

      1. Proof of this interest is the 1980 synod of bishops.

      2. The bishops, gathered in synod, made some propositions and asked the Pope "to be a spokesman before humanity" on the Church's interest in family life.

   F. The family was willed by God in his creative act.

   G. But family life is interiorly ordained to fulfillment in Christ.

   H. The family can realize itself only by accepting Christ.

   I. Further, it is only in accepting Christ that the family can be restored to the full realization of God's plan.

      1. Men and women cannot live family life as God planned because of original sin.

      2. Only the grace of Christ restores the family to what it should be.

I. BRIGHT SPOTS AND SHADOWS
    FOR THE FAMILY TODAY

    A. This part defines the problems of the family in our age.

    B. God's plan for marriage and family life is not an abstract, theoretical concept, but applies to families in their concrete existence.

    C. Some very appealing ideas are proposed in our age to questions about family life.

    D. However, many of these are contrary to the gospel.

    E. The church wishes to offer the entire truth about humanity and family life to the modern world.

        1. The Church is not just the hierarchy, but includes all the baptized.

        2. Christian married couples have a very special obligation to proclaim the gospel to other families.

    F. There are certain modern negative phenomena which threaten the family.

        1. Divorce.

        2. Abortion.

        3. Sterilization.

        4. A contraceptive mentality.

    G. At the root of these phenomena is a false idea of freedom based on selfishness.

        1. There is a conflict between two loves: love of self and love of God.

        2. The Church proclaims the freedom and love of the gospel, which are not in conflict because both find their source in God.

    H. The faithful are not immune to these false ideas.

I. A new culture is emerging which is characterized by advanced technology.

   1. These developments are good.

   2. But we must recover an awareness of moral values.

J. Everyone needs a permanent conversion to Christ.

II. THE PLAN OF GOD FOR MARRIAGE AND THE FAMILY

A. This section teaches the world what the family is, i.e., its identity.

B. The first article of Part Two summarizes the *Theology of the Body* series.

   1. The human person, as an image of God, is made to love.

   2. This love is expressed in and through the human body.

   3. Human love must reflect the total self-donation of God in the creation and the redemption.

   4. The gift of a married couple to one another must include the possibility of children. Couples should exercise "responsible fertility".

   5. Sexuality and procreation are not something merely biological.

   6. If a man and a woman love one another and wish to express their love through their sexual powers, this must occur in marriage.

   7. Virginity and celibacy also represent a gift of love in and through the body.

C. Marriage is a sign of God's love for his people.

D. Christ restores family life and makes it possible even after sin.

   1. Christian married couples are a sign of Christ's love.

   2. They are called to love as Christ loved us on the Cross.

E. Children are a precious gift of marriage: the fruit of the mutual gift of the spouses to one another.

F. The family is a communion of persons, which builds up society and the Church.

G. The family also is the means by which the child enters society and is introduced into the life of the Church.

H. Conversely, the Church finds a way to the hearts of all people, especially children, through the family.

I. Virginity and celibacy are embraced as another way of expressing love.

   1. Virgins and celibates testify to the goodness of marriage and family life.

   2. Further, it is only when family life is held in high esteem that virginity and celibacy make any sense.

III. THE ROLE OF THE CHRISTIAN FAMILY

A. This third part discusses the mission of the family.

   1. As a miniature mystical person of Christ, the family must realize itself and know itself in and through its proper acts. It must become what it is, a domestic church, through its proper acts.

   2. The acts of the family, i.e., the mission of the family, correspond to the mission of the Church.

B. The first division considers the building of the communion of persons in the family.

    1. The familial communion of persons is based on love, the mutual self-donation of all the family members to one another.

    2. Grace, especially that given through the sacrament of matrimony, makes this self-donation possible.

    3. A marital union must be exclusive. Thus, polygamy contradicts the familial communion of persons.

    4. The marital union is total and therefore indissoluble.

    5. All members of the family are called to live in love with the other family members.

        a. The Holy Father discusses the role of women in the family.

        b. He also discusses men.

        c. He treats the children.

        d. He concludes with some remarks on the elderly.

C. The second division of Part Three discusses the family's obligation to serve life.

    1. The Pope divides this topic into two areas.

        a. The first is the transmission of human life.

        b. The second is the education of the children.

    2. The power of transmitting life is an extraordinary gift. Men and women are called to share in the divine love, which is always fruitful.

        a. The Church teaches that the love of spouses must always be open to the transmission of life.

        b. The Church stands for life and supports life against all those who would attack it.

    c. The Magisterium asks theologians to explain the teachings of the Church regarding life.

    d. Contraception is accepted because sexuality is separated from the person.

    e. The Second Vatican Council affirmed the teaching of the Church against contraception as did Pope Paul VI.

    f. Contraception is a manipulation and degradation of human sexuality. The couples who practice it are living a lie.

    g. There is no contradiction between love and morality.

    h. Fertility awareness is unequivocally recommended and encouraged.

    i. All people must always strive to live according to the moral norms. They will grow in holiness and as they grow in holiness, they will find it easier to follow the moral precepts.

    j. All those who investigate the fertility cycle are commended, thanked, and urged to continue.

3. The spouses have a grave obligation to educate their children.

    a. Parents should teach by word, but even more importantly, by example.

    b. They should prepare the children for love, not neglecting education in sexuality, i.e., in discipline and self-control according to Christian values.

    c. Parents teach by virtue of the sacrament of matrimony.

    d. Parents have a grave obligation to ensure the Christian formation of their children. They should teach the children prayer, assist them to grow in holiness, and enable them to receive the sacraments at the proper times. They should teach the Christian truths by example and help their children exercise the Christian virtues.

   e. Church, state, and other Christian families should assist the family in its role of education.

   f. Those families which do not have children witness to their fruitful love by reaching out to others.

D. The third division of Part Three considers the role of the family in participating in society.

   1. The family serves society by giving society new members.

   2. The family also serves society by reaffirming the dignity of each and every human being.

      a. The family does this within itself when all members give themselves in love to all the other members.

      b. The family also does this by extending hospitality to all other human beings.

   3. Families should engage in political activity in order that the government would support and defend family life.

   4. The state has obligations to the family.

      a. The government should not appropriate familial tasks to itself.

      b. The state should assist families in shouldering their responsibilities.

   5. Article forty-six has the charter of the rights of the family.

   6. Christian families, in the exercise of Christ's kingly

office, have a very special obligation to participate in the development of society.

   a. Christian families will offer a very special witness to human dignity by cultivating a preference for the poor, the hungry, and those without a family.

   b. Some issues need to be solved on a worldwide basis. Christian families will unite with other Christian families around the globe in defense of human dignity.

   c. Christian families will give witness to human dignity primarily through education.

E. The last section of Part Three considers the family's obligation to share in the life and mission of the Church.

   1. The Christian family is a domestic church called to exercise the priestly, prophetic, and kingly offices of the Lord.

   2. The Christian married couple exercises the prophetic office by receiving the teaching of the Church with faith.

      a. The couple exercises Christ's prophetic office through the celebration of the sacrament of matrimony.

      b. The ritual of the marriage rite should be a "moment of faith".

      c. The couple should exercise Christ's prophetic office throughout the marriage as they give living witness to the Christian truths.

   3. The couple also exercises Christ's prophetic office by teaching the Faith, especially to their children.

      a. This task of evangelization often causes suffering if the children reject the Faith.

        b. At such times, parents should keep in mind the suffering of the apostles when they proclaimed the Faith.

    4. Spouses also exercise Christ's priestly office.

        a. The priestly office is activated through the sacrament of matrimony.

        b. However, it also requires refreshment through the sacraments of holy Eucharist and penance.

    5. Once activated through the sacraments, the priestly office of the spouses is exercised in prayer and through teaching the children to pray.

        a. The prayer of the family should include liturgical prayer.

        b. Family private prayer should include the usual prayers of the Church, and especially the Rosary.

    6. The parents also exercise their priestly office by presenting the children for reception of the sacraments at the appropriate times.

    7. The family also exercises Christ's kingly office.

        a. Spouses must govern themselves (integration) and this occurs through the exercise of the kingship of Christ.

        b. Such self-rule is necessary for true love.

        c. Spouses must also strive to uphold human dignity and this is an exercise of Christ's kingship in its second aspect: the restoration of the created order as God intended "from the beginning".

IV. PASTORAL CARE OF THE FAMILY:
    STAGES, STRUCTURES, AGENTS, AND SITUATIONS

    A. This part of the exhortation is very practical and applies the principles learned previously to concrete situations.

B. It is in four divisions: stages, structures, agents, and situations.

C. The stages of pastoral care of the family are threefold: preparation, celebration of the rite, and the married life.

   1. Preparation is divided into three areas: remote, proximate, and immediate.

      a. Remote preparation occurs in the family when the child is young and learns about love from his parents.

      b. Proximate preparation occurs during the adolescent years and should include fertility awareness and other practical areas necessary to married life.

      c. Immediate preparation includes the canonical inquiry and a preparation for the actual rite. This should be a journey of faith.

      d. Even though such preparation is the norm, those who refuse to engage in such preparation should not, for that reason alone, be refused marriage.

   2. The actual celebration of the rite is also a stage of pastoral care.

      a. The ritual should be sanctifying. It must be fruitful, valid, and worthy.

      b. Even couples without strong faith may be married in the Church because they are conforming themselves to the will of God as expressed in Genesis.

      c. If a couple explicitly rejects what the Church intends by marriage, the marriage cannot take place. Otherwise, the priest should witness the marriage.

   3. The last stage of pastoral care follows the marriage.

        a. The Church should support the newly married.

        b. Older families should help the younger ones.

        c. There should be Christian associations of families.

D. The second division of Part Four considers the structures of the pastoral care of the family.

    1. The most important structure is the diocese.

    2. However, for most people, the contact with the Church is through the parish.

    3. The family, itself, as a miniature church, is an agent of pastoral care.

    4. Finally, there are associations of families, which should act as agents of pastoral care.

E. The third division of Part Four considers the agents of pastoral care.

    1. The family is an agent of pastoral care.

    2. However, in a diocese, the bishop is a primary agent for the pastoral care of the family. The bishop should take a personal interest in the support of families.

    3. Priests assist the bishop and they should receive training for the family apostolate before accepting parish assignments.

    4. Theologians should assist the Church and families by explaining the teachings of the Church.

    5. Religious orders should try to devote some personnel and resources to the family apostolate.

    6. Lay experts of every type and description extend the Church's pastoral care.

    7. Finally, those in the media should be mindful of their influence on families. Not only should they

discourage programming harmful to families, but they should strive to incorporate family values in the development of new shows.

    a. Families should encourage such programming.

    b. The Church supports those Catholics who undertake such arduous work.

F. The final division of Part Four treats difficult cases.

    1. The Pope first considers families with special needs.

       a. He mentions many such cases, but discusses the families of migrant workers, interfaith families, and families in special situations, e.g., birth, death, and marriage. The Pope also includes elderly families among those with special needs.

       b. The Church wishes to offer such families a special solicitude.

    2. The Pope also discusses the special care which both the couple and the Church must take when there is a marriage between a Catholic and a non-Catholic Christian, or a marriage between a Catholic and a non-Christian.

    3. The Holy Father also considers irregular situations.

       a. Trial marriages violate the dignity of both the man and the woman.

       b. Free unions also violate the dignity of the man and the woman.

       c. Sometimes young people enter these for lack of money and other necessities. Civil authorities should do what is possible to make true marriage a viable option in all societies.

       d. Civil marriages of Catholics are forbidden. Catholics in civil marriages cannot receive the sacraments until the marriage is validated.

e. Divorced or separated spouses should receive the Church's constant support. They are to be encouraged to forgive their spouses.

f. When the divorced and separated live without entering a new union, they give a powerful witness to the whole Church.

g. Finally, the Pope discusses the divorced and remarried.

h. These men and women have chosen a way of life contrary to the gospel. The Church offers prayers on their behalf.

i. There are differences among this group. Those who were abandoned by their spouses or those who remarried for the sake of children are in a different category from those who left their spouses and remarried.

j. The divorced and remarried cannot be admitted to the sacraments, but if they persevere in prayer, God will grant them the grace of repentance.

4. The Pope extends the hospitality of the Church to all those without a family.

CONCLUSION

A. *"The future of humanity passes by way of the family."*

B. The Holy Father expects a special care for families on the part of the baptized because they know the full revelation of God concerning family life.

C. The Holy Father invokes the protection of the Holy Family on all families.

D. He ends this long document with a prayer to Joseph, Mary, and Christ.

Introduction to the Document

Paralleling the English title of the second constitution on the Church of the Second Vatican Council, *Pastoral Constitution on the Church in the Modern World*, John Paul begins his *Role of the Christian Family in the Modern World* with the words "The family in the modern world". Immediately, at the very beginning of this document, the Pope indicates that his exhortation on the family will be set in a contemporary and not a historical context. Under previous pontiffs, most Church documents have begun with a historical survey of the teachings of the Church on the particular issue addressed by that document. However, this Holy Father wishes to discuss the concrete situations of people and families today. His direct approach to contemporary situation may stem from his phenomenological background. Generally speaking, phenomenology begins with the experience of individuals in the concrete situations in which they exist. Phenomenologists tend to direct their attention to current and lived situations rather than to previous historical situations which are somewhat removed from current lived experience.

The Holy Father finishes his first sentence with the thought that the family has been changing rapidly and profoundly in our modern world. In his view, this is the lived experience of modern families. It is in the context of this situation that the entire document is written. Obviously, then, the Holy Father is well aware of the changing times. Often, the Church is accused of maintaining the status quo even in the face of change. Here, in the very opening words of the document, the highest authority in the Church dismisses a static view of family life in our age.

In the first paragraph, the Holy Father recognizes that many families, despite the changes, are adhering to "those values that constitute the foundation of the institution of the family". With this thought, it is quite clear that the Holy Father, while acknowledging the speed of change, still holds to certain values which are at the center of family life in our own era and, by implication, in all eras. There is something about the family which must perdure throughout time if it is to be what it is. Again, this is hardly surprising. It is equally true to maintain that there is something about all businesses which must perdure throughout time, even in the midst of change, if they are to be what they are. In this latter case, the characteristic might be making a profit. In this document, the Holy Father wishes to define the values which make a family what it is.

In addition to those families who are struggling to remain faithful to the "values that constitute the foundation of the institution of the family", there are other families which are "uncertain and bewildered" about the "ultimate meaning and truth of conjugal and family life". Here, the major problem addressed by the document is posed very succinctly. The rapid changes have caused some to forget the values essential to family life. The Holy Father is addressing the classic problem of change and lasting truth. For some, the rapid pace of constant new developments has obscured reality, i.e., truth. Of course, God is Truth and therefore, when the truth is obscured, God is also obscured. Since the Church exists to reveal God, the Truth, the Church has the responsibility to affirm the truth and to assist all in maintaining it even in the face of our rapidly changing world.

A third group of families is rendered incapable of responding to their environment because their most fundamental rights are denied. Since "man is the way for the Church",[1] the Church is interested in every violation of human rights. Therefore, the Church lends its voice to those crying out against the violation

---

[1] See RH, no. 14.

of human rights. In this document on the family, the Pope will be especially conscious of the violation of familial rights wherever in the world this atrocity is occurring.

Having defined the two basic problems: the conflict between enduring values and rapid change; and the violation of familial rights; the Holy Father in the next paragraph of this first article affirms that "marriage and the family constitute one of the most precious of human values". He also indicates that the Church wishes to offer help and assistance to all three groups mentioned in the first paragraph. The Church earnestly desires to support the first group in their efforts to live their lives in accord with the lasting values of marriage and family life. The Church wishes to illumine those families who are "searching for the truth". Finally, the Church wishes to assist the third group of families whose rights are violated.

In light of what we already know of John Paul's understanding of the Church's mission, his promise of support, illumination, and assistance is most interesting. Primarily through the exercise of its priestly office, the Church can support those families attempting to live according to the truth of family life. The family is based on a mutual self-donation of a man and a woman to one another in a lifelong commitment. This sincere giving is possible only through the exercise of Christ's priestly office. This office is given in baptism, a sacrament of the Church. It is activated in a very special way through the holy Eucharist and the sacrament of penance, and receives a specification through matrimony. By celebrating the sacraments, a function of its priestly office, the Church certainly supports families intending to live according to the true value of family life.

The illumination of the second group occurs through the prophetic office of the Church. For this group, the many changes in society have obscured transcendent values of the family. These people no longer understand the truth of family life. Since "marriage and the family constitute one of the most precious of human values", these people no longer understand themselves. Christ came to reveal man to himself, and the Church has the same mission. In teaching the truth of family life to these people, the Church reveals to them their awesome dignity as creatures made in the image of God. In teaching them this precious value of family life, the Church is carrying on the mission of Christ through its prophetic office.

It is most interesting to note that the Holy Father adds that the Church illumines those who are uncertain and "searching for the truth". In other words, the Church's exercise of its prophetic office is effective for those who are uncertain if they are at least open to the truth. The baptismal prophetic office of those who are bewildered disposes them toward the truth taught by the Church.

Finally, the offer of assistance to those families unable to exercise their fundamental rights is clearly an activity of the Church's kingly office. The second function of the Church's kingly office enables it to struggle for the restoration of the proper order in creation. This office gives the Church a responsibility to ensure, as far as possible, that all men and women are accorded the rights and privileges proper to creatures made in the image of God. John Paul is assuring families deprived of fundamental human rights that the Church will exercise its kingly office on their behalf. These are not idle words from the Church, especially in light of this Holy Father's record on human rights.

Finally, the first article concludes with reference to the young. John Paul not only wishes to address existing families, but also those, i.e., the young, who are preparing for marriage. He wishes that his exhortation on the family would give them "new horizons" and help them "to discover the beauty and grandeur of the vocation to love and the service of life".

In the second article of this long document, the Pope cites the 1980 synod of bishops, which discussed the family and its problems, as evidence for the Church's interest in family life. He comments that this synod on the family was a logical outgrowth of previous synodal topics: catechesis, the ministerial priesthood, and justice in the modern world. Of course, the family as a miniature church is called to announce the gospel as Christ did. In other words, the family is called to show human persons who they are by revealing their dignity and their proper activity to them. Since the activity proper to human beings is primarily revealed to them through the exercise of Christ's priesthood, the synodal topic on the ministerial priesthood is directly related to the domestic church. Similarly, because the incomparable dignity of the human person is revealed to him through the Church's prophetic office, the synod on catechesis, the means of handing on revelation, is vital to the family. Since the kingly office enables the exercise of the priestly and prophetic offices, the synodal topic on justice in the modern world pertains directly to the family and its participation in Christ's kingship.

After noting the connection between the synod on the family and previous topics, the Holy Father repeats that the family must fulfill the mission of Christ through its exercise of Christ's triple offices. "The family must help man to discern his own vocation [priestly office] and to accept responsibility in the search for greater justice [kingly office], educating him from the beginning [prophetic office] in interpersonal relationships, rich in justice and in love."

In the last two paragraphs of this article, the Holy Father indicates that the bishops present at the synod on the family presented him with proposals and asked that he act as a spokesman for them on this vital topic. He thanks the bishops for their work and indicates that he has entrusted their proposals to the Pontifical Council for the Family for further study.

In the third article, the last of this introduction, the Holy Father affirms that "the Church is deeply convinced that only by the acceptance of the gospel are the hopes that man legitimately places in marriage and in the family capable of being fulfilled." With these words, the Pope asserts that genuine family life is impossible without the gospel. He makes the mission of Christ, the redemption, necessary to the fulfillment of God's creative act. God instituted the family when he said, "Be fruitful and multiply."[2] But the mutual self-donation of a man and a woman in marriage became almost impossible because of sin. Therefore, Christ came to make the will of God, expressed in the creation, possible. As the Pope writes, "Willed by God in the very act of creation, marriage and the family are interiorly ordained to fulfillment in Christ and have need of his graces in order to be healed from the wounds of sin and restored to their 'beginning,' that is, to full understanding and the full realization of God's plan."

Original sin caused the human race to lose the gift of original innocence. There was now a "constitutive break within the human person"[3] so that the faculties of mind and will no longer governed the body. No longer did individual human persons have control over their bodily desires and passions. Lacking that control, people could not give themselves in a selfless donation to others because the demands and desires of the body always made themselves felt. The body was no longer the " 'trustworthy' substratum of the communion of persons".[4] Further, the human intellect was darkened so that people no longer knew their incomparable dignity or their proper activity.

The human person, made in God's image, was made to love as God loves. However, after original sin, this self-gift was impossible. After sin, the human being was the most pathetic of creatures, made for one activity (love) and now incapable of it. After the fall, people were not fully human because they could not love, the act for which they were made. Since family life is founded on a mutual selfless donation of a man and a woman to one another in and through their bodies, the effects of original sin destroyed true family life. Not only were men and women incapable of a mutual self-donation, they did not even understand it as a fulfillment of their incomparable dignity as

[2] See Gen 1:28.
[3] See TB, no. 28.
[4] Ibid., no. 29.

creatures made in the image of God. Christ restored humanity by restoring, through his grace, the possibility of acting as God intended from the very beginning and the possibility of knowing the truth. In the second and third paragraphs of this short third article, the Holy Father has summarized much of the material from his *Theology of the Body* addresses.

In the final paragraph of this third article, the Holy Father returns to the theme of the document's beginning. He writes that the Church feels the need to proclaim the gospel to all families in our own age because there are forces seeking to "destroy . . . or in some way to deform" the family. Since the gospel of love is the true foundation for family life, by proclaiming this gospel, the Church hopes to be a voice against those who would irrevocably alter or destroy family life. The preaching of the gospel, the mission of the Church, is thus a service to humanity. However, when the Church supports and encourages family life, the Church also reaps rewards. Since "man is the way for the Church"[5] and "*the future of humanity passes by way of the family,*"[6] the good of the Church is "intimately tied to the good of the family".

The first three articles of *Familiaris Consortio* indicate that it is addressed to all people. After all, everyone can be described as a family member. Secondly, these introductory articles describe the occasion for this document, the recent synod of bishops and the forces arrayed against the family. In the following section of the exhortation, Part One, "Bright Spots and Shadows for the Family Today", the Holy Father defines the current difficulties families are facing.

[5] See RH, no. 14.
[6] See FC, no. 86.

I. Bright Spots and Shadows for the Family Today

Part One of *The Role of the Christian Family in the Modern World* is in effect a second introduction, which defines the problem addressed in the document. While the first three articles of the apostolic exhortation on the family spoke of "numerous forces that seek to destroy . . . or in some way to deform"[1] the family, these forces were not delineated. In the first part, the Holy Father analyzes some of these forces.

The Holy Father begins Part One with a reminder that God's plan for marriage applies to husbands and wives in their particular situation, including their particular culture and environment. God's plan is not an abstract theoretical construct to be discussed among theologians. The gospel must meet the needs of contemporary families in their concrete existence.

John Paul notes that the unchangeable gospel of Christ must be ever new in its application to new historical situations. In other words, the mission of Christ is the same: to reveal human dignity (which does not change) and the activity proper to human persons (which does not change). However, the constant message of the gospel must be proclaimed in a matter suitable to each age. By studying the human situation in every age and, above all, by listening to the people of each age, the Church discovers how the gospel might be preached in that era. This process leads to a new presentation of the gospel. In formulating a new presentation of the Faith, the Church understands the gospel better and better. "The call and demands

[1] See FC, no. 3.

of the Spirit resound in the very events of history, and so the Church can also be guided to a more profound understanding of the inexhaustible mystery of marriage and the family by the circumstances, the questions, and the anxieties, and hopes of the young people, married couples, and parents of today." The Holy Spirit leads the Church to a more profound comprehension of the gospel every time the Church proclaims the gospel to a new age.

Of course, as we have seen, John Paul is one of the leading figures in the development of the new synthesis of faith and reason proclaimed in the documents of the Second Vatican Council. This new synthesis makes the gospel understandable for people of our own age. The Holy Father knows from personal experience that the Church understands the gospel more profoundly when, from the gospel, it formulates answers to the essential questions asked in different ways in every age.

Having assured his readers that through the gospel and its modern presentation the Church does have the answers to modern questions, the Pope notes that some very appealing (false) ideas and solutions are offered through "the powerful and pervasive organization of the means of social communication". However, these ideas and solutions are contrary to the gospel and "obscure in varying degrees the truth and the dignity of the human person".

The Church wishes to offer the entire truth of the dignity of marriage and family life to all people of the present age. In noting that this is an obligation of the Church, the Holy Father quickly adds that it is not merely the task of the pastors and bishops, or even of the pope. It is an obligation of the entire Church, laity together with pastors. The Holy Spirit has made all the baptized prophets and therefore all have a responsibility to the truth and a responsibility to proclaim it. The laity proclaim the gospel by example in their daily lives. They have the obligation of applying the gospel in the historical situation in which they are living.

With the responsibility of the baptized acknowledged, the

Pontiff reminds us that the "supernatural sense of faith" of the baptized "does not consist solely or necessarily in the consensus of the faithful". The truth is not to be equated with "majority opinion". In other words, the prophetic role of the baptized must be activated through the teaching office of the hierarchy, i.e., the bishops in union with the Holy Father. The Magisterium develops the sense of responsibility to the Faith which the baptized have and it judges the "genuineness of its expressions". Of course, the bishops and the Holy Father have the obligation of employing whatever information is available from the human sciences, e.g., sociology, so that the gospel might be proclaimed effectively to people of our age.

In the last paragraph of this fifth article, the Pope reminds married couples that they have a very special gift from God for the discernment of family values. He asks them, by virtue of their own special sacrament, matrimony, to give testimony to the precious value of family life found in the creation and in the redemption.

The Pope has clearly indicated that the Church must fulfill its mission to preach the gospel. He has also indicated that this responsibility lies with all baptized Christians, who, nevertheless, must be activated through the Magisterium of the Church. Finally, he has explained that it is impossible to preach the gospel to men and women of our age unless the present situation is understood. The next section of Part One describes the papal view (and the view of the synodal fathers) of the family's position in our modern world.

John Paul II sees in family life today "a sign of the salvation of Christ operating in the world". He commends the "lively awareness of personal freedom and greater attention to the quality of interpersonal relationships in marriage". He points to the promotion of the "dignity of women, to responsible procreation, to the education of children" as very positive signs. The Pope also notes favorably the consciousness of the need for "interfamily relationships, for reciprocal spiritual and material assistance" and he cites approvingly a "rediscovery of the ecclesial mission proper to the family and its responsibility for the building of a more just society".

However, there are also certain modern negative phenomena which threaten the very existence of the family in modern society. Among these are: a mistaken concept of the independence of spouses from each other, a breakdown of the proper relationship between parents and children, the difficulties encountered by families in the transmission of values, the growing number of divorces, the scourge of abortion, the increased frequency of sterilization, the the growing "contraceptive mentality."

Many of these negative forces can be traced to a fundamental corruption of the idea of freedom. For many, freedom exists "for one's own selfish well-being". However, this view of freedom destroys it because only in an unselfish gift of love is our freedom realized. God made us to love, to give ourselves unselfishly to him and to others, and he also made us free. Unselfish love and freedom cannot be in conflict because they both rest on the God-given dignity of the human person. We are made in the image of God to be like God and to do what he does. He is free and he does love. When he loves, he does not surrender his freedom. Similarly, when we, as his images, love, we do not give up our freedom. In fact, it is only in doing what he does, i.e., love, that we become more like him. In other words, it is only in and through love that we realize the Godlike freedom that we should have as beings made in his image. Selfishness, contrary to the popular notion, does not enhance freedom, but destroys it. It makes us less Godlike and therefore less free. What is needed to restore family life and reduce the "negative phenomena" attacking family life is a conversion from a selfish notion of freedom to the freedom proclaimed in the gospel. This, in turn, presumes an educational process. John Paul has begun that education in this apostolic exhortation.

The false and selfish notion of freedom is fueled in the poorer countries by the lack of the means of survival: food, housing, work, and medicine. The need for these basic necessities leads to a certain selfishness. Those who have a little will hoard what they have for fear of losing what they do have. In the richer countries, selfishness is encouraged by prosperity and the consumer mentality. The more consumers have, the more they want, if only to be like everyone else. In both instances, new life becomes a threat: a threat to the few necessities which families in the poor countries might have; a threat to the families of rich countries because a child demands resources which must be diverted from material things.

The current situation of the family then shows a "conflict between two loves: the love of God to the point of disregarding self, and the love of self to the point of disregarding God". It is the latter which is causing the negative phenomena. It can be eliminated only through education in true love founded in faith. This is the task of the Church, which it accomplishes through the exercise of the triple offices of Christ. The Church educates people (prophetic office) and enables them to govern themselves (kingly office) for love (priestly office).

Having explained the current circumstances, John Paul II notes that the faithful are not immune to the situation in which they live. More and more of the faithful divorce and remarry. More and more accept a mere civil ceremony as sufficient for marriage. More and more marry without a living faith. Finally, many marry and reject the moral norms necessary to family life. The Holy Father suggests that these practices show the influence of the "negative phenomena" on the faithful.

In the eighth article, the Pope observes that science and technology can be the cause of these negative phenomena. In the context of a newly emerging technological culture, the Church is especially obliged to fulfill the mission of Christ: to preach the gospel and to reveal men and women to themselves. If the gospel is preached and each individual person realizes his incomparable dignity and proper activity, the new developments will be christianized.

The Pope is at pains to assure his readers that scientific advances are good. They arise from the application of human reason to the created world. They are the fruit of human labor, the results of humanity's participation in the creative work of God. As the fruit of work, these advances are for humanity. However, through political decisions, these scientific and technological breakthroughs are sometimes turned against the human person who is the very reason for their existence. "It becomes necessary, therefore, on the part of all, to recover an awareness of the primacy of moral values, which are the values of the human person as such." If these values are lost, then the human person would become subject to the things of this world. Such a culture would not facilitate the development of its members, but would stifle and even (ultimately) destroy them.

In this section, the Holy Father is outlining the Church's exercise of Christ's kingly office in today's world. The goods of creation and the fruits of human labor must be integrated into a proper order, the order intended by God in his creative act. That order is threatened by certain views which use modern scientific developments. It is only, as the Pope has said already, through an education (prophetic office) in love (priestly office) that human beings can realize themselves. It is Christ's kingly office in its second aspect, i.e., dominion over creation, which enables all people to find the strength and courage to restructure society and culture according to those transcendental human values known and experienced in the prophetic and priestly offices of Christ. This task in our own day is more difficult than in past ages because of the scope and rapidity of change.

In the ninth article, the Pope reminds us that a permanent conversion to Christ is needed. Sin makes it difficult for men and women to maintain the truth, to love in an unselfish donation, and to restore order within themselves and in the exterior world. It is only in the crucified Christ that all can find themselves and the strength necessary to live as they should, as beings made in God's own image.

Finally, in the tenth and last paragraph of Part One, John Paul returns to the theme of the beginning of this section: the

Church learns from all cultures. It is in answering the questions posed in their various forms by the different civilizations that the Church deepens the understanding of the gospel. The Holy Spirit works in the hearts of men and women and guides the Church. One must also add, as the Pope immediately does, that in this process of proclaiming the gospel in various ways to different people, the bishops must remain in communion with the successor of Peter and with each other. As the Holy Father wrote earlier in Part One, the gospel is not subject to "majority opinion".[2] The Holy Father also notes that the Church is enriched by all cultures, not only by the technically advanced ones.

In this first part of the document, John Paul has outlined the need of the Church to know the current situation in order to proclaim the gospel to the men and women living today. He has clearly indicated that the mission of making Christ known is the task of the whole Church. In today's world, family life shows positive and negative phenomena. At the basis of the negative phenomena is a false notion of freedom, which permits and even encourages selfishness. This (false) understanding of freedom has in some cases led to the loss of the most fundamental values of family life. In other cases, it has led to the nonobservance of these values, even though they might still be theoretically acknowledged. The task of the Church is to educate (prophetic office) men and women of our day in self-dominion (kingly office) so that they might love (priestly office). The people of our era will then reform themselves and their culture. However, this is only possible in and through Christ and especially through his Cross.

[2] Ibid., no. 5.

II. The Plan of God for Marriage and the Family

In many ways, this second part of the apostolic exhortation on the family is the heart of the entire work. It is in this section that John Paul outlines the fundamental values of family life, which, at least in some quarters, are under attack today. Even the title of this part betrays its content: "The Plan of God for Marriage and the Family". The first article in this section is perhaps John Paul's most brilliant and most concise summary of his entire theology of the body and of the family. It deserves to be quoted in full.

God created man in his own image and likeness: calling him to existence *through love*, he called him at the same time *for love*.

God is love and in himself he lives a mystery of personal loving communion. Creating the human race in his own image and continually keeping it in being, God inscribed in the humanity of man and woman the vocation, and thus the capacity and responsibility, of love and communion. Love is therefore the fundamental and innate vocation of every human being.

As an incarnate spirit, that is a soul which expresses itself in a body and a body informed by an immortal spirit, man is called to love in his unified totality. Love includes the human body, and the body is made a sharer in spiritual love.

Christian revelation recognizes two specific ways of realizing the vocation of the human person, in its entirety, to love: marriage and virginity or celibacy. Either one is, in its own proper form, an actuation of the most profound truth of man, of his being "created in the image of God."

Consequently, sexuality, by means of which man and woman

give themselves to one another through the acts which are proper and exclusive to spouses, is by no means something purely biological, but concerns the innermost being of the human person as such. It is realized in a truly human way only if it is an integral part of the love by which a man and a woman commit themselves totally to one another until death. The total physical self-giving would be a lie if it were not the sign and fruit of a total personal self-giving, in which the whole person, including the temporal dimension, is present: if the person were to withhold something or reserve the possibility of deciding otherwise in the future, by this very fact, he or she would not be giving totally.

This totality which is required by conjugal love also corresponds to the demands of responsible fertility. This fertility is directed to the generation of a human being, and so by its nature it surpasses the purely biological order and involves a whole series of personal values. For the harmonious growth of these values a persevering and unified contribution by both parents is necessary.

The only "place" in which this self-giving in its whole truth is made possible is marriage, the covenant of conjugal love freely and consciously chosen, whereby man and woman accept the intimate community of life and love willed by God himself, which only in this light manifests its true meaning. The institution of marriage is not an undue interference by society or authority, nor the extrinsic imposition of a form. Rather it is an interior requirement of the covenant of conjugal love which is publicly affirmed as unique and exclusive, in order to live in complete fidelity to the plan of God, the Creator. A person's freedom, far from being restricted by this fidelity, is secured against every form of subjectivism or relativism and is made a sharer in creative Wisdom.

The very first sentence of this article establishes the key point of the new synthesis of faith and reason developed by John Paul and the Lublin/Cracow school: man is made in the image of God. This scriptural truth is the glue which binds the personal and individual insights of phenomenology to the objective truth of the gospel. The emphasis on our creation in God's image gives John Paul's new synthesis its subjective turn, i.e., its emphasis on the individual while maintaining the reality of the order established by God.

Completing the opening sentence of this article, John Paul writes that God created man *through love* and *for love*. Love is the self-surrender of one person to another. When God created man and woman, he gave them being. However, since God is Being, in giving man and woman existence, God shared himself (Being) with them. Therefore, when God created man and woman, God loved them, i.e., he gave himself (Being) to them. We are created *through love*. But we are also created *for love*. As an image of God, a human person is called to do what God does, to mirror and reflect God's acts. God loves, as he did in the creation and even more wondrously in the redemption. We, as his images, can do nothing less. If we fail to love in the way God loves, we fail to be true to our very selves, to our very nature given to us by God in his creative act.

Having reminded his readers of the basic principle of his new synthesis, the Holy Father, in the second paragraph of this article, explains more fully what the love of God is. Without specifically citing the Trinity, John Paul teaches that God lives a "mystery of personal loving communion". A communion can exist only if there are at least two persons who have entered into a union. In God, there is a communion because there are three Divine Persons. Arguing from God to us, the Holy Father remarks that because we are made in God's image, the love of human persons should form a communion in imitation of the Trinity. The Pope could have also approached the subject from our point of view. There is both a downward movement (from God to the human person) and an upward movement (from the human person to God) possible in the new synthesis. The study of God, in whose image we are made, will teach us about ourselves (downward movement). Similarly, the study of man and woman made in the image of God will teach us about God (upward movement). In this article, the Holy Father has chosen to derive the truths about man and woman from a study of God (downward movement).

Anticipating his next point, as he often does, John Paul included in the second paragraph a reference to both men and women. Since the differences between male and female lie in the bodily differences between masculinity and femininity, the Pope, in referring to men and women, very carefully (and slyly) introduced the human body into the discussion. In the third paragraph, he outlines the relationship between the soul and the body. We find here the very familiar and fundamental idea that the body expresses the person. Underlying this concept is the entire *Theology of the Body* series given at the Wednesday papal audiences from September 1979 to May 1981.

In that series the Pope taught that we are persons made in the image of God. Although we reflect God primarily in our interior structure of mind and will, the body also becomes a physical image, a sign or sacrament of God when it expresses the proper activity of a human person, i.e., love. Of all the persons in the universe, only we have bodies. Of all the bodies in the universe, only our bodies are informed by an immortal, rational soul. Therefore, only we can manifest in the physical world how a person acts. Only we can be a physical image or sign of how God acts, i.e., how God loves. We are called, by our creation, to be images of God in our interior and exterior structures.

In the same series, the Pope repeatedly emphasized that our bodies are part of the gift of life. He gave them to us just as they are so that they might express our persons *as they are*. To alter our bodies (unless some medical procedure is indicated by disease) is to claim the rights of the Creator. In effect, when we presume to alter our bodies (except for the medical reasons indicated) we presume to make ourselves better than God made us. This is pride *par excellence*. Further, when we alter our bodies, we treat them as though we owned them. But, our bodies are us and, as our life, they are not things which we own or, even worse, inhabit. We do not own our bodies any more than we own our lives. Our bodies are given to us to express our persons. When we alter our bodies, we attack our lives. Therefore, an unnecessary alteration of a major, healthy, functioning part of the body is an insult to God and a self-destructive act.

The innate vocation of every human being is to love, to surrender oneself to another person. But since a human person is an incarnate spirit whose body expresses his person, he is called to love in and through his body. "Love includes the human body, and the body is made a sharer in spiritual love." In this passage, the Holy Father begins to lay the groundwork for his theology of marriage and the family. In his view, marriage is the expression of a mutual self-donation of a man and a woman to each other in and through their bodies. If his principle that the body expresses the loving self-donation of one to another is denied, there will be a totally different view of marriage. Of course, as he demonstrated in the *Theology of the Body* series, to deny that the body expresses the person leads to absurdities that no one could accept.

The fourth paragraph of this eleventh article is perhaps somewhat perplexing. The very first words, "Christian revelation", denote the change. Up to this point, the Holy Father had not specifically referred to Christian revelation. He had been arguing from the reference in Genesis to our creation in the image of God. Since all men and women are created in God's image, the papal arguments based on this premise apply to the entire human race. Further, it is possible for everyone, even those who are unaware of Genesis, to realize that they are different from the animals and have a different task (vocation) from the other beings on this earth. However, in this fourth paragraph, by beginning with Christian revelation, the Holy Father indicates that the thought he is about to express can be seen only through the eyes of faith.

Of course, this move is completely justified within the context of the new synthesis. We are images of God, but we do not know who we are unless we know Christ. Christ, the God-man, reveals the Father to us and in so doing, he reveals who we are as made in the image of the Father. It is impossible for us to know who we are unless we know Christ and what he came to reveal. Therefore, unless we have faith, we cannot accept those things which are absolutely necessary if we are to know who we are and how to act. Christian revelation is absolutely necessary if our transcendental value and dignity are to be understood. Since the Holy Father is attempting in this article to discuss the values of family life, he not only has the option of introducing Christian revelation, he must, if these values are to be understood.

The Pope notes that Christian revelation teaches that there are two ways everyone can realize his vocation to love: marriage, established by God in his creative act and restored by Christ, and celibacy or virginity. It is quite clear that marriage pertains to human nature, to the way God made us. However, celibacy and virginity seem contrary to human nature and to its basic needs of companionship and continuance. As Christ taught, nonmarriage for the sake of the Kingdom is a fulfillment of the call to love. Both marriage and celibacy or virginity fulfill "the most profound truth of man, of his being 'created in the image of God'". Of course, only faith allows us to see that celibacy or virginity fulfills our vocation to love. John Paul includes a reference to virginity or celibacy in this fourth paragraph as a foundation for the later discussion of those who make themselves eunuchs for the sake of God's Kingdom.

In the fifth and remaining paragraphs of article eleven, John Paul discusses the fulfillment of our vocation to love in the married state. The first sentence of the fifth paragraph is absolutely crucial in John Paul's entire theology of the body and the family. He writes that "sexuality . . . is by no means something purely biological, but concerns the innermost being of the human person as such." Although this point is made here somewhat cryptically, it is an absolutely compelling conclusion from the previous principles. John Paul has established that our vocation is to love. He has also established that the body is called to express that love. Now, the Holy Father logically concludes that the bodily differences between a man and a woman, i.e., sexuality, are the bodily means by which the personal selfless donation of a man and a woman to one another is accomplished. We are enfleshed persons called to love, called to give ourselves in and through our bodies to one another. When a husband and wife give themselves to one another in and through their sexual powers, they give their very persons, not merely their biological powers.

If God had not made us male and female, we would be in an impossible situation. We would still be enfleshed spirits, persons called to love in and through our bodies, but we would be without the bodily means of expressing that love. Of course, this was precisely Adam's situation before the creation of Eve as recorded in the second account of creation in Genesis. Adam was alone. There was no other human person with whom he could establish a mutual selfless communion of persons. His loneliness was the most profound possible for a human being. Called to love in his totality, i.e., in and through his body, he could not because there were no other incarnate spirits present. There was no woman. Finally, when God created Eve, Genesis records Adam's cry of joy, "This at last is bone of my bones and flesh of my flesh."[1] With the creation of Eve, Adam's loneliness ended. Finally, he had someone he could love in and through his body.

Sexuality is, in a sense, the window to the soul. Every act of the human person is contained in his consciousness. We, in a sense, create ourselves through our acts. When we love in and through our sexual powers we truly become what we are: images of God, because we do what God does. By the same token, when we employ our sexual powers in acts which are not selfless donations, these acts are also contained in our consciousness. Through these acts we shape ourselves into something opposed to God. Thus, we no longer reflect God as we should. Although there are many acts which tarnish our reflection of God, sexual acts which do not express love affect us, i.e., tarnish us, more

---

[1] See Gen 2:23.

profoundly because they employ our sexual powers given to us for love in acts opposed to love. They are absolutely contrary to our most fundamental and innate vocation: love. Sexuality is indeed the window to each person's very heart, i.e., his likeness to God.

As we have noted, the papal view of human sexuality depends on the principle that the body expresses the person. In other words, when a man and a woman unite in the sexual embrace, they, as persons, give themselves to one another. Their bodily union is the sign and fruit of a personal self-donation each has made to the other. As the Pope remarks, their sexual union is not merely something biological.

Biology studies the workings of living bodies. When biology applies itself to the human person, it studies the human body. The biologist abstracts from the mystery of the human person, as such, and examines only a small aspect of our totality. Of course, this abstraction is legitimate. Biology and many other sciences would cease to benefit us if this were not a legitimate method of inquiry. No human science can examine man in his totality. Such a task must be divided among many different branches of human knowledge.

However, it must always be remembered that the study of a human being's biology is an abstraction from his total being as it exists in the concrete reality of individuals. The conclusions of the biologist are valid in his own abstracted realm. However, when this knowledge is applied to reality, to the individual human person, biology must not only take account of its own rules and discipline, but also of man and woman in their total reality as God made them. When the conclusions of biology are applied in reality, these results become subject to the order of existence, to the created order as God made it. It is clear then that in the created order, the order of being, God gave man and woman their sexual faculties so that love might be expressed. It is also true that our sexual faculties have interest to the biologist. But, we cannot explain our sexual powers solely from the conclusions of the biologist. There is the order of existence established by God to consider. Therefore, in examining the mystery of sexuality and the sexual embrace, we must realize that the biologist understands the mystery of human love only from one, narrow, point of view. To reduce sexuality to a mere biological act is a terrible impoverishment and trivialization of the act of love and it is a misuse of biology. The sexual embrace is not merely two biological beings coming together (as it is in the animal kingdom). Rather, it is an expression of a personal, mutual self-donation of a man and a woman to one another.

In the next sentence the Pope teaches that sexuality (and here he obviously means the sexual act) "is realized in a truly human way" only if it is the expression of love. He then defines marital love as a total and complete self-donation of a man and a woman to one another. This self-donation is not total and complete if it is bounded in time or extent. In very strong terms the Pope calls the sexual act a lie when it is not the "sign and fruit of a total personal self-giving".

Here, again rather cryptically, the Holy Father is citing what he called the personalistic norm in his book *Love and Responsibility*.[2] This principle holds that persons cannot be the objects of use. They transcend the order of material creation, of things, and are of such infinite and incomparable dignity that they can only be the recipients of love. Love is a self-gift for the sake of the other. The lover wishes the best possible good for his beloved.

There are two possible ways for people to relate to one another: love and use. Love is a complete and total self-gift. If supposed lovers refuse to give themselves in all their potentialities, they are seeking something from the other, e.g., pleasure. The relationship is no longer one of love, but of use. It no longer fits the definition of love. It is also possible for supposed lovers to give themselves only for a limited period of time. Quite clearly such a relationship is one of use. We throw things

[2] See LR, p. 41.

out when they cease to please. We dare not throw people out for any reason! Of course, a relationship of use is contrary to the dignity of the one using and the one used. It is a terrible violation of human dignity.

The sixth paragraph of this article expands somewhat on the concept of love as a total self-gift of one person to another. The Holy Father teaches in this passage that conjugal love requires "responsible fertility". As we have seen, for John Paul, responsibility means the ability to respond to the order established by God. Thus, if a couple is to be responsible, they need to have an awareness of their own fertility. Natural family planning gives men and women the knowledge necessary for "responsible fertility". Any attempt to suppress fertility with contraceptive devices is to reject God's established order and is, for that reason, highly irresponsible. In addition to knowledge, couples exercising "responsible fertility" do not employ their fertility awareness selfishly, but have sufficient reasons for conceiving or not conceiving a child. Of course, the awareness of one's fertility leads one to an understanding of the human person. In turn, this knowledge encourages virtue, i.e., responsibility.

In this sixth paragraph, the Holy Father also emphasizes that procreation is not merely something biological. Just as the sexual act itself is not purely biological, so procreation is also much more than a biological result of the sexual act. This thought echoes what he wrote many years previously: "A relationship between spirits which begets a new embodied spirit is something unknown to the natural order."[3] When a new human being is conceived, a new person is created. The relationship between the child and the parents is a relationship of persons. As such, this relationship involves "personal values". First and foremost, the parents must love the child for his own sake. The new human person must be educated in the Faith and the knowledge necessary for life. Neither these tasks nor the many other ones necessary for the child's proper development can be accom-

[3] Ibid., p. 55.

plished without the "persevering and unified contribution" of both parents. (Of course, the death of a parent creates a special situation. In this case, another adult often acts as a father or a mother figure in place of the deceased parent. Certainly, the Holy Father does not intend to suggest that a child who loses a parent is, for that very reason, deprived of the proper nurturing. He himself lost his own mother at a very young age.)

In the final paragraph of the article, Pope John Paul II teaches that the only "place" where the personal values of conjugal love, fertility, and procreation can be preserved is marriage. Marriage is a freely chosen lifelong commitment of two spouses to one another and to any children God would give them. Marriage thus satisfies the temporal requirement of love, i.e., the gift of love cannot be bounded by time. Further, the lifelong commitment of the two spouses satisfies the need for preserving the necessary personal values inherent in procreation. Children require the constant love and care of both parents. This can only be assured within the marital bond.

There are those who would claim that marriage is an unjust interference with their freedom. Having already noted some of the false ideas surrounding the concept of human freedom, the Pope explicitly addresses this objection to marriage. Unequivocally, he teaches that marriage is not an imposition of a form by some outside authority. "Rather it is an interior requirement of the covenant of conjugal love which is publicly affirmed as unique and exclusive, in order to live in complete fidelity to the plan of God, the Creator." It is important to notice that the Pope argues that it is an interior requirement, i.e., it flows from the kind of being a human person is. No human person may ever be treated as a thing, as something to be used. However, in failing to love, people use other people. Conjugal love requires a total self-surrender of the two spouses. Anything less than this total self-donation is not love. When love is not the basis for a mutual relationship between two people, then selfishness (use) is. But use, of course, is opposed to human dignity. Conjugal love does not exist if the gift of the man and the woman is not until death do them part. Without this timeless mutual gift, their love is not love, but a mutual using. Marriage ensures that their gift is timeless. Therefore, marriage is an institution which flows from the very dignity of the human person. It is the "place" where the total self-giving of love occurs.

There is a further objection. Some would argue that a timeless gift could be made without a public act. In the not so distant past, many couples scorned the public rituals both of the Church and civil society. These couples claimed to be married, to have vowed their love in an irrevocable private act. But marriage is a public act. They were not married, but they claimed there was little or no difference. In fact, there is a difference.

Marriage requires two decisions. The first decision each spouse must make concerns himself or herself. Each must search his or her heart to determine if he or she really does love the other. This decision has two aspects: present and future. Each must ascertain whether he or she loves the other not only at the present time but also whether he or she will love the other during the whole course of married life. Secondly, each must be morally certain that the other has made the same decision about him or her. Love is a mutual self-donation. No one may risk his or her God-given incomparable dignity in a total self-surrender unless he or she is morally certain that the other intends to make the same self-donation.

Only a public act can assure both spouses that each is sincere in his or her self-gift. First, it is often only when faced with a public act, with a commitment witnessed by family members, the Church, and civil authority that each spouse searches his or her heart sufficiently. In other words, the public ritual assists each spouse in making the personal decision about his or her own state of mind regarding the other. However, even more importantly, it is only in and through the public commitment that each spouse can be morally certain of the intentions of the other. Private promises are easily broken. In such acts, neither spouse can even be reasonably certain of the other. However, with the civil and church authorities, and the family as witnesses, each spouse can be morally certain that the other would not enter such a union unless he or she intended to abide by his or her promises to the best of his or her ability. Of course, the practice of civil divorce has weakened the force of the public promises. Perhaps this is the reason for some rejecting the public rituals. If the marriage ceremony does not represent anything more than the private promises, then it is not fulfilling its purpose. (Of course, this argument for marriage abstracts completely from the marriage of Christians. In and through the public ritual of Christian marriage, the sacrament of matrimony is celebrated. The sacrament of matrimony is such an incredible blessing from God that it is difficult to understand why anyone would reject it.)

The final sentence of this key article restates one of the major themes of the document. It is only in living and acting in accordance with our very nature, in accordance with our dignity as created in the image of God, that we are truly free. To act against our own dignity does not enhance freedom but destroys it. As images of God, we are like God in our dignity and freedom. But if one is tarnished, so is the other. Fidelity to the plan of the Creator thus results in true freedom.

With this conclusion, the Pope has explained the covenant of marriage as established by God in his creative act. The next article discusses the marital union as a sign of God's love for his people. Since we are images of God, we are called to do what he does. When a man and a woman enter into a lifelong union of love, they are acting as God acts. They have promised to surrender themselves to one another as God gives himself to his people. Since their love is a physical manifestation of the divine love, they together are a physical sign of God's communion with his people.

Offenses against the marital covenant of love are signs and symbols of the offenses of God's people against him. Prostitution is a symbol of the idolatry of the Israelites. Adultery is a symbol of the people's infidelity to their God. However, just as the people's sins against the covenant God has made with them do not destroy that covenant, so the sins of one spouse against the marital covenant of love should not destroy it. God's love is a forgiving and merciful love. Spousal love must also be forgiving and merciful. "The ever faithful love of God is put forward as the model of the relations of faithful love which should exist between spouses."

In the thirteenth article, the Holy Father summarizes the fulfillment of the Old Covenant in and through Christ. Just as spousal love was the symbol and sign of the Old Covenant, so it is now a symbol and sign of the New Covenant in and through the sacrament of matrimony.

One of the most important points made in this article is found in the second paragraph. Christ "reveals the original truth of marriage, the truth of the 'beginning,' and, freeing man from his hardness of heart, he makes man capable of realizing this truth in its entirety". Since marriage is to be founded on an act of love similar to God's act of love, it is in knowing God and how he loves that we know what marriage is. Christ revealed God and his love, and thus, he revealed the truth about marriage. This truth of marriage corresponds to what God established in his creative act when he commanded Adam and Eve to "be fruitful and multiply".[4] Christ comes and reveals God's will expressed in his creative act.

The Holy Father also teaches in the above quote that Christ frees man "from his hardness of heart". As John Paul wrote in preparation for the synod on the family, after original sin there was a "constitutive break within the human person".[5] Before original sin, the highest faculties of man and woman, their minds and wills, governed them. In other words, Adam and Eve, before the fall, were integrated. However, after original sin, the bodies of our first parents were no longer subject to their minds and

[4] See Gen 1:28.
[5] See TB, no. 28. The *Theology of the Body* series was given as a preparation for the synod on the family. See no. 1.

wills. Their minds no longer grasped the truth as easily and their wills were no longer always able to subdue and govern their bodily passions.

By God's creative act, each human person is made to love, i.e., to give himself to another through a free will choice based on a knowledge of the truth. The loss of clarity of mind and strength of will meant that it was no longer possible for those suffering from the effects of original sin to give themselves in love. After original sin, our minds and wills no longer govern our bodies. In the person tainted with original sin, the free gift of love chosen in the will and known in the mind is contradicted by the bodily passions, which desire satisfaction. The bodily demands are opposed to love because they seek something, whereas love is a gift. Thus, after sin, it was virtually impossible for a man and a woman to give themselves to each other in love.

In this state, we were in an impossible situation. We were called to love as God loves and we could not do it. We could not even function as human beings. In his mercy, God took pity on us and redeemed us from our self-inflicted situation. Christ died on the Cross to open the gates of heaven, but also to make it possible again for us to do what we were made to do, i.e., love. Even the person tainted with original sin and its effects can give himself to another in a total self-surrender if he is blessed with God's life won for him by Christ on the Cross. Grace makes it possible for us to live as Adam and Eve in the Garden of Eden. Grace does not restore the dominance of the mind and will, but grace does give each human person the potential to know the truth and through his will to govern his bodily passions. Even with grace, it is not easy, as it would have been for Adam and Eve. We are not restored in Christ to the *state* of original innocence, but only to the possibility of living as God made us to live.

The next paragraph has two points. The first is that Christ in becoming man and dying on the Cross revealed to each and every one of us how God loves. Saint Paul writes that God took "the form of a servant".[6] God emptied himself for us. He had nothing to gain because he was (and is) God, and yet he became man, a creature. The Incarnation is a stupendous act of love. And still, there was more. He embraced one of the most terrible deaths imaginable. On the Cross, God suffered horribly and died. There was absolutely no selfishness in his death. There can be no greater act of love. As John Paul wrote in the retreat he preached to Pope Paul VI in 1976, "Pilate says '*Ecce homo*': 'Look what you have done to this man!' But there seems to be another voice speaking as well, a voice that seems to be saying: 'Look what you have done, in this man, to your God.'"[7] The one perfectly just, sinless man, God himself, accepted his Passion and death for us. Thus, he showed us what love is.

The second point of the third paragraph is that married couples are called to love as Christ loved us on the Cross. As images of God, we should love as God loves. Christ showed us what love is. Couples should totally surrender themselves to one another and to their children as Christ gave himself for us. This gift of love, corresponding to the intent of God in his creative act when he created us in his image, is made possible through the gift of the Holy Spirit poured forth into the souls of Christians through baptism and the other sacraments, including matrimony. With this divine life, a man and a woman are "capable of loving one another as Christ has loved us. Conjugal love reaches that fullness to which it is interiorly ordained, conjugal charity, which is the proper and specific way in which the spouses participate in and are called to live the very charity of Christ who gave himself on the Cross."

After a quotation from Tertullian, which expresses the beauty and joy found in Christian marriage, the Holy Father turns to the mystery of the sacrament of matrimony. First, he repeats the teaching of the Church that marriage of the baptized is one

[6] See Phil 2:7.
[7] See SC, p. 186.

of the seven sacraments of the New Covenant established by Christ. Second, he remarks that by baptism we are inserted into the "spousal charity of Christ" toward his people, i.e., the human race. As other Christs, those who have received baptism love God and they express their love for God by loving all their neighbors. Matrimony does not destroy baptism, but rather specifies it. Matrimony makes the relationship with the spouse the most important human relationship. In Christian marriage, the love of God is expressed primarily by loving the spouse. Married couples freely bind themselves to one another as Christ freely bound himself to the Church. In their union, Christian couples are "a real representation . . . of the very relationship of Christ with the Church". The spouses are called to give themselves to each other and to the children as Christ gave himself to us on the Cross. Christian married couples are then a "permanent reminder to the Church of what happened on the Cross".

John Paul explains that matrimony, as all the other sacraments, is a memorial, an actuation, and a prophecy. Since spouses are a "permanent reminder to the Church of what happened on the Cross", the sacrament is a memorial of Christ's love expressed in his sacrifice. It is an actuation of that self-gift of Christ in the very lives of the couple and their children. As a prophecy, the sacrament holds the promise and hope of sharing eternal life with Christ in heaven.

In the final paragraph of this thirteenth article, the Holy Father teaches that "the first and immediate effect of marriage (*res et sacramentum*) is not supernatural grace itself, but the Christian conjugal bond, a typically Christian communion of two persons." In other words, the sacrament creates a union of a man and a woman with each other which reflects the union in the three Persons of the Trinity and the union of Christ and the Church. In the third part of this document, the Pope describes the family as the "domestic church".[8] As a domestic church,

[8] See FC, no. 49.

the union of the spouses is as close as the union of the Church and Christ. But the Church is the mystical person of Christ. The family, as a domestic church, is a miniature mystical person of Christ. The couple is joined in Christ to one another and they become one flesh, indeed one mystical person, just as the Church is one (mystical person) in Christ.

Marriage involves a total self-gift of one person to another. This gift includes the "appeal of the body and instinct, power of feeling and affectivity, aspiration of the spirit and of will". This passage seems to echo the discussion of sensuality and sentiment found in *Love and Responsibility*, written many years before John Paul was elevated to the chair of Peter.[9] The union of a married couple is personal and total. It is "beyond union in one flesh" and "leads to forming one heart and soul". As the Pope concludes, "In a word, it [Christian marriage] is a question of the normal characteristics of all natural conjugal love, but with a new significance which not only purifies and strengthens them, but raises them to the extent of making them the expression of specifically Christian values."

In the next article, number fourteen, the Holy Father briefly reminds his readers that the self-surrender of a spouse is not only directed to the partner, but also to new human persons, i.e., to children."The couple, while giving themselves to one another, give not just themselves but also the reality of children".

John Paul expanded on this point many years ago. Our sexual powers are personal faculties, but they also belong to the order of existence, to the created order. They are not merely for us, but are a gift from God that we might share in his creative act.

> In the sexual relationship between man and woman, *two orders meet: the order of nature*, which has as its object reproduction, and *the personal order*, which finds its expression in the love of persons and aims at the fullest realization of that love. . . . When a man and a woman consciously and of their own free will choose to

[9] See LR, pp. 101–18.

marry and have sexual relations they choose at the same time the possibility of procreation, *choose to participate in creation* (for that is the proper meaning of the word procreation) . . . Sexual relations between a man and a woman in marriage have their full value as a union of persons only when they go with a conscious acceptance of the possibility of parenthood. This is a direct result of the synthesis of the natural and personal order.[10]

In the second paragraph of article fourteen, John Paul refers to the "reciprocal 'knowledge'" which the spouses learn through their mutual self-gift. This biblical term for sexual intercourse was discussed at some length in John Paul's *Theology of the Body* series. In one of the addresses of that series the Pope outlined three levels of knowledge gleaned from the conjugal relationship. In the sexual embrace the spouses experience one another. In that total gift of each to the other, both spouses know the other. Further, through the gift of the spouse, each partner in marriage knows humanity in a much fuller way. Secondly, the hidden treasures of humanity are revealed in motherhood and fatherhood. The woman, whose femininity is hidden by her body, is revealed in motherhood. Similarly, the new relationship of the male to the child, fatherhood, reveals an aspect of humanity previously not experienced. Thirdly, in the new life, the child, both the husband and the wife see themselves. They know themselves in the child. Clearly, the reference to knowledge includes the reality of children because the mutual knowledge of husband and wife is not complete without children. Thus, in cooperating with God in the order of existence, spouses not only receive the infinitely precious gift of new life, but also learn about themselves and about humanity.

The third paragraph of this article notes that parents have a grave obligation to teach their children about God's love. Since spousal love is a visible sign of the love of God, the children learn about God's love through the loving relationship they see

[10] Ibid., pp. 226–27.

in their parents. Children learn more by what parents do than by what they say. It is crucial that children see God's love in and through their parents' Christ-like self-gift.

The concluding paragraph of this section reminds everyone that while children are a precious gift and a natural result of the conjugal bond, marriage does not lose its value if procreation is impossible. Infertility can be a stimulus to many forms of community service, especially adoption. Love reaches out to others. When procreation is possible, the love of the spouses is directed outward to the children and to others. When infertility is present, there is still a need for the spousal love to be directed outward, and this need can be the motive for a very valuable service to society.

In article fifteen, John Paul teaches that it is through the family that each individual person is introduced to the larger family of humanity and to the family of Christ, the Church. The Christian family, as all human families, builds up society because through it new members are born. These are then educated in the family so that they might take their rightful place in the larger society at the appropriate time. But beyond this noble undertaking, the Christian family "builds up the Church" because through it, the children are incorporated, by means of baptism, into the mystical person of Christ, the Church, and into the miniature mystical person of Christ, the family. (It is only in baptism that a child can be joined to Christ either in the universal Church or in the domestic church.) Once joined to Christ, it is the Christian family which nurtures the Christian faith and life of the child. At the appropriate time, the child will take his rightful place in the Church, fulfilling the work which God destined for him since the foundation of the world. And finally, he, by God's grace, will find eternal happiness in heaven. Procreation in Christian marriage, "builds up" the Kingdom of God, both on earth and in heaven.

The Holy Father notes that it is not only the family which introduces the child to the Church, but also the Church which finds its entrance to human hearts through the family. This thought echoes a later expression found at the very end of the document: *"The future of humanity passes by way of the family"*.[11] Since "man is the way for the Church",[12] it is true to say that the future of the Church passes by way of the family. The family prepares the children to enter into the full life of the Church and allows the universal Church to enter the lives of the new generation.

In the final article of the second part, the Pope takes up the essential question of celibacy and virginity. If we fulfill ourselves as images of God in and through the total self-gift of spousal love, it would seem that everyone should enter the married state. As we have seen, the Pope has laid the foundation for these remarks already in the first article, the eleventh, of this part of the document.

In the first paragraph of this article (16), the Pope remarks that no one would renounce matrimony for the sake of the Kingdom of God if marriage were meaningless or without value. It is only when marriage is valued that celibacy and virginity are held in high esteem. The Holy Father also teaches that virgins or celibates do express a covenantal love for God. It is not only married couples who love. Virgins and celibates also love. They do fulfill their humanity as made in the image of God, but in a different mode from that of married people. Further, as the Pope notes later in this same article, the love of celibates and virgins is fruitful as God's love and spousal love are fruitful. Virginal or celibate love is not procreative as spousal love is, but, nevertheless, it bears fruit in the spiritual realm. The one who has renounced marriage for the sake of the Kingdom of God is called to bear fruit in God's family, the Church. The celibate or virgin becomes a spiritual father or mother to many, many people.

After a quote from Saint John Chrysostom supporting the point that celibacy and virginity are viable ways of life only

---

[11] See FC, no. 86.
[12] See RH, no. 14.

when marital love is held in high esteem, the Pope gives three reasons for the practice of celibacy and virginity. He notes that not only does a proper estimation of marriage make the life of virginity or celibacy a viable alternative, but also that virgins and celibates, in and through their lives, testify to the incomparable value of marriage. When people observe a virgin or a celibate, they realize that he or she has renounced marriage for the sake of the Kingdom. Often it is only in the lack of something that we appreciate its value. In seeing unmarried people, married couples come to appreciate the inestimable value and dignity of their state in life. In this way, virgins and celibates testify to the great value of marriage.

Secondly, celibates and virgins anticipate the full flowering of the Kingdom of God. In their bodies, they express their hope for the return of the Lord and their expectation of the joys of heaven. Through this hope, expressed in and through their bodies, they are a living testimony, a witness, to the faith and hope of the Church. In their flesh, they are a sign and a sacrament of the Church's belief in the promises of Christ.

Thirdly, celibates and virgins perfect themselves in the love of God. "Virginity or celibacy, by liberating the human heart in a unique way, 'so as to make it burn with greater love for God and all humanity' bears witness that the Kingdom of God and his justice is that pearl of great price which is preferred to every other value no matter how great, and hence must be sought as the only definitive value." Celibates and virgins should choose their state in life for the love of God. With the firm conviction that God is infinitely more valuable than any other good, virgins and celibates should surrender themselves directly and totally to God. When virginity or celibacy is embraced for this reason, the love of God is intensified in the heart of the virgin or celibate.

Married couples give themselves to God. They express their love for God in and through their married partner, i.e., in the domestic church. Virgins and celibates give themselves to God. They express their love in the universal Church. As the

Holy Father clearly indicates, virginity and celibacy, as well as marriage, are gifts from God. They are charisms. While the Church has always taught that the gift of celibacy or virginity was a superior charism, the credit for this superiority rests primarily with God, the one who gives the gift. As a happily married couple should acknowledge that God has blessed them with the gifts necessary for a good marriage, so the virgin or celibate must daily give thanks to God for the gifts he has given him or her.

In the seventh paragraph of this article the Holy Father teaches that married couples "have the right to expect from celibate persons a good example and a witness of fidelity to their vocation until death. Just as fidelity at times becomes difficult for married people and requires sacrifice, mortification, and self-denial, the same can happen to celibate persons, and their fidelity, even in the trials that may occur, should strengthen the fidelity of married couples." Celibates and virgins are called to witness to the intrinsic value of marriage and to the Church's anticipation of the resurrection. They are also called to personal holiness in and through their special charism. From the viewpoint of married couples, the viewpoint of this document, the most important contribution of virgins and celibates is the testimony they give to the incomparable dignity of marriage.

As the final note to this article and to the second part of the exhortation, John Paul voices the hope that his (brief) reflections on virginity and celibacy will help those who, for one reason or another, have been unable to marry. He suggests that these people, if they can embrace their state in life through a freely chosen will-act, can be of significant service to society and to the Church.

It is clear that articles eleven to sixteen, the second part of this document, contain the major principles of John Paul II's thoughts on the body, sexuality, marriage, procreation, and virginity and celibacy. However, these articles and their contents cannot be fully understood without a clear view of the previous works of John Paul II, especially the *Theology of the Body* series and his book *Love and Responsibility*. Part Three of *Familiaris Consortio* takes the description of the family given in Part Two and applies it to the mission of the family, i.e., to the proper activities of the family.

III. The Role of the Christian Family

In Part Two of his apostolic exhortation on the family, John Paul established the identity of the family, i.e., what a family is. However, "the family finds in the plan of God the Creator and Redeemer not only its *identity*, what it *is*, but also its *mission*, what it can and should *do*". As we have seen, the Christian family forms a miniature mystical person of Christ, a domestic church. Since persons do not merely exist, but choose particular acts (will) on the basis of truth (intellect), the family is an actor. The proper acts of the family comprise its mission, but they also lead the family to determine itself, i.e., to shape itself, and to know itself better and better.

As a person, the family has a consciousness, an awareness of its known and freely chosen acts. Consciousness has two functions. First, it is through specific acts that persons determine themselves. Since every personal act is "contained" in the consciousness of the person, each conscious experience forms and shapes the person. The family is called to form itself through its proper activity into a true domestic church. Every family has the power to shape itself into what it is or to destroy itself by destroying what it is. Pope John Paul challenges each family "to *become* what you *are*". In other words, he challenges each and every family to choose only those acts which fulfill the mission of Christ. Any other acts are self-destructive to the family because they form it into something other than what it is.

Further, consciousness has a second function. Since persons possess an intellect, they have a responsibility to know the truth.

First and foremost, they are called to know themselves in truth. They should know themselves as they are, as God made them. It is through the awareness (consciousness) of conscious acts that persons come to know themselves. Consciousness allows persons to observe their own acts and in seeing themselves acting they come to know themselves. However, if they act contrary to the truth, contrary to their very selves, they will not know themselves in truth. The more a person chooses activities opposed to his very self, the less true self-knowledge he possesses. Families, as mystical persons, are called to know themselves in truth and they accomplish this task through their awareness of their proper activities. "Accordingly, the family must go back to the 'beginning' of God's creative act, if it is to attain self-knowledge and self-realization in accordance with the inner truth not only of what it is but also of what it does in history."

The emphasis on self-determination and self-knowledge through an awarenesss of personal acts is a hallmark of the phenomenological method and of John Paul II's synthesis of faith and reason. It may seem surprising that John Paul applies this analysis to a mystical person. However, in his study of the Church and the Second Vatican Council (*Sources of Renewal*), the present Holy Father spoke of the self-knowledge and self-realization of the Church, the mystical person of Christ. In the first half of his volume, the Pope outlined the Church's self-knowledge, which was enriched through the Second Vatican Council. Through the Council, the Church observed itself in its act of knowing. The Pope examined the Church's more profound self-knowledge acquired through its self-observation in the Council. In the second half of the volume, the Holy Father spoke of the self-realization of the Church through attitudes, i.e., will-acts.[1] The Church realizes itself through its acts. Persons, mystical persons included, determine and know themselves through their consciously known and cho-

[1] See SR, pp. 205, 218.

sen acts. These acts may be without bodily expression, e.g., the act of knowing, or they may be expressed through the body.

John Paul defines the proper activity of the family when he writes that "the family has *the mission to guard, reveal, and communicate love*". Of course, as images of God, all men and women are called to do what God does, i.e., to love. The family as a communion of persons should reflect the union of the three Divine Persons in and through love, the mutual self donation of all three to one another. Obviously, as a miniature church, the family is called to imitate the bond of love which binds Christ and the members of the Church into one mystical person. This bond is the grace, the love, of God given in and through the Holy Spirit.

"Every particular task of the family is an expression and concrete actuation of that fundamental mission", the mission to love. Following the synod fathers, the Pope suggests that the mission of love is actualized in four different areas. First, the members of a family should constantly strive to live with fidelity and to intensify the union which they have entered. The familial communion of persons always can be strengthened and perfected. Secondly, the family is called to serve life because life and love are always linked as they are in God. Thirdly, the family should participate in the development of society and, fourthly, it should have a role in the life and mission of the universal Church. John Paul considers each of these areas in turn.

Pope John Paul devotes ten articles to his remarks on the first area: the struggle to perfect the conjugal communion of persons. In article eighteen, the first of this division, the Holy Father teaches that the family is founded in and through love. However, this love must constantly grow if the family is to perfect itself. The Pope suggests that the motive for carrying on this admittedly difficult task is that without love life is senseless. He quotes his own first encyclical, *Redemptor Hominis, The Redeemer of Man*: "Man cannot live without love. He remains a

being that is incomprehensible for himself, his life is senseless
if love is not revealed to him, if he does not encounter love,
if he does not experience it and make it his own, if he does
not participate intimately in it."[2] Human life has no meaning
without love because the human person exists to love, to do
what God does. This love has to be revealed to each of us
because we cannot know how God loves unless God tells us
and shows us. We must love because this is our activity, the
act we were created to do. When family members fail to make
the effort to love as God loves, they not only risk the loss of
true family life, they also risk the loss of all meaning in their
own lives. Without love (and if love does not grow, it dies; it
cannot remain static), human life is absolutely senseless.

In article nineteen, the Holy Father notes that the familial
communion of persons rests on the mutual self-donation of
a husband and a wife to one another. They join and become
one flesh or, as we have seen, one mystical person. They make
this total self-donation and are willing to share with each other
what they are and what they have because of the "natural complementarity that exists between man and woman". Spouses
are called to love and to express this love in and through their
bodies. The "natural complementarity", given to them by God
in his creative act, should give them the joy that it gave Adam
when he first saw Eve. It is this gift which enables them to
fulfill their most basic need, the need to love and to express
love in a bodily way.

However, for Christians, human love is drawn into the
mystery of divine love through divine grace. The union of
a man and a woman in marriage is taken up into the very
love of God by a special sacrament, matrimony. Those who
have received baptism love God and they express their love
for God by loving all their neighbors. Baptism establishes
the relationship with God as the primary one. Matrimony
does not destroy baptism, but rather specifies it. Matrimony

[2] See RH, no. 10.

makes the relationship with the spouse the most important human relationship. In Christian marriage, the love of God is expressed primarily by loving the spouse. Since matrimony showers God's graces on the spouses, they are able to love one another as they each love God. The basis for the spousal relationship and the relationship with God are the same, divine grace.

Grace makes it possible for spouses to love one another as the members of the Trinity love one another, i.e., by making a true self-donation to one another. With the effects of original sin, human persons lost the ability to give themselves in a total self-donation. The "constitutive break within the human person",[3] i.e., the loss of the dominance of the mind and the will, made it almost impossible for any human being to make a true self-donation to another. Now, with grace, creation is restored and we are able to make a true self-donation, if we are in the state of grace. As the Pope writes, "the gift of the Spirit is . . . a stimulating impulse so that every day they [the couple] may progress toward an ever richer union".

A marital union must be total and, therefore, exclusive. Polygamy is a radical denial of the mutual and total self-donation. The one who has more than one spouse does not totally give himself to any one of them. He must, at the very least, spend time with all of them and thus he withholds a complete self-donation to any one of them, at least in terms of time. Without a total self-gift, love does not exist and therefore the relationship is based not on love, but on use.

Not only does the polygamist not make a complete self-donation to any of his spouses, but he usually is seeking something from them, e.g., gratification. However, love is a mutual self-donation of both for the sake of the other. The lover desires nothing but the good of the beloved. In seeking something from his spouses, the polygamist is using them. Although the polygamist may claim to love his spouses, he does not and can-

---

[3] See TB, no. 28.

not love the spouses because the relationship is one of use. Polygamy thwarts a true loving bond because the polygamist does not give himself and because the polygamist treats his spouses as objects for his enjoyment and gratification.[4]

In article twenty the Holy Father considers the other requirement of true love: indissolubility. The husband and the wife must give themselves totally to one another. This gift is not complete unless it is unbounded either in terms of their potentialities, e.g., their fertility, or in terms of time. If a man were to give himself to a woman just for a few years, the relationship would not be founded on true love, but on use. We may discard things which no longer function as we would like, but we may never discard people. To give oneself only for some years, reserving the right to break the relationship, is to treat the other person as a useful object which can be discarded as soon as it is no longer useful. Of course, it is also necessary, as the Holy Father suggests, that marriage be indissoluble as long as both spouses are living for the sake of the children. Through procreation, parents freely take upon themselves grave obligations. These responsibilities cannot be fulfilled without a lifelong commitment of the spouses to one another.

However, the major part of this article grounds the indissolubility of marriage in the specifically Christian obligation to bear witness to the faithful love of God for his people and to Christ's love for the Church. God is always faithful and Christ will never abandon the Church. (How could he? The Church and he form one mystical person!) "The gift of the sacrament [of matrimony] is at the same time a vocation and commandment for Christian spouses that they may remain faithful to each other forever". Since this sacrament is a vocation from God, God also gives the means through which this call may be lived, i.e., his grace. Only his life, as we have seen, makes this absolute fidelity possible for the husband and the wife.

[4] See LR, pp. 211–13.

Through the sacrament, the couple share in Christ's love and are "able to overcome 'hardness of heart' ".

The Holy Father calls this teaching of the Church "good news" for our age. It corresponds to our very humanity because it is the truth about ourselves. The truth is always "good news". With this in mind, the Pope asks all Christian couples to "bear witness to the inestimable value of the indissolubility and fidelity of marriage". He views this task as "one of the most precious and most urgent tasks of Christian couples in our time" because many in our age consider such a lifelong union too difficult or even impossible. Christian couples should be witnesses to the truth about humanity and marriage. The Pope also challenges those who have been abandoned by their partners to be faithful to their vows by not entering a new union. Such people testify to the truth and are witnesses for the rest of us. Acknowledging the difficulty of this path, the Holy Father asks pastors and the faithful to be particularly supportive and helpful to those deserted by their spouses.

Having described the conjugal bond of love, the Pope begins in article twenty-one to outline the relationships among all the members of the family, e.g., parents and children, brothers and sisters, and other members of the familial household. Just as the parents' relationship is founded on divine love, all the family members must be united with one another through the grace of the Lord. The building of the familial communion of persons rests not just with the parents, but with all members of the family. Each family member should know the truth about his need to love and he should freely choose to love the other members of the family. Such love is possible only through divine grace given by Christ through the sacraments. Therefore, all family members, at the appropriate times, have an obligation to receive the sacraments, especially the sacraments of penance and holy Eucharist.

The intensification of love among the members of the family (priestly office) will occur if there is a tenderness toward the little ones, the sick, and the elderly of the family. Love will grow if all serve all through a mutual sharing of the resources which the family has (even if these be minimal). Love also grows through the mutual exchange of joys and sorrows common to human life everywhere. Secondly, love in the family is nurtured through the exchange of knowledge. When the parents teach the children (prophetic office), the parents, through the interaction, realize the inestimable value of the gift of new human life, which God has given them in their children. The children receive the most vital knowledge from their parents: the knowledge that they are images of God called to know and to choose through truth and freedom. Thirdly, familial love will intensify only if there is a spirit of sacrifice (kingly office) present among all the family members. "There is no family that does not know how selfishness, discord, tension, and conflict violently attack and at times mortally wound its own communion: hence there arise the many and varied forms of division in family life. But, at the same time, every family is called by the God of peace to have the joyous and renewing experience of 'reconciliation,' that is, communion reestablished, unity restored." Only a frequent recourse to the sacraments of holy Eucharist and penance will enable all family members to cultivate a spirit of sacrifice and of penance necessary if the divisions found in family life (because of original sin) are to be overcome.

The remaining articles in this first division of Part Three consider the various members of the family. In articles twenty-two, twenty-three, and twenty-four, the Pope considers the role of women. In twenty-five, husbands and fathers are discussed, while the final two articles treat children and the elderly, respectively.

As is his practice, John Paul states the principle underlying his topic at the very beginning of the discussion. In article twenty-two, the Pope reminds his readers that the family should promote, in and through love, the dignity of its members. He next notes that men and women possess the same human dignity. The history of salvation confirms the equal status of men and women. First, God created both men and women in his image. Secondly, "God then manifests the dignity of women in the highest form possible, by assuming human flesh from the Virgin Mary". Womanhood could hardly be more greatly honored than it was in and through the Blessed Mother. Finally, our Lord Jesus Christ demonstrated his profound respect for women when he invited them to be his disciples, when, after his Resurrection, he appeared to a woman before anyone else, and when he asked women to carry the message of his Resurrection to the Apostles. As Saint Paul wrote, "There is neither Jew nor Greek, there is neither slave nor free, there is neither male nor female; for you are all one in Christ Jesus."[5] Thus, both the husband and the wife have an equal dignity and they also have equal responsibilities. Both give themselves in a reciprocal self-donation to each other and to their children.

In the next article, twenty-three, the Holy Father considers the relationship between women and society. He acknowledges that the topic is complex, but he wishes to discuss some basic points. First, he demonstrates his awareness of the long-standing tradition that women have almost exclusively had the role of wife, homemaker, and mother. With such a role assigned to them by society, public functions have sometimes been closed to them and reserved only for men. Such a situation is contrary to human dignity and to the proper position of women in society.

"On the other hand, the true advancement of women requires that clear recognition be given to the value of their maternal and family role, by comparison with all other public roles and all other professions." Since the work of a wife and mother is directly for persons, it is not only vital, but it is noble. The work of a mother is not merely a job, but is an expression of love, the "fundamental and innate vocation of every human being".[6] For the wife and mother, the familial work is first of all a vocation, a path to heaven. The father's

[5] See Gal 3.28.
[6] See FC, no. 11.

familial work is also a vocation for him. His work in the family must take precedence over his work (his job) in the market-place. However, it is important to emphasize that it is not only the husband and father who has a job. The wife and mother remaining in the home does much physical labor. She has a job in the same sense as her husband. But her job coincides exactly with her vocational work, i.e., her familial work. In other words, for her, the familial communion of persons corresponds to the communion of persons in the marketplace, i.e., the mother's job is directly related to the family.

However, the mother's job is not valued in society because generally there is a misunderstanding of work in most industrialized societies. For many, work (the job) is not for people, but people are for work. But we were not created for work. Rather work was created as a means for us, as images of God, to share in the divine creative act. Work, then, is *for* man. However, when most believe that we are for work, human dignity suffers. With this view in place, a worker is not measured by his infinite and incomparable dignity, but by how much he produces or how much he earns. Human beings become subject to things, the opposite of God's plan established in his creative act.

Two conclusions founded on the (false) principle that people are for work tend to devalue the primacy of the familial work of the mother, but also of the father. First, if human persons are for work and for the family, there is a competition between the family and work. Given this view, both mothers and fathers will wish to work in the marketplace and they will value their jobs more than their familial work. As a result, both mothers and fathers will neglect their familial roles. But it is wrong for either the father or the mother to neglect his or her primary vocation, the familial work, for the sake of his or her job. The only solution to this problem is a restoration of the proper view that work (the job) is *for* man and not the other way around. The second problem is that if people are measured by how much they earn or produce, it is apparent that the job of a wife and mother (or that of a husband or father) in the home will be thought worthless. With this job, she (or he) is not earning any money, nor producing anything tangible. Society regards this job in the home as meaningless. This view must change. The job of the wife and mother (or that of the husband and father) in the home is, in the true sense, even more important than any job in the marketplace.

In this document on the family, the Holy Father calls for a new theology of work. In fact, he has developed a theology of work in his third encyclical, *Laborem Exercens, On Human Work*. Through an examination of Genesis (one of the hallmarks of John Paul II's theological system), the Holy Father establishes beyond a shadow of a doubt that work is *for* man. He suggests a completely new approach to work in the world and asks all men and women to consider his thoughts. One of his suggestions, as we have already seen, is that the job of wives and mothers in the home should be recognized by society, either through special grants to them or through a family wage. John Paul expresses the same thought in article twenty-three of his apostolic exhortation on the family: "The Church can and should help modern society by tirelessly insisting that the work of women in the home be recognized and respected by all in its irreplaceable value."

Still, the Pope is also quite emphatic that women are equal in dignity to men and not only have a right to work (job), but, to fulfill their very humanity, i.e., to participate in God's creative work (which they are called to do as images of God), they must work. This work (job) may be in the home or in the marketplace. However, the Holy Father states categorically that wives and mothers should never be "*compelled* to work outside the home". Further, equal in dignity does not mean the same. As John Paul writes: "Clearly all of this does not mean for women a renunciation of their femininity or an imitation of the male role, but the fullness of true feminine humanity which should be expressed in their activity, whether in the family or outside of it, without disregarding the differences of customs and cultures in this sphere." Of course, in this statement, the same foundational principle, i.e., that jobs are *for* man, is operative. Men and women are *for* the family. No work (job) should ever interfere with the primary vocation of husbands and wives: familial love. This familial love is possible because God made us male and female. Therefore, no woman should ever be engaged in work (job) which is offensive to femininity.

In article twenty-four, the Holy Father confronts the basic problem which leads to a denigration of women. Many societies fail to uphold the incomparable and infinite dignity of the human person. Women are the first to suffer when human beings are reduced to the status of things. They become objects of use first because they are viewed as the means to pleasure. "This mentality produces very bitter fruits such as contempt for men and for women, slavery, oppression of the weak, pornography, prostitution—especially in the organized form —and 'all those various forms of discrimination that exist in the fields of education, employment, wages, etc." Further, in many societies, certain groups of women—widows, divorced, childless wives, unmarried mothers—are treated even more shamefully than women in general. The Church stands in firm and unyielding opposition to all attacks on human dignity. In articles twenty-two through twenty-four of this document, John Paul has clearly taught that men and women are equally made in the image of God and are equal in their dignity. He has repeatedly emphasized that women may not be degraded and treated as things. Nor may they be regarded as second-class beings of lesser dignity than men.

In article twenty-five, the Holy Father considers the role of a husband and father in the family. In the very first paragraph of this article, John Paul cites his basic principle and starting point. Not surprisingly, it is Genesis. He suggests that every husband should respond to his wife as Adam did to Eve: "This at last is bone of my bones and flesh of my flesh."[7] Each man

---

[7] See Gen 2:23.

experiences the joy of Adam when he discovers the one he can love. Human persons are made to love. Adam was made to love. Until Eve was created, there was no other human person he could love. However, because he was made for love, he experienced a profound solitude. But when Adam saw Eve, he was released from his agonizing loneliness. Similarly, each man is alone until he finds the one he can love. When he finds her, he must experience something similar to the joy Adam felt at seeing Eve. In and through his wife, a man understands his own being, i.e., that he was made to love and through that love to participate in God's own divine activity. In other words, through his wife, the husband understands God's plan found in his creative act.

A husband is called to treat his wife as his equal. The marital relationship is not that of a master and a slave. The husband and wife should develop a very intense and unique personal friendship. For the Christian married couple, the affection and tenderness toward one another should be comparable to the unequaled love of Christ apparent on every page of the gospel. The love of a Christian husband and father should not be effeminate, but should be strong and gentle as Christ's love: strong enough to meet any obstacle; gentle enough to forgive any offense. Similarly, the husband and father is called to love his children. He should not cultivate an attitude of benign neglect as though family matters were beneath his dignity. It is imperative that the father assist in the education of the children. If the father is absent or if he neglects his proper role, difficulties arise. Neither a haughty superiority over wife and children, nor benign neglect of them, is acceptable for a father. Only through a Christlike love will a father fulfill his vocation.

The father has the specific responsibilities of ensuring the proper development of all the members of the family. He accomplishes this task through a "generous responsibility for the life conceived under the heart of the mother", through education of the children (a task which he shares with his wife), through his work (job) undertaken according to the proper principles and priorities, and by "the witness he gives of an adult Christian life which effectively introduces the children into the living experience of Christ and the Church".

There is no doubt in most people's minds that John Paul has a very special place in his heart for all children, especially the very young and those who are in any way sick or handicapped. His affection for the little ones is expressed repeatedly in the relatively brief twenty-fifth article of this document. In the first of four paragraphs, he teaches that each family should devote particular attention to the children. The younger they are or the more in need they are, the more care all the family members should lavish on them.

This responsibility toward children exists in every family. However, it exists in Christian families and in the Church in a very special way. The Church exists to fulfill the mission of Christ: to reveal man to himself.[8] This task must be renewed for each and every human being. The work of revealing Christ begins when we are children. Since the Christian family is a domestic church, it carries on this mission of Christ for each child. Secondly, Christ expressed an extraordinary regard for the little ones when he said, "Let the children come to me and do not hinder them."[9] The Church and the family, in fulfilling the mission of Christ, express this same generosity toward the children.

In the next paragraph, the Holy Father turns his attention to the relationship between children and society. No culture or civilization can survive if it does not regard new human life as a precious treasure. Every society's future is tied to its children. From this point of view, a healthy attitude toward children is a matter of survival for any nation. However, beyond this necessary concern, all people should find an incomparable joy in the gift of new life. Speaking for all human beings of good will the Holy Father writes, "I wish to express the joy that we

[8] See GS, no. 22.
[9] See Lk 18:16.

all find in children, the springtime of life, the anticipation of the future history of each of our present earthly homelands." Children have a fresh new life and usually they have a firm hold on it. We see in them the reflection of our own life. We should then be attracted to this incomparable gift from God.

The Pope also writes that "concern for the child, even before birth, from the first moment of conception and then throughout the years of infancy and youth, is the primary and fundamental test of the relationship of one human being to another." It is a measure of our estimate of human life. Secondly, and even more importantly, if we cannot relate to these innocent little ones with affection, it will not be possible for us to relate to their fathers and mothers, brothers and sisters, who are not always so innocent. If we do not love the children, we will not love anyone else. Furthermore, for the Christian a tender and loving attitude toward children is the expression of Christ's love, God's grace, given at baptism. Thus, love of children is not only characteristically human, but also distinctively Christian.

In the final article, twenty-seven, of this first section of Part Three, John Paul considers the role of the elderly in the family unit. He encourages and commends those cultures which have traditionally held their older members in honor and esteem, providing for their needs and allowing them to lead useful lives as much as is possible. The Holy Father notes that there are some societies, particularly industrialized and urbanized ones, which "set the elderly aside in unacceptable ways". Of course, such attitudes cause immense suffering. While asking the elderly not to interfere in the families established by their children, John Paul suggests that "the elderly often have the charism to bridge generation gaps . . . how many children have found understanding and love in the eyes and words and caresses of the aging! And how many old people have willingly subscribed to the inspired word that the 'crown of the aged is their children's children'!"

The second division of Part Three, "Serving Life", is organized in two subdivisions. The first is entitled, "The Transmission of Life", and the second is "Education". The second division of Part Three includes articles twenty-eight to forty-one. The first eight articles are in the "The Transmission of Life" subdivision and the other six are in the "Education" subdivision. As we have seen, all of Part Three discusses the mission of the family. The first division of Part Three considers the mission of the family to strengthen the familial communion of persons. The second division of Part Three considers the mission of the family in serving life through procreation and in providing education for the children.

In the first article of this second division of Part Three, John Paul explains that God, when he bestowed the power of procreation on men and women, gave them an extraordinary participation in his own love. Not only did God make them in the divine likeness, but he did not hesitate to allow them to participate in the divine activity: love. God's love is always fruitful as it was in the creation and in the redemption. By God's holy will, human love, like God's, is also fruitful. When a couple procreates, they cooperate in God's creative act. They love as God loved us in creation. The incomparable dignity of human persons as made in God's image could hardly be more highly respected. A mere creature is given a share in creation! However, the Holy Father also notes that the fruit of married love is not only and, obviously, not always, new life. Married love gives rise to spiritual, moral, and supernatural fruits, which parents must extend to the next generation.

In the next article, twenty-nine, the Holy Father clearly and unequivocally states the position of the Church on procreation. The very first sentence of this article reads: "Precisely because the love of husband and wife is a unique participation in the mystery of life and of the love of God himself, the Church knows that she has received the special mission of guarding and protecting the lofty dignity of marriage and the most serious responsibility of the transmission of human life."

In the next paragraph, the Pope bases his teaching on the

prophetic tradition of the Church, the Second Vatican Council, and Pope Paul VI. Finally, in the third paragraph, John Paul quotes the synodal declaration: "This Sacred Synod, gathered together with the Successor of Peter in the unity of faith, firmly holds what has been set forth in the Second Vatican Council (cf. *Gaudium et Spes*, 50) and afterward in the encyclical *Humanae Vitae*, particularly that love between husband and wife must be fully human, exclusive and open to new life."

Some claim that the above statements constitute an infallible teaching of the Church. The Church teaches infallibly on faith and morals in its extraordinary and ordinary Magisterium. Most of the infallible teachings have been promulgated through the extraordinary Magisterium, which is exercised in two ways. When the Pope makes an *ex cathedra* statement on faith and morals, he exercises the extraordinary Magisterium and teaches infallibly. Secondly, the extraordinary infallible Magisterium is exercised when a doctrine or moral norm is defined as infallible by the bishops gathered in a general council in union with the Holy Father. The ordinary infallible Magisterium is exercised when a doctrine or moral norm has been taught by the popes and the bishops throughout the history of the Church and is universally accepted. Some regard the Church's teaching on the transmission of life as infallible by the ordinary Magisterium.[10]

Of course, the attempt to defend the teaching of the Church against contraception as infallible is a response to those many voices in and out of the Church which claim that this teaching is not binding because it is not infallible. However, if those who wish to uphold this pronouncement of the Church begin quarreling on the question of infallibility, they have already granted the major premise of the opposition, i.e., that non-

---

[10] See John C. Ford and Germain Grisez, "Contraception and the Infallibility of the Ordinary Magisterium", *Theological Studies*, vol. 39, no. 2 (June 1978), pp. 258–312. In this article the authors make a strong case for the infallibility of the teaching against contraception. See also William Smith, "The Role of the Christian Family, Articles 28–35", in *Pope John Paul II and the Family*, ed. Michael J. Wrenn (Chicago: Franciscan Herald Press, 1983), pp. 79–80.

infallible teachings are not binding. This is precisely the point which cannot be granted. For this reason, it seems better not even to enter such a discussion. The situation is similar to a Catholic confronted with a fundamentalist who wishes to know where in the Scriptures a particular doctrine is found. The question itself is loaded because implicit in its formulation is the fundamentalist doctrine that revelation is found only in the Scriptures (not in Tradition). If the Catholic discusses such a question, he has already granted a premise opposed to the teaching of the Church. The only prudent choice in this case is to change the context of the discussion, to ask a different question.

Some may believe that if the teaching of the Church on the transmission of life can be established as infallible, more will accept and practice it. However, it does not seem plausible to assume that those who have rejected the Church's official position will suddenly abandon their long-established practice just because a number of theologians involved in a rather technical theological discussion have agreed that this teaching should have the theological note of infallibility attached to it. Once a person has rejected an authoritative (but not necessarily infallible) teaching of the Church, it is a small, but logical, step to a rejection of other teachings, including infallible ones. Further, the argument from conscience could apply as much to infallible teachings as to other authoritative announcements.

For these reasons, it seems better not to enter the discussion of infallibility regarding contraception. Such a dialogue is useful within academic theological circles. However, in pastoral practice, the teachings of the Church should be based on the mystery of the Church. As we have seen, the Church is the mystical person of Christ. When the Church acts, it is Christ who acts. Christ acts in the most solemn pronouncements and in the homily given by a bishop at a parish confirmation. Both should be accepted as the acts of Christ (providing, of course, that the bishop is teaching in union with his brother bishops and the Holy Father). Will anyone reject the voice of Christ?

If anyone chooses to reject this voice, he is rejecting the only one who can teach him the truth about himself. In addition to this argument from authority, i.e., that the Church speaks with the mind of Christ, it is necessary to show by reasonable arguments that opposition to the Church's teachings causes more problems and difficulties than accepting them does. This path is the one chosen by Pope John Paul II in his *Theology of the Body* series and in this document on the family.

In the next article, thirty, the Holy Father asserts that the Church is for life. The Church treasures human life in all its aspects. However, this teaching of the Church is proclaimed today in a context hostile to life. Some believe that it would have been better if they had never been born and that children should not be conceived because of the evils present in the world, especially the evils stemming from our advanced technologies, e.g., pollution. Others are selfish and wish to keep for themselves material possessions, i.e., the goods of the earth and especially the goods which are the fruit of human labor. With more people, these goods will be less available to any one person. Thirdly, there are those who cannot see the infinite worth of spiritual goods, e.g., new life. They only measure value in terms of material progress. In a bold statement the Pope writes that "the ultimate reason for these mentalities is the absence in people's hearts of God."

From these ideas and their cause, the lack of the love of God, an antilife attitude arises, which manifests itself in many different ways. The Pope gives only one example: the panic derived from the dire predictions about uncontrolled population growth. In spite of this current milieu, John Paul firmly proclaims that the Church is for life. As Christ, the Church responds to the "No" of the world with the vehement "Yes" of Christ. Every life, no matter how poor, or how sick, or how weak, is of infinite (spiritual) value, transcending all material goods. Finally, the Holy Father reiterates the Church's condemnation of governments which attack human dignity by attempting to force contraceptives, sterilizations, and procured

abortions on their people or, which, because of their economic
resources, aid other nations, but only on the condition that
these other nations accept contraceptives, sterilizations, and
procured abortions.

In article thirty-one, the Holy Father makes an urgent appeal to theologians to study the Church's teaching regarding
the transmission of life. The Pope acknowledges the difficulties
many couples around the world have in following this teaching and he is sympathetic to social difficulties, e.g., population
growth. Nevertheless, he reaffirms the Church's unwavering
conviction that "consideration in depth of all the aspects of
these problems offers a new and stronger confirmation of the
importance of the authentic teaching on birth regulation re-
proposed in the Second Vatican Council and in the encyclical *Humanae Vitae*." In other words, the proposed "cure" for
the difficulties is more harmful than the difficulties themselves.
Theologians, united with the Church's Magisterium, should
study "the biblical foundations, the ethical grounds, and the
personalistic reasons behind this doctrine". When such an endeavor is properly undertaken, people of good will around the
world will understand the Church's teaching and will put it into
practice. However, it is absolutely necessary that theologians
begin this work in union with the Magisterium.

This work is vital not only for the sake of salvation, but
also because "doubt or error in the field of marriage or the
family involves obscuring to a serious extent the integral truth
about the human person". Our sexuality, as noted above, is a
window to the soul. When this is falsely understood, people
have a mistaken notion about themselves, i.e., they do not know
who they are. Secondly, with this false understanding, many
act contrary to their very selves and thus, shape themselves
into something other than images of God. They cease to know
themselves as human beings and cease to function as the images
of God that they are. In other words, they destroy themselves.
The Church's teaching is for salvation, but it is also for all
men and women in the sense that it teaches them who they

are as Christ did. The task of theologians then is to develop arguments persuading the people of our era that the teaching of the Church is correct. Men and women of our age deserve the best efforts from theologians. This work is particularly urgent in our society because of the dominant culture which has already adopted many beliefs and practices contrary to human dignity.

Having reaffirmed the teaching of the Church, explained the positive aspects of it, and asked the theologians to support and defend it, the Holy Father, in article thirty-two, marshals some arguments in its defense. Not surprisingly, in the very first paragraph of this article, the Pope suggests that the difficulty in accepting the Church's position regarding the transmission of life lies in our culture's mistaken notion that sexuality can be separated from the human person. In opposition to this widely held view, John Paul asserts that the Church presents "sexuality as a value and task of the whole person, created male and female in the image of God". This principle is a restatement of the major theme of article eleven of Part Two. The next two paragraphs cite the teaching of the Second Vatican Council and Pope Paul VI. The council taught that the means of "harmonizing" conjugal love and procreation must be judged not merely by the intentions and sincerity of the spouses, but by *objective standards . . . based on the nature of the human person and his or her acts*". Pope Paul VI affirmed that the unitive and procreative meanings of the conjugal act may never be separated.

These arguments are familiar to many. However, John Paul adds his own contribution to the discussion in the fourth paragraph of this article. He writes that spouses who practice contraception "act as 'arbiters' of the divine plan and they 'manipulate' and degrade human sexuality—and with it themselves and their married partner—by altering its value of 'total' self-giving. Thus the innate language that expresses the total reciprocal self-giving of husband and wife is overlaid, through contraception, by an objectively contradictory language, namely, that of not giving oneself totally to the other." The Pope's argument should be familiar to us. In this passage, he teaches that couples who practice contraception are lying to one another. In the midst of an act of total self-surrender, of love, they refuse to give themselves to each other. Their sexual union, the spousal language of love, is not for them a language of love because it no longer represents their total self-donation. There are two possible ways for human beings to relate to one another: love and use. Since couples practicing contraception do not love, they are using one another. Therefore, they attack one another's dignity.

Further, since the Christian family united in Christ is a reflection of the trinitarian *communion of Persons*, the conjugal union is a sign or sacrament of the love of the Trinity. It is therefore a holy and blessed act similar to the priest's consecration of the Eucharist at Mass. When a couple engages in this holy act while, at the same time, not giving themselves in love, the conjugal embrace is no longer a reflection of the love of the Trinity. A holy, sacred sign is desecrated. Such desecration, if knowingly and willingly done, is a sacrilege. It is comparable to a priest's desecration of the holy Eucharist. Thus, contracepting couples act contrary to the familial communion of persons and in so doing they give grave offense to God and to each other.

However, the Holy Father commends those couples who, while respecting both the conjugal and procreative meanings, responsibly and prudently make use of the periods of infertility. Such couples do not alter or manipulate their sexual powers.

With this thought, John Paul introduces his other argument against contraception. As we have seen, for him, contraception is not only unacceptable because it is an offense against God and the familial communion of persons, it is also a grave attack against the body, against one's own life. The Holy Father developed this argument in his *Theology of the Body* series. In *Familiaris Consortio*, he has already outlined this argument in article eleven of Part Two. In the thirty-second article, he repeats some of the main theses of his argument. He writes that the difference "between contraception and recourse to the rhythm of the cycle . . . is much wider and deeper than is usually thought, one which involves in the final analysis two irreconcilable concepts of the human person and of human sexuality." The Church holds that the body is an expression of the person. The other possible position is that it is a machine, which the person owns and uses. If the body is a machine, anyone can do exactly what he wishes with it or to it. However, if the body is part of the gift of life, it is not ours and it cannot be altered or changed because God gave it to us to express our persons *as it is*.

If spouses responsibly employ the infertile periods in order to space children, they are doing something quite different from spouses who contracept. The contracepting couple claims implicitly, if not explicitly, absolute control over their bodies. They claim ownership and use over their bodies as though they were machines. The noncontracepting couple, employing the infertile periods, respects their own flesh and blood realizing that their bodies are a gift from God over which they neither have absolute control nor ownership. Since each accepts his or her own flesh and that of his or her married partner and since the body is the expression of the person, each also accepts the other fully in his or her personhood. On the other hand, contracepting spouses, while treating their bodies as machines, do not accept each other's bodies, even as machines. They alter them and thus, again implicitly, reject each other's "hardware". Further, for those who claim use and ownership over their bodies, sensuality and sentiment, tenderness and affection, become mere machine reactions unexpressive of the individual person. Of course, for those who accept the Church's position, these emotions can be expressive of the person as well as a positive aspect of human love. As the Pope writes, in "breaking the personal unity of soul and body, [man] strikes at God's creation itself at the level of the deepest interaction of nature and person".

In the thirty-third article, John Paul reminds his readers that the Church is both a teacher and a mother. As a teacher, the

Church never ceases to announce the truth. However, almost in the same breath, the Pope notes that the Church is not the "author or the arbiter" of what is proclaimed. God is Truth and he is the source of what the Church teaches. As a mother, the Church is well aware of the difficulties many married couples experience not only in practicing the teachings of the Church, but even in comprehending them. However, as the Pope clearly states in the next paragraph, it is the same Church which is both teacher and mother. There can be no conflict between these roles of the Church. It is only in proclaiming the truth that the Church shows genuine affection for its members. Only one who has a genuine love for another will tell the truth, even if it is difficult. Therefore, the Church shows a true love even in teaching the hard sayings of the gospel. The Holy Father also notes that there can be no conflict between the truth and true conjugal love. God is Truth and is Love. There is no conflict in him. There can be no conflict in us, his images, made to know the truth and to love in and through the truth.

Nevertheless, true love in imitation of the Trinity is surrounded with difficulties. With the effects of original sin, it is impossible for us to love as we are made to do. The sin of Adam and Eve caused a "constitutive break within the human person".[11] No longer do the mind and will dominate as they should. Since love is primarily a union of wills, when our will choices cease to be expressed adequately in and through our bodies, we fail to love as we should. Unable to do what we are made to do, we are, in a sense, subhuman. But God did not leave us in this pathetic situation. He sent us a Redeemer. With the grace of Christ, it is now possible for us to love as we should. Grace does not restore the *state* of original innocence, but it does make it possible for us to function as true images of God. Thus, the Holy Father teaches that virtue is required to live the married life, i.e., to love. Further, it is absolutely essential that married couples frequent the sacraments

[11] See TB, no. 28.

of penance and holy Eucharist. Without these, the divine life of spouses would grow weak and perhaps die and they would be unable to love as they should. As he writes, "the gift of the Spirit, accepted and responded to by husband and wife, helps them to live their human sexuality in accordance with God's plan".

Grace completes nature. For a true loving union, couples must not only receive the sacraments and live a good life, but they must help themselves by learning whatever the human sciences offer as aids to married life. "The necessary conditions [for marriage] also include knowledge of the bodily aspect and the body's rhythms of fertility. Accordingly, every effort must be made to render such knowledge accessible to all married people and also to young adults before marriage." This papal statement is an absolutely extraordinary mandate for those who teach and wish to learn about natural family planning. Not only does the Pope, the highest authority in the Church, ask that married couples learn about their fertility, but he also expressly states that such knowledge is *necessary* to young adults before marriage.

Natural family planning is a tool for understanding and examining human fertility, i.e., it is fertility awareness. There is a distinction between knowledge of fertility and its application. Through natural family planning, married and unmarried adults learn about their fertility. They then use this knowledge in accordance with their state in life. Within the context of marriage, married couples must apply the knowledge of their fertility responsibly. They should have sufficient reasons for avoiding a pregnancy. The circumstances should be appropriate for having a baby. John Paul II, following in the footsteps of his predecessors, insists that only when there are reasonable grounds to avoid a pregnancy may a couple have recourse to the infertile periods only. This caution by the Pope only concerns the *use* of natural family planning, i.e., fertility awareness, within marriage and does not mean that one must have reasonable grounds to study natural family planning. Outside of marriage, men and women should learn natural family planning. They apply this method responsibly when they abstain.

John Paul II mandates natural family planning because it is a method of teaching the profound mystery of the human person. Natural family planning is the study of the body's fertility. The human body is more than the sum of its biological functions. Through these apparently understandable functions, the mystery of the human person finds expression. Thus, in themselves these biological functions are intriguing. If they were not, they could not express the mystery which each human being is. The body fully expresses the person when it participates in the most proper activity of the human person, i.e., love. Love is the most notable human activity because it is the most Godlike. The bodily expression of this love occurs through our sexual powers. These are the most fascinating of our bodily capabilities because through them the human person is revealed most fully as an image of God. Thus, in studying these powers, men and women will see the mystery which is expressed in and through these faculties. Men and women will perceive the dignity of the body and its sacramental value as a physical image of God. Through fertility awareness, people will realize that the body is not a machine. They will begin to respect it and hold it in awe and reverence. For John Paul II, fertility awareness is the means to teach the world the incomparable dignity of the human body as the expression of the human person. When men and women understand the truth about themselves, they will be more inclined to act responsibly, i.e., in accordance with their truth and value. But it is impossible to act responsibly if one is unaware of the truth. Natural family planning teaches the truth about fertility. As such, natural family planning will usually lead to virtue. Thus, the Holy Father encourages its use as a means of developing a holy life. John Paul II has elevated natural family planning to an apostolate, a tool for all to use on the path to holiness.

This view is confirmed by pastoral experience. Many, including the Holy Father, can testify to couples who, while at first not wishing to have any children or just one or two, have, after some years of marriage, a number of children. Their fidelity to natural family planning led them to appreciate the profound mystery of human love and procreation. Their newfound comprehension of the mystery of conjugal love and procreation led them to desire more children, i.e., to be unselfish in their gift of life. Secondly, a number of studies have been done which demonstrate that fertility awareness, if taught with a reverence and awe of the body to young adults, lessens premarital activity and pregnancies in the unmarried.[12] Natural family planning encourages virtue. This is the Holy Father's theoretical principle which has found confirmation in the lives of many married couples and even in the unmarried.

However, some authors continue to confuse natural family planning with its use to avoid a pregnancy. They not only equate knowledge and its application, but they fail to understand that natural family planning encourages virtue even among those couples who may, at first, use the knowledge of their fertility selfishly. One author has even written that natural family planning can become "Planned Barrenhood", a kind of "underground Catholic cousin of Planned Parenthood".[13] In this passage, this author clearly equates natural family planning with one of its uses, i.e., avoiding children. However, in this same passage, he does not seem to allow the possibility that fertility awareness encourages virtue and attacks the "contraceptive mentality". The same author believes it is strange that Pope John Paul II does not mention in his exhortation on the family the grave reasons necessary for spacing or postponing births. But the exhortation considered fertility awareness. It did not take up the application of this knowledge in the sexual act. Again, this moralist fails to distinguish between knowledge of

---

[12] See "Teen Fertility Awareness/Billings Method Study", *Fellowship of Catholic Scholars Newsletter*, vol. 7, no. 2 (March 1984), pp. 11, 15.

[13] See Smith, "The Role of the Christian Family", pp. 95–96, in *Pope John Paul II and the Family*, pp. 73–107.

fertility and its application. The distinction between knowing
one's fertility and the application of that knowledge in the sexual act is absolutely crucial if one is to understand John Paul II's
teaching. There is no question that married couples must act
responsibly in deciding about spacing their children. But not
to investigate their own fertility, i.e., natural family planning,
is the height of irresponsibility.

The final paragraph of article thirty-three is a long quote
from Pope Paul VI's encyclical, *Humanae Vitae, On Human Life.*
Pope John Paul II demonstrates with this quotation that his
predecessor taught that periodic abstinence is not harmful to
conjugal love because it develops self-control, i.e., a dominance
of the will. Since love is primarily a union of wills which is
then expressed in and through the body, the more each spouse's
will dominates his or her body, the better the couple is able to
express love to each other. Further, since we become what we
do, the more we express love, the more we become like God.

The next article, thirty-four, continues the theme of the
previous article. It discusses the moral progress of the married.
The Pope teaches that it is necessary to understand clearly the
moral norms given to God for humanity. He emphasizes that
the moral order is not something hostile to people, but is for
them. We are created in a certain way and for a specific activity.
The moral norms describe who we are and what we are to do.
The moral norms reveal us to ourselves. They are thus for
us. While God's plan can be known, it is accomplished in us
through gradual stages of growth.

Married people are called, as all the baptized are, to holiness.
They should strive always to understand the commandments of
God more and more, and to practice them more perfectly each
day. "They cannot however look on the law as merely an ideal
to be achieved in the future . . . 'The law of gradualness' or step
by step advance cannot be identified with 'gradualness of the
law,' as if there were different degrees or forms of precept in
God's law for different individuals and situations." The moral
order always binds, but we can gradually grow to observe it

better. For example, contraception is always evil and never justified. However, when a couple (unjustifiably) resorts to it, they may, through the sacrament of penance and a growth in understanding and holiness, comprehend that it offends married love as well as God and they may have the strength not to use it again. The Holy Father is well aware that the moral order is difficult to observe. However, he reminds his readers that there is no Christian love without the Cross. If we hope to rise with Christ, we must also share some suffering with him.

Finally, the Holy Father concludes this article with another plea to pastors and theologians to educate the faithful in the teachings of the Church. He also pleads with them to maintain a unity with the Magisterium "in order that the faithful may not have to suffer anxiety of conscience". This is the second appeal in this document to theologians and pastors to teach with the Church.

In article thirty-five, the Holy Father commends those who have scientifically investigated the fertility cycle. He asks that this work continue. Secondly, he reminds everyone that doctors, counselors, teachers, and other experts, as well as married couples should assist families in living their lives with respect for conjugal love in all its aspects, especially procreation. "This implies a broader, more decisive and more systematic effort to make the natural methods of regulating fertility known, respected, and applied." Finally, in this short article, the Holy Father congratulates those couples who, through the practice of periodic continence, "have reached a more mature personal responsibility with regard to love and life." They can be a powerful witness to other married couples.

The next six articles, thirty-six to forty-one, consider the family's role in serving life through education. Married couples share God's creative activity: giving life. New human life has the potential for growth and learning. Parents, in giving life, "take on the task of helping that person effectively to live a fully human life." The right and obligation of parents to teach their children is essential to their parental role because it is directly tied to procreation. Further, the role of the parents is primary, i.e., others teach children only at the request of the children's parents and with parental approval, which may always be withdrawn. Parental education is irreplaceable and inalienable. Children have a right to parental guidance. The parental role cannot be completely delegated. Finally, the Pope reminds parents that their educational role presumes that they love their children. Love is the *"animating principle"* of their guidance of their children.

In the next article, the Holy Father begins to specify the proper spheres of parental education. First and foremost, parents should teach children by word and by example that "man is more precious for what he is than for what he has." Secondly, parents must educate their children in true love because this is the "fundamental and innate vocation of every human being".[14] The children should see in the lives of their parents unselfish love. The children should learn and practice this unselfish love within the family so that it may be extended to others outside of the family. Especially in times of difficulties and joy, children will realize the immense spiritual value of love. They will understand that the unselfish donation of themselves to others fulfills their very humanity.

Since the body participates in the expression of love, parents cannot neglect teaching their children the knowledge and the discipline necessary to the expression of love in and through their bodies. This education is commonly called sex education. Primarily such education is the responsibility of the parents, but it may be carried out by other institutions with parental approval and guidance. In this passage, the Holy Father gives his approval to sex education in the schools, provided it has the consent of the parents and provided it is sex education in the proper sense.

John Paul makes quite clear that sex education, in the sense

[14] See FC, no. 11.

of the Church, must be education for love, for a total self-donation of one spouse to another. It must counteract the commonplace opinion that our sexual powers are given to us for pleasure. It must be an education in chastity, for only when the sexual powers are under the control of the will, can they be a means of expressing true love: a self-donation chosen in the wills of the two parties. Sex education must teach the children moral norms, which are the "guarantee for responsible personal growth in human sexuality." Christian parents will also teach the children that true love may be expressed either in the married or celibate state.

In article thirty-eight, the Holy Father reminds Christian parents that their mission to educate their children is not only rooted in their parental participation in God's creative activity, but also in the sacrament of matrimony, which they have received. Through this sacrament a miniature church is formed, which continues the mission of Christ as expressed in his offices of priest, prophet, and king. Each sacramentally married couple forms a domestic church, a specification of the universal Church, which continues the mission of Christ and exercises his triple offices within the universal Church. Therefore, the Holy Father teaches that the exercise of the prophetic office in the family is a ministry of the Church. "Thus, in the case of baptized people, the family, called together by word and sacrament as the Church of the home, is both teacher and mother, the same as the worldwide Church."

In the next article, John Paul continues his discussion of the content of proper Christian education. Parents of the baptized aim not just at human maturity, but also at an understanding and, above all, a practice of the gospel. Christian parents will introduce their children to prayer, particularly liturgical prayer. They should present their children for the reception of the sacraments at the proper times. In other words, they will assist their children to practice the priestly office of the baptized. Further, parents will aid their children in giving witness to the Faith, an exercise of the prophetic role. In supporting their children's growth in holiness, the Christian father and mother help the children attain self-control, an exercise of Christ's kingly office. In addition, parents will teach their children that the world must be restored to God's original plan, an exercise of the kingly office of the Lord in this second aspect. The motive for this admittedly laborious task is that Christian parents together with God bring new life into the world, which is destined for eternity. Parents give life to men and women called to be saints, called to share heaven forever with God. As the Pope writes, Christian parents become fully parents because "they are begetters not only of bodily life but also of the life that through the Spirit's renewal flows from the Cross and Resurrection of Christ." Finally, in this article, the Pope gives voice to the synod's request that a catechism for families be developed that could aid parents in their awesome vocation to teach their children.

In article forty, John Paul discusses the agents which support the parents in their mission of teaching their children. The parents and family have the primary but not the exclusive role in education. The Holy Father suggests that Christian families should work together with pastors and civil officials to promote the best possible education. While the Church and the state have an obligation to provide educational institutions, which families have a right to demand, both Church and state recognize that the parents have the primary role. But the parents must cooperate with civil and ecclesiastical authorities. In a closing note, the Holy Father suggests that associations of Christian families should be formed in those societies which are hostile to the Christian Faith. Such Christian family associations can offer mutual support to parents and children so that the young will not "depart from the Faith".

In the last article of this second division of Part Three, the Holy Father reminds everyone that love is a self-gift to others. Within the family, this self-gift is usually expressed through procreation and education of children. However, any act of true love toward another human being "bears witness to and perfects the spiritual fecundity of the family". Such a broad conception of familial love should comfort those families unable to transmit life because of sterility. They are not excluded from familial love because of their physical problem. On the contrary, when they respond generously to the children of other families, they give themselves in love. Many children whose parents often must struggle to provide the barest necessities would benefit from the helping hands of other adults. When parents without children, and even those who have children of their own, "adopt and foster" children, they enrich their own lives with spiritual values. Of course, this is an incomparable service to the children they take under their care. Finally, every act of charity toward the outcasts of society, the elderly, the sick, the disabled, drug addicts, and former prisoners, is an expression of the love of Christ, of proper familial love. As the Holy Father wrote in another context, "The Savior leaves his imprint on every single act of charity, as on Veronica's handkerchief."[15]

The third major division of Part Three of this document considers the expression of familial love toward society. It is titled, "Participating in the Development of Society". This division has seven articles and is the shortest of the four divisions of Part Three. In article forty-two, the Holy Father bases the role of the family in civil society on God's creative act. He quotes the Second Vatican Council: " 'Since the Creator of all things has established the conjugal partnership as the beginning and basis of human society,' the family is 'the first and vital cell of society.' " It is through the family that new members of society are conceived and nurtured. All cultures and societies should be vitally interested in the life of their families. For its part, the family serves society by giving it new members and by educating those members for their proper role as adults.

In article forty-three, John Paul suggests that it is the total self-surrender of family members to one another according

---

[15] See SC, p. 189.

to the incomparable personal dignity of each member which constitutes the most significant contribution of families to society. It is in the family that the personal dignity of human beings is affirmed. Each family member surrenders himself or herself to the other family members because each knows and understands the infinite dignity of all human beings. This value taught and affirmed in family life should be extended to other human beings. As John Paul puts it, "The family is . . . the most effective means for humanizing and personalizing society." Of course, our age is threatened with dehumanization as is evident from the many forms of escapism: alcoholism, drugs, and even suicide. The family reminds all people of their personal dignity and enriches them "with deep humanity" and places them in their "uniqueness and unrepeatability within the fabric of society". Of all the institutions in society, the family is most vital in teaching all people that they have an incomparable dignity which is realized in and through a selfless donation to others.

In the forty-fourth article, John Paul considers the social and political roles of the family. Since families affirm the incomparable dignity of their members and, by extension, of all human beings, they should reach out to all those who are in need of assistance, especially the poor. Concretely, this task can be accomplished through hospitality, the willing acceptance of others into one's home, but even more importantly, into one's heart. The practice of hospitality will not go unrewarded: "Whoever gives to one of these little ones even a cup of cold water . . . shall not lose his reward." The family, in its social role, seeks to guarantee the rights of all and this goal cannot be accomplished without some political activity. "Families should be the first to take steps to see that the laws and institutions of the State not only do not offend but support and positively defend the rights and duties of the family . . . otherwise families will be the first victims of the evils that they have done no more than note with indifference."

Having outlined the family's manifold service to society,

the Pope, in article forty-five, admonishes the state about its obligations to the family. The government must recognize that "the family is a society in its own original right." First and foremost, the state may not appropriate or give to other social institutions the duties and obligations proper to the family. Secondly, the government should assist the family to shoulder its responsibilities by offering aid in the economic, social, educational, political, and cultural spheres.

In the next article, forty-six, the Holy Father promulgates his now well-known charter of family rights. Clearly, this charter was aimed at those societies and governments which do not respect the rights of the human person or of the family. The Holy Father places the full weight of the universal Church behind the rights of the family to exist, to transmit, and to educate new life. They have a right to intimacy and privacy in the conjugal communion, and a right to a stable marital bond (supported, of course, by the civil authority). Families have the right to believe and profess their faith and the right to raise their children in accordance with their traditions. They should have physical, social, political, and economic security, adequate housing, free speech, and representation. The family has the right to associate with other families, the right to protect the young from drugs, pornography, and alcoholism, the right to wholesome recreation, and the right to emigrate. Finally, the elderly of the family have a right to a worthy life and death. This charter of family rights, together with other statements of the Church, formed the basis for the *Charter of the Rights of the Family* promulgated by the Holy See on October 22, 1983.[16]

At the beginning of this third division of Part Three, John Paul indicated that his starting point was God's creative mandate. As such, everything he has written applies to all families, Christian or not. However, in articles forty-seven and forty-

---

[16] See *Charter of the Rights of the Family, The Wanderer*, vol. 116, no. 52 (December 29, 1983), p. 6.

eight, he turns his attention to the role of Christian families in developing society. In article forty-seven, the Holy Father suggests that Christian families have a very special obligation to remake all things according to God's original plan. Christian families will offer a self-effacing witness to the dignity of all through a very special preference for the poor, the hungry, and those without families. This is part of their mission as a domestic church. However, they also receive from God the necessary graces to undertake this monumental task.

In article forty-eight, John Paul calls attention to the international scale of some issues. "It is only in worldwide solidarity that the enormous and dramatic issues of world justice, the freedom of peoples, and the peace of humanity can be dealt with and solved." Christian families, united together, can be a powerful witness to the proper order in society, i.e., to the solution of the worldwide problems in accordance with human dignity. Far from suggesting that Christian families leave hearth and home for other parts of the world, the Holy Father suggests that the proper way for Christian families to contribute to the solution of large-scale international problems is through education. If Christian married people would inform themselves and, particularly, their children about the worldwide difficulties, they would be exercising their prophetic and kingly offices in accordance with the values of the gospel. They would be contributing to the solution of the world's problems.

With these last comments about the Christian family's role in the development of society, John Paul concludes the third division of Part Three. In article forty-nine, he turns his attention to the fourth division of Part Three entitled, "Sharing in the Life and Mission of the Church", which considers the family's vocation to love within the universal mystical person of Christ. Having discussed the family's vocation to love within itself, in procreation, and in society, the Pope now devotes some remarks to the Christian family's role within the Church.

In article forty-nine, the Holy Father calls the family a "domestic church". John Paul writes that it is the Church which "gives birth to, educates, and builds up the Christian family". The Church gives birth to the family by dispensing God's grace through the sacraments. Secondly, as we have seen, it is the Church which reveals man to himself as Christ did. By extension, then, it is the Church which educates the family by revealing to the family what it is. Thirdly, it is the Church which builds up the family by guiding "the Christian family to the service of love".

The domestic church does not merely receive from the universal Church, but, "grafted into the mystery of the Church", the family has the responsibility of continuing the mission of Christ. Once activated through the hierarchy of the Church, the family has the vocation of communicating love through its participation in Christ's triple offices. The family should reveal man to himself, as Christ did, by manifesting to each and every human person his incomparable dignity and proper activity, i.e., love. Thus, the family is a "living image and historical representation of the mystery of the Church".

In article fifty, the Holy Father teaches that the family carries out its mission given to it by Christ as a community of life and love. Thus, it is the husband and wife, together with the children, who "must live their service to the Church and to the world". The family members do not accomplish the mission of Christ as isolated individuals, but rather as a familial community, as a communion of persons. Further, the Pope teaches that the mission of Christ is undertaken by the family through *"the love between husband and wife and between the members of the family"*. In and through this familial love, the priestly, prophetic, and kingly offices of Christ are exercised and expressed. Thus, the family does not accomplish the mission of Christ through unusual or newsmaking activities. Rather, the domestic church continues Christ's mission in and through the familial bonds of life and love, which are, in themselves, quite extraordinary.

Finally, he writes, "Having laid the *foundation* of the participation of the Christian family in the Church's mission, it is now time to illustrate its *substance in reference to Jesus Christ as Prophet, Priest, and King*". In the remaining articles of this fourth division of Part Three, the Holy Father considers the family's exercise of each of these dominical offices.

In articles fifty-one through fifty-four, John Paul discusses the family's participation in Christ's prophetic office. The family must first welcome the word of God as announced by the universal Church. The Pope speaks of the "obedience of faith" which spouses should offer the word of God as taught by the universal Church. In other words, the family's share in Christ's prophetic office needs to be activated by the Magisterium.

The preparation for marriage is often a journey of faith. "It is a special opportunity for the engaged to rediscover and deepen the faith received in Baptism." The celebration of the sacrament of matrimony should also be a moment of faith. The word of God reveals and " 'fulfills' the wise and loving plan of God for the married couple". This moment of faith must be lived continuously in the marriage. "In and through the events, problems, difficulties and circumstances of everyday life, God comes to them [the couple], revealing and presenting the concrete 'demands' of their sharing in the love of Christ." In other words, the couple must always welcome the word of God spoken by the Church, who is Christ. Their reception of God's word, which reveals man to himself, helps them to know themselves.

Once activated by the bishops in union with the Holy Father, the family's participation in Christ's prophetic office enables it to proclaim the Faith to others. The domestic church becomes, as the universal Church, an evangelizing community. In article fifty-two, John Paul teaches that "the future of evangelization depends in great part on the Church of the home". The task of evangelization is assumed by all at baptism, but through the sacrament of matrimony the couple's baptismal task of evangelization is strengthened and specified. The Christian married couple is called primarily to evangelize their children.

Especially under governments hostile to Christianity, it is only in the family that the children can learn about the Faith.

In articles fifty-three and fifty-four, the Pope discusses two spheres open to the family's work of evangelization. First and foremost, the parents are called to educate their children in the ways of the Faith. They must transmit the gospel to their own children. This is an education in knowledge, but also, and more essentially, an education in the practice of the Faith. Mothers and fathers must guide their children to live according to the transcendent spiritual values taught in the gospel. This teaching must be done by word, but, even more importantly, by example. If the parents live what they teach, it is likely that their children also will live well, i.e., according to the teachings of Christ. Further, it is only from a domestic church living the values of the gospel that young men and women find the strength to follow a vocation to the religious and spiritual life.

The Holy Father is well aware of the pain and difficulties which parents suffer when the adolescent or young adult challenges the faith and the lifestyle of the family. "In the Christian family, parents must face with courage and great interior serenity the difficulties that their ministry of evangelization sometimes encounters in their own children." The sufferings of parents occasioned by their work of evangelization are comparable to the sufferings of the apostles. These sufferings, as all sufferings, have value when they are united with the sufferings of Christ.

In the last paragraph of the fifty-third article, the Pope reminds us that the family's work of evangelization occurs within the universal Church and must always remain in union with the evangelizing activities of the official ecclesiastical structure. One thinks of the proper cooperation which should exist between the families of a parish and the parish school.

The second sphere open to the family's work of evangelization is the world as is described in the fifty-fourth article. Christ commanded, "Go into all the world and preach the Gospel to the whole creation." This command was given to all the baptized. It certainly pertains in a special way to the domestic church, which exists to carry out Christ's commands. The Pope first suggests that the family undertake missionary work within itself when one or more of its members do not practice the Faith. Those practicing are sent, are missionaries, to the nonpracticing members. Those who follow the teachings of Christ fulfill their mission to the others primarily by example: a good and holy life. Secondly, each Christian family gives testimony to the Faith to those "far away", to those families who have abandoned their Christian practices, and to those families or individuals unaware of the Faith. In our pluralistic society, often families do not realize that their testimony to the Faith is the impetus for others to seek instruction and baptism or to return to the Christian life. "The Christian family is called to enlighten 'by its example and its witness . . . those who seek the truth.'" In addition to their missionary activities toward their own nonpracticing members and to families unassociated with the universal Church, Christian families may also decide to work in missionary lands. This generous offer may be given for a couple's entire life or, more likely, for a part of their lives. Finally, Christian families contribute to the missionary work of the Church by raising men and women who will gladly undertake a vocation as a foreign missionary.

In articles fifty-five through sixty-two, the Holy Father discusses the family's participation in Christ's priestly office. Through the sacrament of matrimony, the priestly office of Christ in the man and the woman, now joined in marriage, is activated for expression within the family. Still, the priestly office of the domestic church continuously needs to be refreshed through the sacraments of the Church, especially penance and holy Eucharist. Within the family, the priestly office is expressed through the offering of one's life to God in the marriage. The priestly office, when activated through the hierarchical priestly office, is a means of sanctification for the couple, their children, and all others who know the family.

After an introduction to this material in article fifty-five, the

Pope considers in the next three articles (fifty-six, fifty-seven, and fifty-eight) the sacrament of matrimony, the sacrament of holy Eucharist, and the sacrament of penance respectively. In the following four articles (fifty-nine, sixty, sixty-one, and sixty-two), the Pope discusses prayer. In these four articles the Holy Father summarizes his views on family prayer, Christian parents as teachers of prayer, the distinction between liturgical and private prayer, and the relationship between prayer and life.

In article fifty-six, John Paul writes that the sacrament of matrimony "takes up again and makes specific the sanctifying grace of Baptism." By baptism people are called to love God, to give themselves to the Holy Trinity in a total self-surrender. This love of God is then expressed through charitable acts toward our neighbors, i.e., all our fellow human beings whom God loves as he loves us. In matrimony, the love of God remains primary, but the expression of that love is specified in a particular way. Those married have a vocation to express their love for God through a specific self-gift to their spouses and to any children born of this conjugal union. The sacrament of matrimony is a sacrament to be lived. It is not exhausted in the celebration of the sacramental ritual.

Of course, as we have seen, it is the sacrament of matrimony which makes the total self-surrender of a man and a woman to one another possible. Grace restores creation, which was disrupted by original sin. After sin, it is impossible for people to give themselves to others in a lifelong total union in and through their bodies because there is a "constitutive break within the human person".[17] Lust seeks something from the other and it is absolutely contrary to a self-gift. The body desires sexual pleasure. In other words, it is subject to lust. With original sin, the human intellect and will no longer dominate the body. Without this control, an act of the will does not necessarily prevail over the bodily passions. Those subject to lust (all of us) cannot give themselves in love to others. It is only grace,

[17] See TB, no. 28.

God's own life, which allows the human will again to dominate the body and its desires. Thus, it is only grace given normally through the sacraments (and when it is a question of marriage, the grace is usually given through matrimony) which enables men and women to make a total self-surrender in and through their bodies to their spouses. The divine life, grace, makes marriage in accordance with God's original plan possible.

Marriage cannot be lived without grace. Grace makes us God-like, that is, makes us holy. Therefore, all married people are called to struggle for sanctity, to become grace filled. Holiness demands sacrifice because we always must struggle against the temptations of the flesh, the world, and the devil. The temptations of the flesh did not exist for Adam and Eve, but they do for us tainted with sin. Even those with grace are tempted because grace does not restore us to the *state* of original innocence but only to the possibility of living as Adam and Eve did. Even with grace, it is a struggle to live as God wishes. Therefore, it involves sacrifice.

In article fifty-seven, John Paul makes some remarks about marriage and the Eucharist. "The Eucharist is the very source of Christian marriage." The man and the woman joined in matrimony love one another in Christ, in God's grace. This grace was won for us by Christ on the Cross. Therefore, the source of Christian marriage is the sacrifice of Christ renewed each time holy Eucharist is celebrated. So intimate is the connection between the sacraments of matrimony and the Eucharist that matrimony should normally be celebrated within the sacrifice of the Mass. Further, it is in the Eucharist that the couple is strengthened to continue their struggle for holiness and to sanctify their family. It is through the Eucharist that their priestly offices are continually activated. The couple's sharing in the Eucharist "becomes a never-ending source of missionary and apostolic dynamism for the Christian family".

In article fifty-eight, the Holy Father considers the sacrament of penance. First, everyone sins. At times, everyone is unfaithful to the vocation given in baptism. Since marriage depends on a vital living of the divine life by each of the spouses, the sacrament of penance, which restores grace after sin, is essential to all married couples. It is through penance that the spouses maintain a healthy and close relationship with the Trinity. Second, in penance, the couple discovers an essential element of divine love: mercy. Since they should live the same divine love in their union, they should experience it in order to live it in their marriage. The sacrament of penance allows them to experience the merciful love of God. Their own love for each other should then be characterized by the same trait: mercy. Of course, it is not enough to experience this mercy once. Rather, the experience must be renewed constantly if it is to be a constitutive element of their own love.

Priests pray. The married couple are priests by their baptism. Their priestly offices are activated in the sacrament of matrimony and especially in the Eucharist. Thus, they should pray. In article fifty-nine, John Paul suggests that the prayer of the married couple must be the prayer of a domestic church, of the familial communion of persons. It should be as a communion, as one flesh, that spouses pray. "Family prayer has for its very own object *family life itself*." All the moments of family life, homecomings, births, deaths, birthdays, wedding anniversaries, and even significant decisions should be occasions for family prayer. Prayers of praise, thanksgiving, petition, and contrition should all be offered at the appropriate times. It is only by prayer that the domestic church can sustain the life of the Trinity it is called to lead.

In article sixty, John Paul teaches that only by prayer can Christian parents "penetrate the innermost depths of their children's hearts and leave an impression that the future events in their lives will not be able to efface." Christian parents "by reason of their dignity and mission" are called to educate their children in prayer. In this task, the parents express their priesthood and begin to activate the baptismal priesthood of their children. The Holy Father concludes this article with a rather extensive quote from his predecessor. Pope Paul VI once asked mothers and fathers if they were fulfilling their role of educating their children in prayer. Pope Paul clearly indicated that parents teach their children to pray by praying with them, not simply by telling them to pray.

The next article considers the relationship between liturgical and private prayer. The prayer of the domestic church should always be a preparation for the liturgical prayer of the Church, especially the celebration of the Eucharist. Thus, the Eucharist activates the priesthood of the baptized for prayer, but the prayer of the baptized develops in them a desire to manifest their priesthood of Christ more fully through the fullest possible expression, the celebration of holy Eucharist. Further, such prayer should also encourage a sharing in the other sacraments of the Church at the appropriate times, especially the sacraments of baptism and confirmation. The Holy Father also reminds couples that the directives of the Council suggested that the family celebrate the Divine Office. Finally, the family should integrate its prayer into the public prayer of the Church by observing the liturgical year and its significant seasons and feasts.

In the next paragraph of this sixty-first article, the Pope discusses the times and the forms of familial prayer. The family should pray in the morning and evening, just as the universal Church does. The domestic church should pray by reading and meditating on the holy Scriptures, by preparing to receive the sacraments, by devoting and consecrating itself to the Sacred Heart, by honoring Mary with the various devotions tradition has bequeathed, by praying grace before and after meals, and by practicing the other popular devotions. John Paul, son of Poland and true son of the mother of Christ, concludes this article with a strong endorsement of the family Rosary. "She who is the Mother of Christ and of the Church is in a special way the Mother of Christian families, of domestic churches."

The Pope concludes this section on the priestly office of the family with a brief article on prayer and life. In article sixty-two, John Paul teaches that "prayer constitutes an essential part of Christian life". It is not a form of escapism, but rather it is an expression of the family's union with Christ. It also builds and nourishes that union. It is only through an ever closer bond with Christ that families can become what they are: a miniature mystical person of Christ. It is only through Christ and his grace that they can live their marital communion of persons because without grace marriage is almost impossible. Further, it is only in union with Christ that they can carry out their calling to transform the world for Christ. Since prayer manifests and builds the family's union with Christ, it is essential and, therefore, hardly escapist. Of course, family prayer will die without the sacramental ministry of the universal Church, especially the sacraments of penance and the Eucharist.

The concluding articles of Part Three consider the family's participation in Christ's kingly office. The first function of a king is to rule himself. Christ demonstrated extraordinary kingly self-rule during his Passion and death. We, through our baptism, share in that self-rule of his kingly office. Therefore, we are called to govern our own desires so that we can offer ourselves totally to God. Since spouses are called to give themselves to one another, they, through their participation in Christ's kingly office, must overcome the selfish desires of the body, which are contrary to a loving self-surrender. True love, made possible through the exercise of Christ's kingly office, should be lived within the family, but also outside of the family. The family should always treat other persons as infinitely precious gifts toward which "the only proper and adequate attitude is love".[18] In other words, the family should never use people. It should observe the personalistic norm. Just as the members of the domestic church are enabled to love God and each other through their share in Christ's kingly office, so they are able to extend that love to others in and through their Christlike kingship.

Further, it is through the exercise of Christ's kingly office

[18] See LR, p. 41.

in its first aspect, self-rule, that we possess true freedom. We are free because the bodily passions do not compel us to act one way or another. However, without this self-discipline, we indeed would be the slaves of our own passions.

In article sixty-four, after repeating the principle that the personalistic norm must be observed toward every human being, John Paul turns his attention to the second aspect of Christ's kingship: the restoration of creation according to God's original plan. Christ's kingship, in this aspect, aims at the rehabilitation of the dignity of all people in the theoretical and practical spheres. Human persons are to be treasured more than things, and therefore people should never lack what is necessary for life. Every man and woman has an infinite value, far transcending any material thing. It is contrary to the dignity of every human being that any one human person should lack the necessities of life. Their baptismal share in Christ's kingship enables all Christians to work ceaselessly for the restoration of the proper order in creation, i.e., that the dignity of all men and women would be respected both theoretically and practically. In this aspect, Christ's kingship aims at a restoration of justice for all.

With the discussion of Christ's kingship in its second aspect, the Holy Father closes Part Three. He has described the family's process of self-realization and growth in self-knowledge through the fulfillment of its mission. The mission of the domestic church is that of Christ and the Church. It is to reveal man to himself through love in accordance with the truth. The love of the family is manifested in its own communion of persons, in its procreation of children, in its service to society, and in its service to the universal Church.

In the fourth and last part of this exhortation, the Holy Father turns to practical affairs. He outlines the pastoral care which the universal Church should offer to the family.

IV. Pastoral Care of the Family: Stages, Structures, Agents, and Situations

The last part of *Familiaris Consortio*, Part Four, is divided into four sections. The titles of these divisions correspond precisely to the four elements in the title of this part: stages, structures, agents, and situations. The first division, "Stages of Pastoral Care of the Family", has five articles. The second, "Structures of Family Pastoral Care", has only three articles. The third, "Agents of the Pastoral Care of the Family", is written in four articles. The fourth, by far the largest of the four divisions, "Pastoral Care of the Family in Difficult Cases", has nine articles.

Unlike any other part of this apostolic exhortation on the family, Part Four is devoted to practical problems. In the introduction to the document John Paul indicated that he was addressing all humanity. The Pope also explained that this document was occasioned by the recent synod of bishops and the modern influences arrayed against family life prevalent in our societies. Part One defined the problems of family life today more specifically. In Part Two, John Paul examined the identity of the family. In Part Three, he studied the mission of the family. Part Four describes the practical implications of the teachings found in the introduction and the first three parts.

In article sixty-five, the Holy Father first notes that the family is a living reality. As such, it develops and grows. The Church is interested in each stage of that growth. The interest of the universal Church in the family is founded on the principle that the Christian family is a miniature mystical person of Christ. "The Christian family too shares, in communion with the Church, in the experience of the earthly pilgrimage toward the full revelation and manifestation of the Kingdom of God." The universal Church and the domestic church have the same life, the same goals, and the same mission. It would be strange if they were not interested in one another.

However, the domestic church also needs the universal mystical person of Christ. The life principle of the domestic church, the divine grace life, is granted through the universal Church. Further, the domestic church cannot fulfill its noble mission, the mission of Christ, unless the triple offices of Christ are activated through the ministry of the hierarchical ecclesiastical offices of deacon, priest, and bishop. "Therefore, it must be emphasized once more that the pastoral intervention of the Church in support of the family is a matter of urgency." For the universal Church, the pastoral care of the family must be a priority both because the family depends on this support and because the future of the universal Church is tied to the domestic church. Of course, the future of the Church passes by way of the family because evangelization depends on Christian families. Therefore, the universal Church also needs the familial church.

John Paul also teaches that the concern of the universal Church will extend to all families, and especially those in difficult situations. The Church's support for family life must be as broad as Christ's love for all men and women. The goal of the universal Church is to assist all families so that "they can come closer to that model of a family which the Creator intended from 'the beginning' and which Christ has renewed with his redeeming grace". Not only must the Church's support for families extend to all, but it must accompany the family in the "different stages of its formation and development".

The next article, sixty-six, discusses the first stage of family life, the preparation for marriage, and the role of the Church in that stage. The Holy Father notes that in some countries it is still the family itself which almost by itself transmits the true values of marriage and family life to the next generation. However, John Paul suggests that the rapid changes in most modern cultures necessitate the increased participation of the Church in the preparation of young people for marriage. He attributes some of the negative phenomena of modern family life to young men and women who found new families without the necessary hierarchy of values and without the proper criteria for behavior. They are thus ill-prepared to face the modern difficulties encountered in the conjugal union. Those who are better prepared are more apt to succeed in their vocation. What is true generally of family life is especially true for Christian married couples. The Church, for the sake of young men and women, wishes to promote family life, eliminating as many difficulties for young couples as possible.

The Holy Father suggests three distinct steps in marriage preparation: remote, proximate, and immediate. Remote preparation is the sphere of the domestic church, the family. All parents have a grave obligation to instill human and Christian values in their children. Parents should teach their children by word and example. In the family, the Child should learn about himself and then about others. Particularly, he should discover his own strengths and weaknesses. The child must be encouraged to practice self-discipline (kingly office). The parents will teach their children how to relate to others, particularly the members of the opposite sex (priestly office). The specifically Christian revelation will include catechetical instruction, which will reveal to the child the vocational possibilities, including that of virginity or celibacy (prophetic office). In short, John Paul, in this remote preparative stage, is asking parents to teach their children all that is necessary for them to love, to fulfill themselves in accordance with their very humanity as created in God's image and redeemed by the God-man.

The second step, proximate preparation, is a "catechumenal process". This involves "a more specific preparation for the sacraments, as it were a rediscovery of them". The young people should come to a more profound understanding of the sacraments so that they might better live the sacrament of matrimony. Clearly, without the other sacraments, the Christian family cannot fulfill the mission of Christ, which is its special charge. Therefore, all Christian married couples need to understand the significance and magnificence of all the sacraments. This religious preparation must be accompanied by a practical education in other aspects necessary to a successful marriage. First and foremost, marriage will be presented as an "interpersonal relationship" and it will include an examination of "conjugal sexuality and responsible parenthood, with the essential medical and biological knowledge connected with it". It is clear from this passage and from what John Paul taught earlier regarding natural family planning[1] that those preparing for marriage should be taught fertility awareness. Since he includes this task under proximate preparation (not immediate preparation) and since he refers to young people in this passage, he wishes this awareness taught in the middle or late teen years, i.e., in the high school years. Other practical matters, e.g., financial considerations, administration, proper care of children, and housekeeping should be taught in this preparative step toward marriage. Finally, the young people should be prepared for the "family apostolate, for fraternal solidarity and collaboration with other families, for active membership in groups, associations, movements and undertakings set up for the . . . benefit of the family".

Immediate preparation occurs in the months and weeks before the marriage and it should give "new meaning, content and form to the so-called premarital inquiry required by Canon Law". This preparation is necessary in every case, but especially needed by those couples who have doubts and difficulties with Christian doctrine and practice. John Paul also calls this step a "journey of faith which is similar to the catechumenate". The couple should come to appreciate more profoundly the

[1] See FC, no. 33.

mysteries of Christ, the Church, grace, and their responsibilities within the domestic church. This step will also involve liturgical preparation so that the couple will take an active and conscious part in the sacramental ritual.

In the next paragraph of this article, John Paul asks that the entire ecclesial community involve itself in the preparation of the young for marriage. He asks that the episcopal conferences publish a *Directory of the Pastoral Care of the Family*, which would establish the minimums required for the marriage preparation course. Finally, in the last paragraph of this article, John Paul, while affirming the necessity of proper preparation for matrimony, adds that its omission "is not an impediment to the celebration of marriage". By baptism, people have a right to the sacraments, including matrimony, and marital preparation cannot be added as an *absolute* requirement for marriage. Still, as John Paul teaches, dispensations from it should not be granted easily.

In the next article, sixty-seven, the Holy Father considers the actual celebration of the sacrament of matrimony. "Christian marriage normally requires a liturgical celebration expressing in social and community form the essentially ecclesial and sacramental nature of the conjugal covenant between baptized persons." The ritual celebration is a sacrament, a sign, and an act of the Church. John Paul examines each of these aspects individually.

As a sacrament, the matrimonial ritual should be sanctifying. As such it must be *"per se* valid, worthy, and fruitful". Pastors must ensure that the requirements of the conjugal covenant are satisfied. Further, the discipline of the Church regarding free consent, impediments, canonical form, and the celebration of the sacrament must be observed. "The celebration should be simple and dignified" according to the norms issued by the Apostolic See. Elements from each culture may be included provided they are in harmony with Christian beliefs and morality.

As a sign, the ritual should include "a proclamation of the word of God and a profession of faith on the part of the community of believers". Pastoral care should be apparent in the careful choice of texts for the Liturgy of the Word and in the catechesis preceding the profession of faith. The catechesis should particularly benefit the two who are to be married.

As a sacramental act of the Church, the celebration of marriage should include the active participation of all the faithful present including the priest, the bride and the bridegroom, the witnesses, relatives, and friends.

In article sixty-seven, the Holy Father examined the celebration of marriage for believing Christians. In the following article, sixty-eight, he considers the pastoral dilemma encountered when nonbelieving, baptized Christians present themselves for marriage. John Paul first notes that a nonpracticing or even a nonbelieving couple can rediscover the riches of the Faith through the marriage preparation process. Priests and those involved in marriage preparation should carefully nourish the faith which a couple does have and "bring it to maturity". However, "pastors must also understand the reasons that lead the Church also to admit to the celebration of marriage those who are imperfectly disposed". Clearly, the Holy Father teaches that every benefit of doubt must be given to the couple wishing to marry.

Since the sacrament of matrimony, unlike all the other sacraments, concerns a reality already established in God's creative act, the decision of a man and a woman to marry "really involves, even if not in a fully conscious way, an attitude of profound obedience to the will of God, an attitude which cannot exist without God's grace". For John Paul, even a couple with a weak faith is blessed with God's grace because in the decision to marry, the couple is cooperating with God's will as expressed in his creative act. Provided the intentions of the bride and the groom correspond to God's intentions in creation, they have "already begun what is in a true and proper sense a journey toward salvation". Through the preparatory stages, but, above all, in the marriage, God's grace will increase and develop and their faith will become stronger. In addition to their cooperation with God's original intentions "in the beginning", the baptized bride and groom are joined to Christ and the Church through their baptism. In accepting God's plan for marriage, they "at least implicitly consent to what the Church intends to do" when marriage is celebrated. Further, the sacrament of matrimony strengthens and nourishes their baptismal faith. Rather than a necessity for matrimony, an increased faith is a result of the sacrament. For these reasons the Holy Father, while acknowledging that many couples approach a pastor wishing to marry for social reasons, teaches that couples may not be refused marriage simply because social motives play a part in their decision.

John Paul is reluctant to establish any firm criteria beyond those already mentioned because these might encourage "unfounded and discriminatory judgments". Further, such guidelines might cause doubts about valid marriages celebrated in previous years. Thirdly, these criteria might question the validity of the marriages of non-Catholic, but baptized, Christians.

However, toward the end of this article, the Pope does state explicitly what has been implicit in his remarks. A pastor may not witness a marriage, even of the baptized, if the bride and the groom "show that they reject explicitly and formally what the Church intends to do when the marriage of baptized persons is celebrated". The Holy Father asks the pastor in such a situation to explain to the couple that the Church is not causing the problem. Rather, it is the man and the woman themselves who are placing an insurmountable obstacle in the way of their proposed union.

In the sixty-ninth article, the Pope reminds his readers that the Church's pastoral care of families does not end with the celebration of marriage. The Church should offer help and support to all families, but especially to the newly married as they face the difficulties in adapting to one another and to children. All members of the local ecclesial community, but especially experienced families, should offer their advice and support to younger families. The Christian community should be a "great family made up of Christian families". The younger families should receive readily the counsels of the older ones and then, in their turn, they should take their rightful place in the ranks of the experienced helping the newly married. Further, the older families will benefit from the " witness of life and practical contribution" of the younger families. The Holy Father believes that an association of Christian families will be the most effective means of transmitting the Christian values which are the chief content of the Church's pastoral care. He cites two Christian values which are of particular importance. First, a husband and a wife should love responsibly, that is, they should love each other in accordance with the marital requirements of communion and service to life. Therefore, after the birth of children, the Pope promises parents that the Church will remain close to them so that "they may accept their children and love them as a gift received from the Lord". Second, the husband and the wife should "harmonize the intimacy of home life with the generous shared work of building up the Church and society". With these remarks on the Church's pastoral care for existing families, the Holy Father concludes the first division of Part Four, "Stages of Pastoral Care of the Family".

After a brief introduction, John Paul begins the second division of Part Four, "Structures of Family Pastoral Care", by noting that the universal Church is "expressed and actuated" in the local church, the diocese, which, in turn, is divided into parishes. The local church, indeed every parish, must take responsibility for the pastoral care of families. In fact, the Pope asks that all pastoral undertakings include the apostolate of family pastoral care. John Paul also notes that it is necessary for priests and religious to be prepared to shoulder the burdens and obligations of extending the Church's support to families. He suggests that during their time of formation, future men and women religious prepare themselves for the family apostolate. He asks that priests enroll in specialized courses before accepting parish assignments. He notes with approval the recent foundation of the John Paul II Institute on Marriage and the Family of the Lateran University. He also mentions some bishops who have established similar institutions. Obviously, many more such institutions will be necessary if priests and religious are to be properly prepared for the family apostolate.

The baptized husband and wife form a domestic church, a miniature person of Christ. As such, they are called to carry on the mission of Christ in the world. They are apostles of Christ formed and called through the sacrament of matrimony. Their apostolic work is, first and foremost, to families. Christian married couples will witness to a holy life and strive to form their children in accordance with the gospel. They will help their children mature in the Faith, educate them in chastity, prepare them for life, protect them from "the ideological and moral dangers with which they are often threatened". Christian parents will carry out their mission and gradually introduce their children to the larger community of the Church and civil society. They will also help their children discern their vocation. Further, the Christian family will reach beyond itself to aid all those in need of the charity of Christ, especially those who are poor, sick, old, handicapped, orphaned, widowed, and abandoned by their spouses. Christian families will extend their charity to unmarried mothers and mothers-to-be who are in difficult situations and who might be tempted to abort their children. The family itself is one of the most important structures of the Church's apostolate to families.

In article seventy-two, the Holy Father discusses associations of Christian families which extend familial pastoral care to those in need. These associations of "spirituality, formation and apostolate" should foster a "sense of solidarity" among all Christians. Such associations, in a small way, should reflect or mirror the communion of persons in Christ, i.e., the Church. The Pope also urges that couples join nondenominational family associations. He mentions especially those which exist to transmit, preserve, and protect "wholesome ethical, and cultural values". He also praises other associations which "work for the building of a more just and human world", and for education. Thus, in addition to the specifically religious associations of families, it is proper for Christian families to be active in more secular familial associations which, nevertheless, promote the dignity and rights of all men and women. With these reflections on associations of families, John Paul concludes the second division of Part Four, "Structures of Family Pastoral Care".

After a one-sentence introduction, which acknowledges that the Christian family is an agent and a recipient of the Church's pastoral care, the Holy Father begins the third division of Part Four, "Agents of the Pastoral Care of the Family". In four articles, he discusses bishops and priests, men and women religious, lay specialists, and agents of social communications, as the agents of the family apostolate. In this division, he does not mention the family as an agent because the role of the Christian family in extending pastoral care to other families has already been discussed in the second division of Part Four.

In the first sentence of article seventy-three, the Holy Father clearly states that the bishop is the one most responsible for extending the support of the Church to families in his diocese. The bishop must devote to this apostolate "personal interest, care, time, personnel and resources, but above all personal support for the families". The diocese, under the bishop, should become a family of Christians, a concrete expression of the ecclesial communion of persons. John Paul notes the foundation of the Pontifical Council for the Family as evidence of the importance he, as the Vicar of Christ, attributes to the family apostolate.

The bishops are aided by their priests and deacons, who should support all families, but especially those experiencing suffering and difficulties. The ordained should help all families "to see their lives in light of the gospel". The priests and deacons will, in turn, if this apostolate is undertaken "with due discernment and with a truly apostolic spirit", be encouraged in their own vocations. Deacons and priests, after the proper preparation, will become fathers, brothers, pastors, and teachers of the truth. However, "their teaching and advice must therefore always be in full harmony with the authentic Magisterium of the Church". This is necessary if the truth is to be taught. Further, with the unity established through fidelity to the Magisterium, the faithful will not be scandalized by different judgments. There will be a unity. This is the third time in this document that John Paul has urged fidelity to the Magisterium by priests and deacons. It is obviously something very close to his heart.

In the last paragraph of this article, the Pope summarizes the share in Christ's prophetic office which the baptized, the ordained, the married, and the theologians have. "In the Church, the pastors and the laity share in the prophetic mission of Christ." The laity witness to the Faith in their lives. The pastors distinguish what is genuine and what is not in harmony with the Faith in this witness of the laity. Families exercise their prophetic office in their unique witness to the plan of God for marriage. Theologians should offer their expertise by explaining exactly the teachings of the Magisterium. However, "the proximate and obligatory norm in the teaching of the Faith . . . belongs to the hierarchical Magisterium." All Catholics must acknowledge the essential prophetic ministry of the Holy Father and the bishops. Without the activation of the prophetic office of the baptized by the hierarchy, Christ's mission cannot be properly fulfilled.

In article seventy-four, John Paul discusses the role of men and women religious in the family apostolate. First and foremost, those who have embraced the evangelical counsels serve Christian families by their example. Their virginal and celibate lives testify to the inherent goodness of marriage. The religious do not remain unmarried because marriage is meaningless, but rather because it is such an unfathomable treasure. They show their love for God in surrendering an inherently good and noble way of life, marriage. Second, they "are witnesses to that universal charity", the charity of Christ, "which, through chastity embraced for the Kingdom of heaven, makes them ever more available to dedicate themselves generously to the service of God and to the works of the apostolate". This charity is also the animating principle of Christian marriage. When couples see the example of religious, they should be encouraged in their own vocations.

Those religious institutes active in the world should develop an apostolate to families. The Pope asks that they be particularly solicitous toward children, especially if they are abandoned, orphaned, handicapped, or unwanted. Religious can and should have a special apostolate to the sick and toward single-parent families. Priests, brothers, and sisters in religious institutes can also offer invaluable assistance preparing young people for family life especially in regards to responsible fertility. Religious houses, in the tradition of Saint Benedict, should offer magnanimous hospitality toward all those seeking a sense of God's presence and a holy way of life. In concluding this article, John Paul urgently asks that all superiors of religious orders, while respecting the proper work of their orders, make the family apostolate an important priority.

In the next article, seventy-five, the Pope considers lay specialists as agents of familial pastoral care. Among lay specialists are lawyers, doctors, psychologists, social workers, consultants, and many others. These experts have a mission to families and since "the future of the world and of the Church passes through the family", the work of these specialists has an effect on all society and on the Church. Their work is truly a mission to the Church and to the world.

In article seventy-six, John Paul discusses the role of social communications as an agent or, as is often the case, a counteragent, of the familial apostolate. While acknowledging the media's potential beneficial effects, John Paul also warns of the dangers inherent in the mass media. The Pope realizes the potential for harm when the mass media are employed to encourage programs and information harmful to human values. He also mentions the media's potential for inculcating "divisive ideologies", i.e., propaganda. There can be little doubt that John Paul, son of Poland that he is, has had firsthand experience of media employed as propaganda weapons. These dangers are enhanced by the modern patterns of life, especially in the industrialized nations. The presence of television and certain publications in almost every home makes it easy for parents to shirk their responsibilities to educate and to entertain their children. Parents have a grave obligation to protect their children from "forms of aggression they are subjected to by the mass media" and to ensure a proper use of the media for education and entertainment. Parents should also seek other entertainment for their children so that they are introduced to a variety of possible activities for recreation. Above all, through a proper and discerning use of the mass media, the children will develop a properly formed conscience in this regard and at the appropriate time, they will be able to make the correct judgments on the programs and information presented to them in the media.

John Paul also asks that families participate in the development and selection of programs for the media. He asks producers and others involved in this process to be aware and attentive to the needs of families. The Pope concludes with a firm endorsement of those working in the media and assures them that the Church relies on their responsibility and good will. At the same time, the Church encourages all Catholics who are interested in such endeavors and possess the requisite talents, to work in this field in support of the mission of Christ, i.e., the mission of the domestic church. With these reflections on the agents of the family apostolate, the Holy Father concludes the third division of Part Four.

Article seventy-seven begins the fourth and last division of Part Four, "Pastoral Care of the Family in Difficult Cases". In nine different articles, the Holy Father suggests pastoral approaches to the difficult circumstances in which families sometimes find themselves.

In the first article of this division, John Paul discusses those families which are in need of special assistance because of economic, juridical, and cultural structures in their society.

In this category the Pope numbers the families of migrant workers and the families of those who must be away for long periods, e.g., sailors, soldiers, prisoners. The Pope includes the growing number of exiled families in this category as well as single-parent families and those with children handicapped or addicted to drugs. He numbers in this group those without homes and those in large cities who, with little or no money, live as outcasts. Families who experience discrimination or who are ideologically divided need some special considerations. Teenage married couples and the elderly also are in need of more specialized pastoral care.

In the next three paragraphs of this article, John Paul considers three types of families from the above list. In the first paragraph, he outlines the Church's proper response to the families of migrant workers. First, the Pope asks that the Church be the home for all migrant workers. In order that these people would feel at home in the Church, he asks that, as far as possible, priests of their own rite and language be assigned to shepherd them. John Paul also assures these people that the Church constantly appeals to the public conscience so that these people can find work at just wages in their own homelands; so that they can be reunited with their families; so that their cultural identity will be respected; so that their children can receive a proper education; and so that they may own the land they need for living and working.

In the next paragraph, the Holy Father discusses the ideologically divided family, i.e., the interfaith family. He asks that personal contact be maintained with all such families and that the faith of the Catholic party be strengthened and supported. Further, Catholic spouses, while not surrendering their faith, must constantly dialogue with their spouses. "Love and respect must be freely shown." In addition, even beliefs directly contrary to the Faith "can stimulate the believing members of the family".

The Church "cannot ignore the time of old age" when married love can be deepened, but when, too, there is often lone-

liness. The elderly suffer profoundly when they are or believe
they are abandoned by their children. Ill-health not only sometimes causes the suffering of bodily pain, but often brings the
psychological suffering of dependence on others. With these
sufferings, it is often pastorally beneficial to remind the elderly of their participation in the death and Resurrection of
the Lord. John Paul also considers a number of special circumstances which occur in many families and which demand tactful
handling on the part of pastors. These occasions include the
children's adolescence, the marriage of the children, abandon-
ment by a spouse, and the death of a spouse or the death of
another family member. The Holy Father concludes this article with the admonition of that prayer, "the source of light
and strength and the nourishment of Christian hope", is always
necessary.

In the next article, seventy-eight, the Pope makes some
remarks about mixed, i.e., interfaith, marriages. First, John
Paul considers the freedom of both spouses. It is imperative
that Catholics remain free to practice their faith, and to baptize
and raise their children Catholic. It sometimes happens that the
religious freedom of the Catholic party is violated by obstacles
placed in the way of a free exercise of the Faith or of the baptism
and education of the children. The religious freedom of the non-
Catholic party also might be violated by an attempt to pressure
him or her into becoming a Catholic. Both these pitfalls should
be avoided.

Second, the canonical and liturgical necessities for marriage
must be observed, but bishops should use their faculties to meet
the pastoral necessities of their dioceses. Particular attention
should be given to marriage preparation so that the problems
noted above do not occur and so that both parties to the
marriage understand Catholic teaching, especially as it pertains
to marriage. Further, the faith of the Catholic party must be
strengthened by the community in order that he or she will
become a powerful witness to the Faith for the spouse and the
children.

Third, the Holy Father suggests that the mixed marriages of Catholics to other Christians, provided both the husband and the wife are faithful to their religious practices, have an ecumenical value. Especially in the sphere of moral and spiritual values, the couple is as united as the Christian churches are. To encourage this ecumenical spirit, a cordial relationship between the priest and the non-Catholic minister should be established, especially before the wedding. Of course, the non-Catholic spouse cannot receive the Eucharist except for the cases cited in the norms on intercommunion promulgated by the Secretariat for Promoting Christian Unity.

Finally, in the last paragraph of this article, John Paul remarks that marriages between Catholics and the nonbaptized are growing in numbers. When the nonbaptized party professes another religion, his or her beliefs must be treated with respect. However, in many cases the nonbaptized person has no religion at all. In these instances, the episcopal conferences and the local bishops should ensure that there are some safeguards for the Faith of the Catholic party. The bishops should assist the Catholic in such marriages not only to practice the Faith, but also to baptize and to educate the children as Catholics. Further, the Catholic party should be assisted in an effort to offer a genuine witness to the Catholic Faith.

In article seventy-nine, the Holy Father introduces the topic of families in irregular marital situations. Increasingly, even Catholics find themselves in these situations.

In the eightieth article, John Paul discusses trial marriages. By this term the Pope apparently means those marriages which are public, but which are not permanent because the spouses only intend to test each other. These are unacceptable as is clear from human reason and from the Faith. A human being cannot be the subject or object of an experiment. The dignity of all human beings requires that they should always be "the term of a self-giving love without limitations of time or of any other circumstance." Further, the Church, for reasons derived from the Faith, "cannot admit such a kind of union". Marriage of the baptized is a true sign of the union of Christ and the Church, which is not a temporary or trial union! Between the baptized, there can exist only an indissoluble union, the very opposite of a so-called trial marriage.

Pastorally, the Pope notes that it is difficult to overcome the situation of those involved in a trial marriage unless the two people involved have been taught since childhood, with the help of God's grace, to control their desires so that each could make a truly free self-donation to another in love. Only a genuine education in love and the "right use of sexuality" introduces the man and the woman to true love. Since Christ's teachings are founded on love, when a man and a woman understand love, they will come to understand Christ. With this understanding, they will know that trial marriages are contrary to true love. John Paul remarks that it would be useful to discover the causes of this phenomenon, including the psychological and sociological causes, so that a proper remedy might be found.

In the next article, eighty-one, the Pope discusses free unions, unions without any publicly recognized bond. The Holy Father outlines the reasons for the increasing frequency of these free unions. Some contend that if they contracted a regular marriage they would lose economic advantages or suffer harm or discrimination. However, others enter such unions because they scorn society, the family, or the social and political order. Others simply are seeking pleasure. Nevertheless, there are those "driven to such situations by extreme ignorance or poverty, sometimes by a conditioning due to situations of real injustice". There are those who are psychologically immature and therefore afraid of a permanent union. In some societies, it is customary for the marriage to be celebrated only after a period of cohabitation.

There are serious religious and social consequences which originate in these free unions. In the religious sphere, there is scandal, the loss of the sacramental grace of matrimony, and the weakening of the concept that marriage is a sign of God's Covenant with his people. In the social sphere, there is the destruction of the concept of the family, the weakening of the sense of fidelity, possible psychological damage to the children, and the increase of selfishness.

Through the activity of pastors and laity, the Church should study each case separately because the circumstances vary with each instance. Once familiar with the situation and its causes, the ecclesial community should patiently and charitably enable the couple to understand the need to regularize their union. However, the Pope asks for a campaign of prevention primarily by teaching the young a sense of fidelity to the spouse and instructing them in the conditions and structures necessary to such fidelity. The young should come to appreciate the sacrament of matrimony as a wonderful gift from God. Further, the public authorities should be approached so that they would hinder the tendencies "which divide society and are harmful to the dignity, security and welfare of the citizens as individuals". In addition, those in public office should try to shape public opinion so that it would support marriage and family life rather than hinder it. Finally, the Pope firmly admonishes civil officials to ensure that young people are not burdened by extreme poverty resulting from unjust social and economic structures. The authorities must provide the circumstances favorable to legitimate marriage, e.g., a family wage, decent housing, and opportunities for work.

In the next article, eighty-two, the Holy Father considers those Catholics who are united in civil unions. "Their situation cannot of course be likened to that of people simply living together without any bond at all because . . . there is at least a certain commitment to a properly defined . . . state of life." Catholics united in a civil union, while often reserving the right to divorce one another, do accept the civil responsibilities and obligations of marriage. Still, these unions are not acceptable to the Church. Pastors should patiently explain to these men and women that there should be a consistency between their choice of life and their faith. Such couples should be invited to regularize their union. But "while treating them with great charity . . . pastors of the Church will regrettably not be able to admit them to the sacraments." In the eyes of the Church, Catholics in a civil union are not married. They are living with someone who is not their spouse. Therefore, they cannot be invited to receive the sacraments until they repent of their sin.

In the next article, eighty-three, John Paul considers those who are separated and those who are civilly divorced from their spouse. Marriages do break apart. Sometimes there is a lack of understanding or an inability to enter into interpersonal relationships. Whatever the reasons, separation should be considered only after all possible avenues of reconciliation have been tried and have failed. After the separation, the two spouses, but especially the innocent party, suffer loneliness and many other difficulties. The Church must offer support and assistance to both spouses so that they might be able to "preserve their fidelity even in their difficult situation". Above all, the Church must help such spouses to forgive so that they might be ready to return to the married life should that prove possible. Those who are divorced and realize that their union was a valid and indissoluble marital bond give a particularly powerful witness to the Church when they do not enter a new union. For these people, the Church's support and assistance are even more important than for separated spouses. Of course, both the separated and the civilly divorced may receive the sacraments as long as there is no attempted second union.

John Paul considers the last and most difficult of the irregular situations in the eighty-fourth article: the divorced and the remarried. Many Catholics who are divorced remarry. "The Church . . . cannot abandon to their own devices those who have been previously bound by sacramental marriage and who have attempted a second marriage." The Church will always try to bring these people the graces necessary for salvation.

The Pope admonishes pastors to discern the various situations very carefully. He distinguishes between "those who have sincerely tried to save their first marriage and have been unjustly abandoned, and those who through their own grave fault

have destroyed a canonically valid marriage". Second, he notes
that there are those who have entered into a second union for
the sake of their children or because they are "subjectively certain in conscience that their previous and irreparably destroyed
marriage had never been valid". The Church must assist the
divorced and remarried, and encourage them to practice their
faith by attending Mass, by praying, by contributing to the
works of justice and charity, by educating their children in the
Faith, by cultivating a spirit of penance, and by imploring God's
grace. For its part, the Church will pray for these people.

However, the divorced and remarried cannot be admitted
to the sacraments. They cannot receive Holy Communion
because "their state and condition of life objectively contradict
that union of love between Christ and the Church which
is signified and effected by the Eucharist". Further, to admit
the divorced and remarried to the holy Eucharist would cause
confusion about the Church's teaching on the indissolubility
of marriage.

The divorced and remarried also cannot receive the sacrament of penance unless they are willing to repent from breaking
"the sign of the Covenant and of fidelity to Christ . . . [and] to
undertake a way of life that is no longer in contradiction to the
indissolubility of marriage". In practice, divorced and remarried
Catholics may be admitted to the sacrament of penance if they
separate from their (second) spouses. If separation is not feasible,
John Paul allows one possibility for the divorced and remarried
Catholic to be admitted to the sacrament of penance. When a
couple cannot separate because of the children or some other
grave reason, they may receive the sacrament of penance if they
"take on themselves the duty to live in complete continence,
that is, by abstinence from the acts proper to married couples."
Of course, once reconciled in the sacrament of penance, the
Catholic may receive holy Eucharist.

In the next paragraph, the Pope indicates that the Church
cannot "perform ceremonies of any kind for divorced people
who remarry". Pastors may not engage in any such ceremonies

because of the respect owed to the sacrament of matrimony, to the couple themselves, and to the community of the faithful. Any such ceremony would give the impression that the Church is celebrating a new and sacramentally valid marriage and this, in turn, would "lead people into error concerning the indissolubility of a validly contracted marriage".

In the next paragraph, John Paul reminds his readers again that the Church is faithful to the truths taught by Christ and that this fidelity to truth is the highest expression of care and concern for all men and women. It is only when we know the truth that we shape ourselves into what we are: images of God. To teach the truth to the divorced and remarried as the Church does is an act of true love and compassion. To deny the truth is not compassion, even when the truth is a hard saying. Those who deny truth deny Christ, who is ultimately our only answer to the most pressing questions of life and death. This is hardly compassion! It leads people away from the only one who can overcome the most pressing difficulties.

The Pope concludes this article with an extraordinary statement. He writes that "those who have rejected the Lord's command and are still living in this state will be able to obtain from God the grace of conversion and salvation, provided that they have persevered in prayer, penance and charity." In this single sentence, John Paul promises salvation even to those who are living in a sinful union. This is an extraordinary promise from the highest authority in the Church. In effect, the Holy Father assures the divorced and remarried that God will find a solution to their particular problem, if they will only continue to pray, do penance, and to practice charity.

In article eighty-five, the Holy Father considers those who are without a family. He believes that they are particularly close to the Heart of Christ and that they should receive affection and solicitude from the pastors of the Church. Some are without a family because of extreme poverty, which causes a host of other difficulties, e.g., promiscuity, lack of housing, irregular and unstable relationships, and the extreme lack of education.

Others have simply been left alone in the world. The Pope reiterates his appeal to the civil authorities to find solutions to the extreme poverty existing in some parts of the world. He also asks families to participate in solving these difficulties.

The Pope assures those without a family, whether caused by poverty or other reasons, that the doors of the Church are open to them. The Church, particularly in its diocesan and parochial expressions, "is a home and family for everyone" especially the homeless.

With this last article discussing those without a family, John Paul concludes Part Four of *Familiaris Consortio*. In Part Four, he has discussed the stages, structures, and agents of pastoral care, as well as some difficult cases. It is an admirable closing section to this immensely rich document on the family. His conclusion to the entire document is found in article eighty-six.

Conclusion to the Document

At the end of this exhortation, as at its beginning, the Holy Father turns again directly to his readers. He assures married couples, fathers and mothers, young men and women (the future of the Church and of the world), bishops and priests, the religious, and all upright men and women who have an interest in the family, that *"the future of humanity passes by way of the family"*. It is urgent, for the sake of humanity, that everyone should "foster the values and requirements of the family". In other words, John Paul is asking everyone to teach others the values which he has described and explained in this document on the family. He asks the sons and daughters of the Church to exert a special effort in teaching familial values because they through the Faith have the full knowledge of God's plan. "They therefore have an extra reason for caring for the reality that is the family in this time of trial and of grace. They must *show the family special love.*" Those who love the family foster the true values of familial life. They help the family overcome the evils which threaten these values and they support and encourage families in the difficult situations of the present age. Christians should love with a special joy because they have the good news of the gospel.

The Holy Father again reminds us that the Church does not impose its teaching on anyone. Rather, the Church, the mystical person of Christ, proposes the truth about humanity as Christ did. The Church reveals man to himself as Christ did. But the truth about us sometimes involves hard sayings. The truth is hard not in and of itself, but rather because it is difficult for historical man, the man tainted with sin, to follow. But the cross is always part of any Christian life. The Christian family will have its crosses, but any attempt to eliminate the cross results not in less difficulties, but in many, many more. Families, domestic churches, must carry their crosses with Christ. True compassion is helping each family bear its crosses. Therefore, the Pope, even in the conclusion, addresses another appeal to all people to work together to benefit families. However, the true values of family life must always be maintained. To deny the truth is not compassion, but rather cruelty. It leads to the destruction of human beings who, as images of God, are made to know the truth.

At the very end of this long document, John Paul invokes the protection of the Holy Family of Nazareth on all families. He notes the hidden life of God at Nazareth as well as the poverty, persecution, and exile which the Holy Family underwent. Having experienced these sufferings, the Holy Family "will not fail to help Christian families—indeed all the families in the world—to be faithful to their day-to-day duties, to bear the cares and tribulations of life, to be open and generous to the needs of others, and to fulfill with joy the plan of God in their regard."

The next three paragraphs are in the form of a prayer addressed to Saint Joseph, the Blessed Virgin, and Christ. The Vicar of Christ calls on Saint Joseph to "guard, protect and enlighten families". The Polish Pope with an authentic and profound devotion to the Mother of God asks her to be not just the mother of the universal Church, but also to be the mother of domestic churches. He asks her "motherly aid" in shaping the family into a true miniature mystical person of Christ animated by the divine life. He suggests that she should be an example to all families in her humble acceptance of the will of God in her life and especially as the mother of sorrows who bore the difficulties and sufferings occasioned by the Passion and crucifixion of her Son. The Pope asks Mary to "comfort the sufferings and dry the tears of those in distress because of the difficulties of their families". Finally, John Paul asks Christ to "be present in every Christian home as he was at Cana". Since this document was promulgated on November 22, 1981, the feast of Christ the King, the Pope asks the Lord to assist all families in furthering the Kingdom of God on earth, "a kingdom of truth and life, a kingdom of holiness and grace, a kingdom of justice, love, and peace".

> I entrust each family to Him [Christ], to Mary, and to Joseph. To their hands and their hearts I offer this Exhortation: may it be they who present it to you, venerable Brothers and beloved sons and daughters, and may it be they who open your hearts to the light that the Gospel sheds on every family.
>
> I assure you all of my constant prayers and I cordially impart the apostolic blessing to each and every one of you, in the name of the Father, and of the Son, and of the Holy Spirit.
>
> Given in Rome, at Saint Peter's, on the twenty-second day of November, the Solemnity of Our Lord Jesus Christ, Universal King, in the year 1981, the fourth of the Pontificate.

With these words, which must come from the heart of His Holiness, John Paul concludes the most significant document on the family ever promulgated by a pope. The authors hope that this commentary will encourage many to study this immensely rich document. Even more it is hoped that the truths and values taught in this exhortation will enable all families to have the joy and peace, even amidst difficulties, which only the truth and deeds in accordance with the truth, can bring.

Bibliography

THE WORKS OF KAROL WOJTYLA (POPE JOHN PAUL II)

The Acting Person. Edited by Anna-Teresa Tymieniecka. Translated by Andrzej Potocki. Vol. 10: *Analecta Husserliana: The Yearbook of Phenomenological Research*. Dordrecht, Holland: D. Reidel Publishing Company, 1979.

Charter of the Rights of the Family. The Wanderer. Vol. 116, no. 52 (December 29, 1983), p. 6.

"A Discipline That Ennobles Human Love." *L'Osservatore Romano*. (English Edition.) Vol. 17, no. 36 (September 3, 1984), pp. 1, 6.

Dives in Misericordia, On the Mercy of God. Boston: Saint Paul Editions, 1981.

Familiaris Consortio, Apostolic Exhortation, The Role of the Christian Family in the Modern World. Boston: Daughters of Saint Paul.

"God Works through the Sacrament of Penance". *The Wanderer*. Vol. 114, no. 15 (April 9, 1981), p. 9.

"Jesus Christ, Living Peace and Living Justice" (Homily of His Holiness at the Mass in Yankee Stadium on October 2, 1979). *The Pope in America*. St. Paul: Wanderer Press, 1979, pp. 25–27.

Laborem Exercens, On Human Work. L'Osservatore Romano. (English Edition.) Vol. 14, no. 38 (September 21, 1981), pp. 1–13.

Love and Responsibility. Translated by H. T. Willetts. New York: Farrar, Straus, Giroux, 1981.

"Peace through Truth and Justice" (Address of His Holiness to the United Nations on October 2, 1979). *The Pope in America*. St. Paul: Wanderer Press, 1979, pp. 11–18.

Redemptor Hominis, The Redeemer of Man. L'Osservatore Romano. (English Edition.) Vol. 12, no. 12 (March 19, 1979), pp. 3–14.

"Remain Faithful to the Universal Magisterium" (Address of His Holiness Delivered in Chicago to a Plenary Assembly of the Bishops of the United States on October 5, 1979), *The Pope in America*. St. Paul: Wanderer Press, 1979, pp. 53–58.

Salvifici Doloris, The Christian Meaning of Human Suffering. Origins. Vol. 13, no. 37 (February 23, 1984), pp. 609, 610–24.

Sign of Contradiction. Translated by Saint Paul Publications. New York: Seabury Press, 1979.

Sources of Renewal: The Implementation of Vatican II. Translated by P. S. Falla. New York: Harper and Row, 1980.

Theology of the Body (A series of sixty-three addresses at the Wednesday audiences.) *L'Osservatore Romano*. (English Edition.) Vol. 12, nos. 37–40, 42, 44–48, 51–53 (September 10, 17, 24, October 1, 15, 29, November 5, 12, 19, 26, December 17, 24, 1979). Vol. 13, nos. 1–3, 5–8, 10–11, 13–14, 16–18, 20, 22–23, 25–26, 30–46, 49–50, 52 (January 7, 14, 21, February 4, 11, 18, 25, March 10, 17, 31, April 8, 21, 28, May 5, 19, June 2, 9, 23, 30, July 28, August 4, 11, 25, September 1, 8, 15, 22, 29, October 6, 13, 20, 27, November 3, 10, 17, December 9, 15, 29, 1980). Vol. 14, nos. 2–3, 5–7, 12, 14–19 (January 12, 19, February 2, 9, 16, March 23, April 6, 13, 21, 27. May 4, 11, 1981). This series can also be found in the two-volume series: *Original Unity of Man and Woman: Catechesis on the Book of Genesis* and *Blessed Are the Pure of Heart: Catechesis on the Sermon on the Mount and Writings of Saint Paul.* Boston: Saint Paul Editions, 1981, 1983.

WORKS OF THE SECOND VATICAN COUNCIL

(The works of the Second Vatican Council are all cited from *Documents of Vatican II.* Edited by Austin P. Flannery. Grand Rapids, Mich.: William B. Eerdmans Publishing, 1975.)

Dignitatis Humanae, Declaration on Religious Liberty. (December 7, 1965), pp. 799–812.

Gaudium et Spes, Pastoral Constitution on the Church in the Modern World. (December 7, 1965), pp. 903–1001.

Lumen Gentium, Dogmatic Constitution on the Church. (November 21, 1964), pp. 350–432.

Presbyterorum Ordinis, Decree on the Ministry and Life of Priests. (December 7, 1965), pp. 863–902.

OTHER WORKS

Ford, John C., and Grisez, Germain. "Contraception and the Infallibility of the Ordinary Magisterium". *Theological Studies.* Vol. 39, no. 2 (June 1978), pp. 258–312.

Gruden, John C. *The Mystical Christ: Introduction to the Study of the Supernatural Character of the Church.* St. Louis: B. Herder Book Co., 1936.

Hogan, Richard. "A Commentary on 'Familiaris Consortio'". *The Wanderer.* Vol. 115, no. 10 (March 11, 1982), supplement, pp. 1–3.

————. "A Theology of the Body: A Commentary on the Audiences of Pope John Paul II from September 5, 1979 to May 6, 1981". *Fidelity*. Vol. 1, no. 1 (December, 1981), pp. 10–15, 24–27.

Krapiec, Mieczylaw. *I–Man*. Translated by Marie Lescoe, Andrew Woznicki, Theresa Sandok, et al. New Britain, Conn.: Mariel Publications, 1983.

Malinski, Mieczyslaw. *The Life of Karol Wojtyla*. Translated by P. S. Falla. New York: Doubleday, 1979.

May, William. *Sex, Marriage, and Chastity: Reflections of a Catholic Layman, Spouse, and Parent*. Chicago: Franciscan Herald Press, 1981.

Muehlen, Heribert. *Una Mystica Persona: Die Kirche als das Mysterium der heilsgeschichtlichen Idenitaet des Heiligen Geistes in Christus und den Christen: Eine Person in vielen Personen*. 3d ed. Paderborn: Ferdinand Schoeningh, 1968.

Patrologiae Latinae. Edited by J. P. Migne. Vol. 76.

Paul VI, Pope. *Humanae Vitae, On Human Life*. Washington: United States Catholic Conference, 1968.

Pius XII, Pope. *Mystici Corporis, The Mystical Body of Christ*. Washington: National Catholic Welfare Conference, 1943.

Pope John Paul II and the Family. Edited by Michael Wrenn. Chicago: Franciscan Herald Press, 1983.

Robinson, H. Wheeler. "The Hebrew Conception of Corporate Personality". *Beihefte zur Zeitschrift fuer die alttestamentliche Wissenschaft*. Vol. 66 (1936), pp. 49–62.

Seifert, Josef. "Karol Cardinal Wojtyla (Pope John Paul II) as Philosopher and the Cracow/Lublin School of Philosophy". *Aletheia*. Vol. 2 (1981), pp. 130–99.

Smith, William. "The Role of the Christian Family, Articles 28–35". *Pope John Paul II and the Family*. Edited by Michael

J. Wrenn. Chicago: Franciscan Herald Press, 1983, pp. 73–107.

Talks of John Paul II. Boston: Daughters of St. Paul, 1979.

"Teen Fertility Awareness/Billings Method Study". *Fellowship of Catholic Scholars Newsletter*. Vol. 7, no. 2 (March 1984), pp. 11, 15.

Thomas Aquinas, Saint. *Summa Theologiae*.

Williams, George. *The Mind of John Paul II: Origins of His Thought and Action*. New York: Seabury Press, 1981.

Woznicki, Andrew. *A Christian Humanism: Karol Wojtyla's Existential Personalism*. New Britain, Conn.: Mariel Publications, 1980.

Index